TRYING TO GET SOME DIGNITY

Trying to Get Some Dignity

*Stories of Triumph
over Childhood Abuse*

Ginger Rhodes
Richard Rhodes

William Morrow and Company, Inc.
New York

Library of Congress Cataloging-in-Publication Data

Rhodes, Ginger.
Trying to get some dignity : stories of triumph over childhood
abuse / Ginger Rhodes, Richard Rhodes.—1st ed.
p.   cm.
Includes index.
ISBN 0-688-14096-3 (alk. paper)
1. Adult child sexual abuse victims—United States—Case studies.
2. Sexually abused children—United States—Case studies. 3. Abused
women—United States—Case studies. I. Rhodes, Richard.
II. Title.
HV6570.2.R49   1996   96-22608
362.7'6'0973—dc20   CIP

Printed in the United States of America

First Edition

1 2 3 4 5 6 7 8 9 10

BOOK DESIGN BY SUSAN DESTAEBLER

For Brooke, Alexandra, and Juliette, the next generation

CONTENTS

TRYING TO GET SOME DIGNITY

Prologue

"Our Voices Are Our Power"

SKYE SMITH (*a pseudonym*): What is there about us? I'm curious, I'm fascinated with that.

LYDIA DEROBERTIS: Why we keep trying?

SKYE SMITH: Why we keep trying and why we really do so well.

We were five, sitting in a Connecticut living room on a summer afternoon. Skye Smith, one of the many survivors of childhood abuse who spoke to us for this book, had driven over from upstate New York with two friends, Lydia DeRobertis and Maria Marewski. Skye used to be anorexic. All of us had stories.

GINGER RHODES: Something that's very powerful for me is a related issue: imagine what we could have done.

MARIA MAREWSKI: I say all the time to my friends, If we hadn't had to spend our thirties recovering, who might we have been?

SKYE SMITH: We did it in spite of, not because of. That's a big distinction.

We had all survived abusive childhoods and we wondered why. After phone calls, letters exchanged, interviews, shared books and manuscripts we found out why. Something of why.

Maria Marewski is German-American, blond, forty.

MARIA MAREWSKI: How many secrets did your parents live with, and their parents? It would be great if you could really piece together your family that way. It would be interesting to see if it was always the same secret.

RICHARD RHODES: Abuse certainly gets passed down from generation to generation, but you wonder how far back it goes.

MARIA MAREWSKI: And what forms it took. I think at some point this stuff that we consider abuse, child-rearing practices, wasn't a secret. I know from my father's family, that was just the way it was. There was no shame about it.

RICHARD RHODES: There was a time when this sort of behavior was in some sense adaptive. It's certainly true when you go back to peasant cultures, where people are living essentially a subsistence life, that the world was a very brutal place. Most of the old fairy tales got cleaned up; they were incredibly violent and pessimistic. The Big Bad Wolf ate Little Red Riding Hood in the original.

SKYE SMITH: That's why you believed in Heaven, too. Because there had to be a better place.

RICHARD RHODES: It meant that anything you could do to get your children ready for the brutality of the world was considered healthy.

MARIA MAREWSKI: Protection. That was my mother's take on the thing. She was a survivor of the Nazi concentration camps and my father was a German soldier who spent time in a Russian prison camp. My mother repeated a lot of the violence because she thought the only thing

Maria Marewski

she could do was to educate us, as she said, so we would be able to take the pain and suffering. And that meant keep doing it—to make you strong now.

SKYE SMITH: As though that makes you strong.

MARIA MAREWSKI: Right, it just makes you crazy.

> *If you hear bravado, it's because we were veterans reminiscing about our wars—exhilarated at reunion, letting down our guard.*

GINGER RHODES: But these adults are the ones who are supposed to teach you how the world works. They're the people saying, This is what love means, this is how a family operates, this is how people negotiate. They're our link to learning how to live.

RICHARD RHODES: And yet I'm struck by child-abuse survivors. We all seem to be savvy in some instinctive way about figuring out strategies.

It may be dysfunctional in the larger world, but at least it gets you through the battle.

MARIA MAREWSKI: That's right, we really learn to perceive other people's feelings.

SKYE SMITH: They don't even need to talk.

GINGER RHODES: Child-abuse survivors have tremendous bullshit detectors.

SKYE SMITH: As a teacher I could sense who was hurting. I could sense what they were all thinking out there. I was very good at managing the big group because I'm able to appraise a situation instantly. You walk into a room, POW!, you've got it figured out, what's going on, where the tension is, where the exits are.

This book began in the aftermath of another book, Richard's personal memoir A Hole in the World *(Simon & Schuster, 1990). Richard received several hundred letters from readers after he published that personal account of surviving childhood abuse. We found compelling the stories people told of their own experiences of abuse and survival. Each story was different, as each life was different, but there were common elements in the behavior of the abusers as well as in the strategies the abused found for coping and for surviving. We wanted to share these personal accounts with other readers, for the insights they offered and the measured, realistic hope they held out that childhood abuse need not be ruinous. We knew Richard had heard only from survivors, not the inhabitants of prisons, mental hospitals, and cemeteries who unluckily had not survived. If we assembled a book of interviews, we understood that such interviews would tell only part of the story of child abuse in America. But hope is crucial to survival in extremity, and worth salvaging. We picked out the most articulate correspondents and began interviewing them as we traveled on other business.*

By the time we began editing, four years later, our chorus of voices numbered twenty.

Unlike our meeting with Skye Smith and her friends, most of our interviews were one on one—two on one, the two of us with one person at a time. Alexa Donath, another survivor, in her forties, intense, with a bad back and multiple illnesses, sat in the same living room with us on another afternoon:

ALEXA DONATH: A friend of mine said, Just get over it. Get over this, already. I said, I'm going to take into consideration what a really bright person you are. And he should know better. I found this from being sick: if you've never been profoundly sick you're not apt to feel real compassion towards somebody who is. You don't want to know about it. My friend had wonderful, wonderful parents. . . . Everything in your life, everything that you do always comes back to square one. You're overcoming this, no matter what you do. If you have a good relationship finally, it's *finally*, it's not *to begin with*. You've had to overcome all the other crap that you've had in your life. This friend was made to feel like he was the most wonderful person in the world. He has no conception of what it means, as a child forming yourself, to grow up thinking that you're a piece of shit.

So when my friend says get over it, I say, Do you understand how many damaged people there are walking around out there? It isn't just that it colors everything in *my* life. As somebody who studied sociology, worked with young children and saw violence, I believe it's what causes violence in our society. It isn't just we who are the walking wounded.

For professional perspective, we interviewed two psychotherapists at the Menninger Clinic in Topeka, Kansas. Alice Brand Bartlett, an attractive woman in her forties, trains therapists at the celebrated midwestern institution:

RICHARD RHODES: I'm struck as you talk about this by something that I've heard many people say: "Well, you survived it, didn't you?" The depreciation of the abuse on the grounds that it wasn't really enormous.

ALICE BRAND BARTLETT: That's the listener's denial. The truth is, repetitive, early childhood abuse shatters your sense of self, your capacity to trust others, even your belief in God. It shatters everything. There's no way that it cannot have an effect on every part of your life.

We met Valorie Butler in Baltimore. Small, open-eyed, innocent, clutching her purse in the doorway, she looks like the actress Sally Field. Her mother called her the "walking siren" because she cried so easily, but her name, she notes, is derived from the word "valor." She is deeply religious:

VALORIE BUTLER: Most people avoid facing it, in my own family at least. There's not been a lot of healing, and I find that sad.

RICHARD RHODES: The tragedy of that is that it often gets passed on to the next generation.

VALORIE BUTLER: Right. There's a verse in the Scriptures that I used to be angry about. Now I understand it in a different light. It's about the sins of the fathers being visited upon the children to the third and fourth generation. I thought, that's not fair of God. Why should they suffer for it? Now I realize if the mother or father does abusive things, the child is going to feel it. We're not separated from one another. It's not that He's inflicting it on us, *we* are carrying it from one generation to another. Of course I'm analyzing this for myself and my daughter, too. I have a sixteen-year-old. She's quite a prize in my eyes, and I don't want her to suffer all the things I've suffered. But I can't say she hasn't been affected, because we're not perfect, we're imperfect. I haven't dealt with her in any of the ways that I was raised. In fact, I might have gone the other way, to leniency, not extremely so but rather more so than punitive.

Barbara Hamilton is a mother, a woman in her seventies, and the sins of the fathers in her family—incest—were visited upon the generations. Barbara wrote a book about it, The Hidden Legacy *(Cypress House, 1992), that led us to her in northern California:*

BARBARA HAMILTON: It's so devastating. Child abuse has been going on for hundreds of years and we're finally getting to the point where it's coming out. It just staggers me that we still have so much going on in the way of denial. I thought we were stronger. I came through World War II, the last patriotic war. We got together and submerged our differences and quit bitching. But we aren't really all that strong. To have such warped priorities that the misery and the devastation of little children can't be incorporated into somebody's sense of horror . . .

Karen Seal is a successful California businesswoman, tall and immaculately groomed, with graying hair and unusual blue-green eyes, a powerful presence who radiates wintry rage:

KAREN SEAL: I think we all chose the same path—immoderation. Half or whatever percentage wind up drug-addicted. I'm beginning to suspect anybody who's a superstar. Sort of, God, what happened to that person? Normal people don't have to prove what we keep trying to. Gotta, gotta, gotta keep running. Society reaps the benefit, because some of us turn out to be such incredible performers and producers. At what cost?

The two sides of the survivor Karen sees—sufferer and achiever—are sometimes paralleled in the two sides of the abuser, Menninger therapist Alice Brand Bartlett told us:

ALICE BRAND BARTLETT: When I'm training therapists, I tell them, Don't *suggest* that there is goodness in abusers, but keep the possibility in mind, because often the patient may eventually find some kernel of value, some positive experience that wasn't abusive. Finding something of value in the abuser can be sustaining. A patient doesn't lose everything that way. At some point, when the pain begins to lessen, the patient can create a broader perspective: "This is probably why my mother did this. This is maybe what she was experiencing at the time. She probably did the best she could. She probably was repeating her own abuse." Whatever their narrative, I don't suggest it, ever. It has to be in the meaning that the person comes to. But you have to allow that work to happen.

And I think many perpetrators fear that patient and therapist alike see only the abuse. They're so often troubled themselves and have such guilt, they think that treaters are only saying bad things and patients are only saying bad things about them, when it's really a much more difficult piece of emotional work.

David Doepel, a Miami-based therapist and documentary filmmaker, interviewed Richard at length for a professional training film:

RICHARD RHODES: When I speak publicly about my childhood, there's one question someone in the audience always asks that I find extraordinarily presumptuous: "Have you forgiven your father yet?" Presumptuous because it assumes that what my father did is forgivable. I didn't have an answer at first, out of sheer apoplexy. Now I say, He didn't apologize; why should I forgive him?

DAVID DOEPEL: And if he had repented?

RICHARD RHODES: I don't much believe in repentance.

DAVID DOEPEL: In the victim movement, there's dialogue about the need to forgive—if not for the abuser's sake, people say, then for yours. That somehow to hang on to hatred is maladaptive.

RICHARD RHODES: Yes, if it were hatred. But I've never felt that I hated my father. I feel enormous anger. And I've found a place to direct that anger—out into the work of the world.

Celia Golden, a beautiful California blonde whose mother raped her, concurs:

CELIA GOLDEN: We survivors are no longer powerless victims. Our voices are our power. And it is children our voices can protect.

1

"It's Just the Kids"

Everyone we spoke with had vivid memories of defining incidents of abuse. Those memories they often recounted first in our conversations, even before they told us the context of their experience—as if they were haunted. Some part of the violence these survivors experienced had receded into the past, but not these memories of outrage.

We talked to Celia Golden in her first-floor apartment in Santa Cruz, California. She recalled one of her sadistic mother's favorite tortures:

CELIA GOLDEN: When I was young, my mother used to cut my nails. I was supposed to come when she told me to come. I was supposed to sit there and calmly give her my fingers. One after the other. Knowing every time what it would mean. The cuticles on two of my fingers grow naturally up the nail. She would purposely cut them real slowly. You could watch her face and she would get this smile. I wasn't supposed to cry, I wasn't supposed to make a noise, I wasn't supposed to move, I wasn't supposed to flinch. It was always with this smile, going to laughter.

I learned to chew off my toenails and fingernails so that there would be nothing for my mother to pretend to cut.

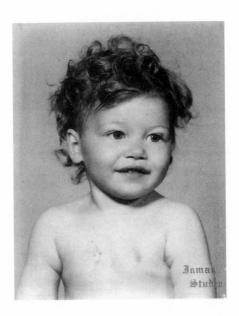

Celia Golden

Valorie Butler lost her father and then her mother while she and her two sisters were still in grade school. An aunt and uncle took the three sisters in and compounded their loss with cruelty:

VALORIE BUTLER: After our father's death, my sisters and I lived with our aunt and uncle. Our aunt punished us by making us stand on the stairs with our hands behind our backs from about seven or eight in the morning until after eleven at night. I remember at eleven-twenty-five this editorial came on the news, and I would look for that, that would be a signal. This was in the summertime, of course. I would look forward to school—I liked school to begin with—but then I could sit down most of the day. Even if we had a couple of hours of standing in the evening, it wasn't nearly like the fourteen-hour days in the summer. I cannot tell you how absolutely exhausted our legs felt. You know how, when you've been carrying something that's very heavy and you put it down, your arm feels like it doesn't exist? That's how my lower half felt—like it didn't exist. When I finally lay down on my bed at night, my legs felt like an enormous weight was lifted off of them.

GINGER RHODES: This happened a lot?

VALORIE BUTLER: Weeks and weeks, day in and day out. It was very depressing. Once I ate a hot dog in three bites. "I saw you eat that hot dog in three bites, you've got another week on the steps." You know, my world was like: They're out to get you, you can't have fun, you must not, you cannot have anything, no matter what happens. Don't look for happiness, it's going to be taken away from you.

RICHARD RHODES: Would she let you sit down for lunch?

VALORIE BUTLER: I don't remember lunches much. I imagine so, but it was quick, you know, you weren't allowed to linger.

GINGER RHODES: It was her version of solitary confinement.

VALORIE BUTLER: Right.

Barbara Hamilton is delicately framed, with a cap of white hair. In her book The Hidden Legacy, *she recalls her experience of incest long ago in childhood at the hands of her father:*

BARBARA HAMILTON: In our new house, the boys shared a large playroom upstairs, over the kitchen. My bedroom was downstairs, across the hall from my parents' room. One night Mother was out of town. After my brothers were asleep, Dad suggested that I sleep in Mother's bed— as a special treat—and I was pleased. . . . That night I had wiggled myself into a sleeping position on my stomach and closed my eyes when Dad came into the darkened room. He spoke my name softly and did not turn on the light. When he sat down on the edge of the bed, I was surprised. "Shhhhh," he said, as he gently turned me over and carefully unbuttoned my one-piece pajamas. I froze. He lifted my arms to remove the top part,

Barbara Hamilton

then pulled them off over my feet. He slid into bed beside me. He was naked. "I want to teach you about your body so that you will be a good wife someday."

Buzzing, buzzing in my head—sinking, sinking—

He stroked, petted, and kissed me all over, while he whispered, snuggled, and caressed me. Although he didn't physically hurt me, I felt frantic and helpless—like when I was drowning. I could hardly breathe. Numbness floated me away from feeling his body, his hands, his lips, his fingers. I turned into a Raggedy Ann doll. I couldn't speak or move. I pretended he was caressing someone else and I was just watching; but I knew it was me inside the Raggedy Ann doll.

He said, "This is our own, special secret and we won't tell anyone."

Oh, Daddy, this is too scary! Who are we? What is happening?

But I couldn't ask him out loud. He had become a stranger I didn't know and didn't want to know. My world had crumbled away.

Afterward, I couldn't think of him as being all bad, because he wasn't. I remembered the good times and helpful lessons that he taught me— memories which distorted reality and fed my confusion.

When his old self returned, periodically, flashes of my devotion rushed in to chase away the nightmare. One time several months later, I clearly recall feeling close to him again. It was like a sudden summer shower—unexpected, warm and pleasant. But it happened in the winter. I was chosen to lead the carolers in our Christmas play at school and we trooped onto the stage singing "Here We Come A-Wassailing." Then I sang "The First Noel" as a solo. It surprised my parents. Later, as we crunched through the snow to our car, Dad said, "When I heard you sing all by yourself, it brought a big lump to my throat." I glowed inside at his praise. My real father was back. I tried not to think about our secret, but when he reminded me, "Always keep it—never tell," I couldn't forget it. I didn't blame him, because I truly believed that my daddy wouldn't do anything wrong. And I trusted him to take care of me. But I hated his latest "lesson" and sensed he wasn't finished.

Barbara arranged for us to talk to her stepson, Dan Hamilton, whose molestation by another member of the family continued the abuse into another generation. A New Yorker now, tall, slim, poised and handsome, Dan is a professional actor and director, most recently of the soap opera As the World Turns:

DAN HAMILTON: My abuser was Barbara's brother—"Lee" in her book, Larry in my world. The first experience was when I was eight or nine, maybe ten. It was a camping trip in the California Sierras with my family. Late one night, in the dark, I woke up to find him entering my sleeping bag, crawling in with me, fondling me. I was very aware of the seduction aspect and the sexual aspect. I was certainly old enough to know this was going on. He was in his thirties or forties. The family was four or five feet away, also sleeping on the ground, in sleeping bags. I remember that sensation of somebody coming into the sleeping bag and my initial reaction—What, what, what? And the need to be quiet—I don't know whether that was a verbal command or simply an understanding on my part. To my knowledge, that was the first time. Then, anytime he was with the family, which was a couple of times every year, holidays and vacations, there would always be some kind of surreptitious approach at night. This happened for four to six years—eight to fourteen or nine to fourteen, somewhere in that range. There was a family ranch, and we would spend summers there. I can remember being taken off to a clump of trees or up to the creek. It was a constant exploration.

Dan Hamilton

RICHARD RHODES: Did he use force? Did he use negotiation?

DAN HAMILTON: I don't recall force. And I don't recall verbal negotiation other than "Don't tell anybody." I would assume what happened was much closer to a physical seduction, because I don't remember ever talking about it. I don't remember. Other than the initial surprise in the sleeping bag episode, the most emotional memory I can remember was one Thanksgiving. I was sleeping in the living room of my grandmother's house and everyone else was in various bedrooms. I had the sofa bed in the living room, and I can remember his coming in in the middle of the night. It was usually just his sucking me or wanting me to suck him. I don't recall any [anal] sodomy. But I can remember that night very strongly screaming *No!* at the top of my lungs in dead silence. But that

No! and the image of that bed with the holiday and the family sleeping in the house. And that *No!*

RICHARD RHODES: That *No!* was inside your head?

DAN HAMILTON: Inside my head, yes. No sound came out. No one ever knew, until we were adults, that anybody else in the family had been touched by the same man. Everybody thought they were the only ones.

> *Anna Lee Traynor is a health professional in New Jersey, a counselor and occupational therapist. She's a single mother of two, petite and intense. The beatings and abuse her stepfather inflicted on her in adolescence left her with inflammatory bowel disease—colitis—severe enough to require a permanent ileostomy:*

ANNA LEE TRAYNOR: We were sitting in the living room watching TV, me and my stepfather. I was ten or eleven years old. He was on the couch and wrestling was on. I remember it was a weekend night, about nine, ten o'clock. I was just sitting there and my stepfather gets up, goes to the bathroom, comes back, and calls my sister and mother into the room. This is one of the things I would never talk about except within the past two years—and I'm the health professional, I'm supposed to be used to anything. He comes back and he's holding something, but I'm not paying attention, I'm watching wrestling. He starts questioning my mother and my sister. He calls them to stand at attention—Hitler was in the room, right? He starts questioning them about something. What it was about was a wrapped-up sanitary napkin. If you think about back then, they were like the size of a tree. I'm still not really paying attention, for one very important reason: I had not started my menstruation at that point. He continues interrogating them, and finally he says, How about you? I said, How about me what? He said, Well, did you throw this into the garbage pail, miss and leave it on the side? You have to understand I was young and was not comfortable with this man, and I'm not talking about this kind of stuff with him. People don't talk about it now in comfort.

I said, No—and I didn't want to deal with this, I was already feeling so violated, and I turned back to the TV. He said, No, you stand up and come before me. I stood there and he was on the couch and he held it up—it must have been twenty minutes or more because the wrestling was going to be over—interrogating me. You did this, this was yours, you threw it, you're a pig, you don't pick up, you don't do this. Over and over connecting me with this sanitary napkin. I just said, It's not mine, it's not mine. It sounds so removed from the pathos of it at this point, but I was a ten- or eleven-year-old girl and he's holding something that I certainly didn't want to discuss with this man or anyone, it was so personal. My mother is there and I'm thinking, is my mother going to say anything, is she going to stop this man and say, It can't be hers? Oh no.

So twenty minutes to a half hour, we go back and forth and back and forth. I said, No, it's not mine, I didn't do it. Well, get out the red-leather-bound Bible. I will never forget this. Get that Bible out, put that Bible on the table, get on your knees and you swear an oath to God that you didn't do this. I put my hand on that Bible and I said, I swear I didn't do this. I have a very strong connection to my faith. I'm just a regular Catholic, but still. I thought—about him!—One of these days *you're* going to put your hand on a Bible and *you're* going to be swearing to God what you did to me. I still feel it will be in a court of law. Very distinctly, as my hand was there on the Bible, I'm doing this and being degraded this way, I'm thinking, *You're going to have to swear an oath to God someday that you did this to me.*

In appearance and presence, Anne O'Neil could be a Mother Superior—and in her young adulthood she was a nun in the congregation of the School Sisters of Notre Dame. She withdrew from the order before she took permanent vows and later married. Today, in middle age, Anne presents herself with reassuring calm and extraordinary openness. Her rich voice

reflects her lifelong interest in music. She was one of seven surviving children
of a pioneer chiropractor and a disturbed, schizophrenic mother:

ANNE O'NEIL: Mother gave us enemas. The enemas were a way she had of purging not only our bodies, but also our minds. Her goal, as she would say, was to rid us of our devils. In her mind the Devil and excrement were the same thing somehow. She used to say, "Cleanliness is next to Godliness."

RICHARD RHODES: Martin Luther used to make the same connection.

ANNE O'NEIL: Yes, right. There may be that German connection there. The enemas were always done in the bathroom. They were always multiple. Never one enema: ten at once.

RICHARD RHODES: You mean in sequence?

ANNE O'NEIL: Yes, over and over and over again. Mother was creative in that sense. She was always looking for a better way; nothing was ever good enough. Instead of just giving multiple enemas, she decided to add molasses. She put molasses in the water and that made the enemas more explosive. They were more colorful, shall we say, they had more odor, they were stronger, they had pizzazz, drama. My mother was extremely dramatic. Looking at me, you can imagine. I'm very dramatic and Mother was very, *very* dramatic.

RICHARD RHODES: Did she use a rubber bag?

ANNE O'NEIL: No, she used a syringe. A large syringe. In and out, in and out, in and out.

RICHARD RHODES: So it was meant to be a washing process.

ANNE O'NEIL: Yes. Around the same time she started using the molasses, she decided that she needed to introduce air to "neutralize the gases." So she would use an empty syringe and pump air in. We were to take as much of that as we possibly could. Now to give you a little perspective, recently I had a sigmoidoscopy. I make a point of sharing something of my personal history with my doctor because I find then we have more of a common bond and I can trust more. So the doctor had to inject air into my bowel for the sigmoidoscopy. Gosh, he said, you're really a good patient—most women are screaming and hollering at me when I do this. I thought, this is nothing. I said to him, Well, I learned to endure.

I spent my childhood with intense intestinal discomfort. The sigmoidoscopy was nothing, it was really nothing by comparison.

RICHARD RHODES: She must have been aware that she was causing pain. Or were you required not to show that pain?

ANNE O'NEIL: Oh never, oh never, never. We could never show that we were sad, that we were unhappy, that we were resentful, that we were in pain. Pain was forbidden. Pain was not allowed. Absolutely not allowed. When she did the air thing she called it "the teeter-totter." I was crazy about teeter-totters; I loved teeter-totters. She ruined them for me. I don't remember that I played on teeter-totters after that.

> *John Wood, a sometime antique dealer who has also been homeless, is a rugged, scattered, angry man who positions himself precariously on the edge of disaster. Responding to Richard's book, he wrote us:*

JOHN WOOD: I come from a good family. If you don't believe me just ask my parents. My mother's mother was Social Register and pretty snooty. Her grandfather had wads and wads of money and made tons and tons of money peddling flour to the Union Army during the Civil War and then he'd buy real estate. Oh, you must see a photograph of that guy. It's a caricature. I mean, it's really an incredible caricature of an angry man. There was always a veneer of gentility. One of the things that I think about doing is going around to schools and talking about being abused as a child. I would love to do it in Newtown School [*in Connecticut*]. I would love to do it while there are still people around who knew my mother, because it would blow them away. I mean, most people would never in this world believe it.

John Wood

I didn't have a wicked stepmother or live in a home for boys [*as Richard did*], but the damage was just as serious. I'm an incest survivor. I don't remember much of my life before age about twenty. Almost nothing before age about twelve. My sewer system★ was fantasizing about living off the land a hundred miles from the end of the nearest road in British Columbia. My chief defense was and is repression. Forgetting. My life has been a shambles, including isolation, emotional and financial highs and lows, jail, college dropout, lots of relationships and jobs, first wife shot herself, second wife was a genuine con artist, I'm agoraphobic, compulsive under-earner, compulsive debtor, and so on. . . .

Incest wasn't the only kind of abuse in our house—there was emotional and mental abuse and tons of it. My mother was an incest survivor, and, like [*Richard's*] stepmother, the only men she felt safe around were men whom she controlled, and so, like you, I suffered the ravages of a full court press for as long as I lived with her. And so did my father and my brother, who were among the male perpetrators of sexual abuse on

★*Richard's brother Stanley explored the big storm sewers under the streets of Kansas City, Missouri, to escape their stepmother's abuse, a story Richard tells in* A Hole in the World.

me. In fact, one can easily build a case for the position that I come from a long line of incest survivors. . . .

Ralph Kessler, a retired proofreader, short and solidly built, approached Richard when he read from A Hole in the World *at Black Hawk Books in Berkeley, California. Ralph wanted to know, he said, how it was possible for a parent to stand by and watch her child being abused, as his mother had done. He had not asked his mother before she died, and the question still haunted him. Ralph sat for an interview later at our home in Connecticut on a trip east to visit his daughter, but decided when he saw the transcript to write his memories for us. His narrative begins:*

RALPH KESSLER: I am a seventy-five-year-old American Jew, living with my wife in a senior housing facility in Berkeley, California. I worked as a newspaper proofreader and retired in 1983 from the *San Francisco Chronicle and Examiner.* I was active in my union, the International Typographical Union (ITU). For more than fifteen years, I have actively produced a volunteer radio program at a local university. Its themes are senior and disability issues. My wife, June, hosts the show. She is a medically retired English teacher.

In the fall of 1990, I read the book *A Hole in the World,* which is Richard Rhodes's story of his own suffering at the hands of his stepmother while his father passively accepted it. It reminded me of my own life. My stepfather beat and mistreated me and my mother said not a word.

Michael Davies (a pseudonym) is an editor for a midwestern publisher, thin and soft-spoken. In his initial letter to us, he wrote:

MICHAEL DAVIES: My family's lives have been so inextricably bound up in secrecy that, until recently, we'd had virtually no access to what we'd hidden. And each door we've subsequently pried open has revealed a dark room leading to another door opening into darker rooms still. . . .

The central fact of my childhood and early adulthood was an extremely violent alcoholic father. On a regular basis, for nearly the first thirty years of their marriage, he beat and berated his wife and terrorized his children. As each of us edged into adolescence, each was also harried into the arena of verbal and physical conflict. Combat, I should say. To this day, I can't hear ice clinking into an empty glass without thinking of my father's demons and the violence they delivered.

He seemed to run a fortnightly cycle, my alertness and dread increasing daily as each eruption approached. Clink. Clink. Mr. Hyde ringing Dr. Jekyll's doorbell. The slow descent into temporary but tenacious madness. The household once again and again and again and again under occupation. A razor-wired concentration camp emerging repeatedly from its incubation in my father's brain. That was the central fact, one we all experienced, one we never forgot.

Louise Hill (a pseudonym) is a writer and university professor. She's Rubenesque and dramatic, with a wry, tongue-in-cheek wit, but the joie de vivre *she radiates doesn't completely disguise an underlying grief:*

LOUISE HILL: My mother died about five years ago. She didn't apologize, she was never one to apologize. She didn't say she was sorry, but in her way she did. A couple of years before she died, she said, Look, I just have to tell you, I was a very angry person and they didn't have psychiatrists in those days. If they did, she said, I would have gone to see somebody. As she explained it to me, this was the reason for her behavior—because she was very angry. She was angry because she was poor. My father was sick. He was ill with heart disease. He wasn't earning a living. But even more, her own mother, my grandmother, was always ridiculing her for the bad marriage she made. So she felt like she had no allies and she, I quote, "took it out on you"—meaning me.

She had very few friends. She had almost no friends. She had a bridge club and they would come and I liked that because now I see in retrospect

I was a very sociable kid. But she had very few friends. Because she didn't trust people. She got a car eventually. She said that if anybody asks for a ride, tell them we have no room, because, you know, then you'll be obligated to them. She was not a person who enjoyed friendships. Yet she was always yelling at me, Don't you have any . . . ah, have any friends? Aha—now I see. Projection.

I now indeed see. It's taken me more than fifty years to understand the word *projection*. In fact, I do remember one incident. I loved to go to the movies on a Saturday afternoon. It was an escape and it was a wonderful world for me. I would come home and put on all the shows in the kitchen for my mother and father. But you didn't go to the movies by yourself. That was one thing you didn't do. The thing was to get a friend every Saturday to go to the movies with. So it would start early in the week, it was like having a date for a Saturday night. One week, I remember, Saturday had come around and my mother asked me, Aren't you going to the movies today? I said, Well, I don't have anybody to go with. She said, What do I have to do, pay Theresa Smith—who was a girl down the street of unsavory reputation—pay Theresa Smith fifteen cents to go to the movies with you?

David Ray is a distinguished American poet who grew up in poverty in Oklahoma in the years during and after the Second World War. Neglect and abuse compounded the effects of his family's poverty on David's childhood. In one of many poems exploring that difficult time, he remembers supplementing his meager rations with wild mulberries:

The Mulberries of Mingo

I brush into a pile
the fallen mulberries,
good for nothing but to make us
slip and break our bones.
And so I give them to my youngest
trees, my linden and my birch,

for food.

I never want my child

to eat mulberries,

because I had to live on them

once, sitting in the branches,

bitterly, having nothing else,

nothing save hate,

and now it is turned into proverbs

as I sweep down the slopes

the fallout-dusted berries

which are good for nothing

in modern times

though the Chinese found them

beautiful for paintings

on silk, and children once

took them into their bellies,

to survive.

Skye Smith and her younger brother, Bob, lived with their divorced mother and their grandparents, who operated a movie theater and a drive-in in Stearns, Oklahoma. When they weren't working, Skye and Bob rattled around an upper floor of the theater, unattended:

SKYE SMITH: There were these huge closets and I used to sit in there for hours by myself, in my misery. I wanted somebody to come get me, but they wouldn't. They didn't come get me. There were no windows. A big linoleum space in the middle of the floor. That's where we tricycled, Bob and I. Of course you could fall down the stairs, but "It's just the kids, so what?" We would go to the drive-in and play on the playground equipment by ourselves—not with the other children, we weren't allowed to play with them. At home, we had to work in the concession stand, so we worked. We were isolated off in the concession stand. We were just working, there was nobody around. "It's just the kids, so what?"

GINGER RHODES: My family had the same attitude. My grandmother would say, Get busy. If you're not busy, you'll be thinking about yourself and then you'll be feeling sorry for yourself—just get busy.

SKYE SMITH: Don't ever think about yourself, ever. It would be very dangerous. You'll want to kill us if you do.

2

"Trying to Make Sense of It"

Since we had already corresponded with the survivors we arranged to meet, and Richard's book had broken the ice, stories came quickly when we sat to interview, often accompanied by family photographs and mementos.

The prosperity of Alexa Donath's Boston-area family made it all the more difficult for outsiders to believe she was being abused:

ALEXA DONATH: I come from an affluent background. Because of that background and because it was the Fifties and Sixties, no one believed anything I told them about what was happening to me. You told a teacher, she said, Yes, yes, dear, your mother's hurting you. My mother looked like everybody's mother wanted to look. She was beautiful, fashionable, my father was successful, and no one believed me.

I had everything. I had a beautiful house in a beautiful suburb, something different to wear every day. I went to religious school three times a week. But before every Seder and before every Jewish holiday, she'd go berserk. [*Opening a photo album:*] Here's a photograph of a birthday party with a caption: "Another wonderful birthday party to share with our friends and family." But this picture is worse than Kafkaesque, because before or after, she would go into a rage.

We had a retarded woman whom my mother used to mistreat terribly. In those days you could have a sort of indentured servant. This woman was given to the family in a way, by the home for the retarded where she'd been raised. Her name was Mary. She was almost my mother and I was her mother. She was my first student. When I was in the fourth grade I taught her to read and write. So she wrote a letter to the home saying that my mother was mistreating her. My mother never forgave me. She screamed, *How did she learn to read and write?—I know who did it!* But of course, the woman who was in charge of Mary at the home adored my mother.

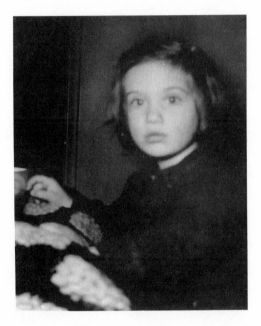

Alexa Donath

I can't even see Mary anymore because it's too hard for me to see her. She's living with a cousin of mine. My parents gave her away. But that's how I knew I could be a teacher.

Valorie Butler slowly relaxed as she settled in to talk in our hotel room in Baltimore. She had driven up from Washington, D.C., where she works for the federal government. She wore no jewelry of any kind, not even a wedding ring:

VALORIE BUTLER: My father was killed in a car accident when he was twenty-five. [*Offering an envelope:*] This little packet was what was taken off of him when he was killed. In this police envelope is his wallet. It's very revealing. It has a card, "The Society for the Rehabilitation of Broken Down Horse Players." My father and my uncle, they loved horse racing. That was his weakness, it was an addiction. They were always poor, they never had any money. They would go to horse races all the time.

My father had his own life. My mother was schizophrenic, unable to meet his needs.

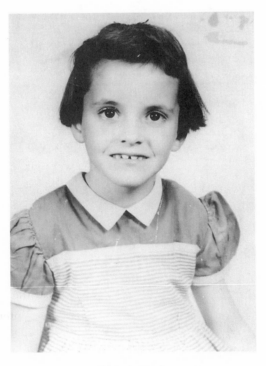

Valorie Butler

I thought he was a very handsome man. He did not spend a lot of time with us. He drank. I believe he was an alcoholic. I remember him wanting Alka-Seltzer a lot, because of upset stomach. When my father would drink, we called his vomiting "can of soup." That's what it looked like. We used to use it like a verb, "can-of-soup." One day he came home and said, Do you want to watch Daddy can-of-soup? He was probably sick from drinking, but at the time I didn't know that. So we lined up in front of the bathroom door and watched him throw up into the toilet. That's kind of gross, but that was the entertainment that we had. It was comical in a way, but sad.

He was killed when I was about six years old, in first grade. I remember the policeman coming to the door; I remember my mother's tears and everything. My father getting killed was devastating for her, he was her crutch. But I do not know at what point I realized that he was dead. I still don't remember that, at what point. I know I was fairly young. But no one discussed these things with us.

GINGER RHODES: You weren't allowed to go to the funeral?

VALORIE BUTLER: It wasn't until later that I realized what a funeral was and that we should have gone.

RICHARD RHODES: You didn't understand that he was dead.

VALORIE BUTLER: I did understand when I was still very young, but I don't remember exactly when that was. We were taken to Tennessee to live near my mother's parents. Then our mother's mental health deteriorated and our health deteriorated along with it. My childhood remembrance of her was of frustration. I was called the "walking siren" because I cried a lot. She was not abusive in the way my aunt would be, but she neglected us. We were not fed properly. She would tune us out. My two sisters and I would sit on the floor. We had these little words and things that we made up. We didn't have a lot of interaction with others at the time. We would sit on the floor and rock back and forth and chant *Maker, maker, maker.* I'd never thought about that until in adult life. I thought, what did that mean? Maker? Then it dawned on me. *Make her*. Make her do what I want. Make her read me a book. Make her, make her do this or do that. That's what we were really feeling at the time.

GINGER RHODES: You lived separately from your grandparents?

VALORIE BUTLER: We lived near them, but the relationship between my grandmother and my mother was not real good. My grandmother tended to be domineering. That may have been part of my mother's problem. She could be very highly sensitive. So that didn't work. But our grandmother, she would pay attention to me. If I wanted her to say something over again she would say it over again. I had more interaction with her than I normally had with adults. I wanted a lot of attention, and she gave me that attention. If she needed to spank us, or wanted to spank us, she did that too. So I was angry at her too.

RICHARD RHODES: Was she religious?

VALORIE BUTLER: Yes, as a matter of fact she was. We went to Sunday school back then, and that was fun. She could quote the Scriptures. I felt sad when we went to live with our aunt later because we never did go back to my grandmother's. She has died, so of course I can't do that now. I have some pretty good memories about her.

But we [*she means she and her sisters*] started to suffer more from diarrhea. We were thin. We lived in a little house my mother rented. Money was very important to her. I didn't realize it until later. She would get three Social Security checks, one for each of us girls, and that would be her subsistence. She was very tight with it. She did not spend it on us. We went around in very little clothing, we had very little food. I don't remember going hungry, but we just were not fed a properly balanced diet. A teacher carried me out on papers because I had diarrhea in first grade. We had diarrhea year-round, constantly. And very few toys. I remember stealing some toys next door, wanting to play with them. Not with the intent to steal but just gathering up things to play with, you know.

Another indication of the depth of their neglect Valorie revealed in an autobiographical essay, "Song of Valorie," published in Adventist Review:

One experience that vividly revealed the lack in my life happened when I was in the first grade. While I was sitting in music class one day early in October, the teacher came to me with a paper crown with six paper candles and asked, "Do you know what day this is?" I did not know what day it was—that it was my birthday. *My* birthday? No one told me that it was my birthday. In fact, I had no recollection of ever celebrating it at any time in the past. Then she asked me to walk around the room in a circle while the children sang "Happy Birthday." But . . . what was a circle? I had never heard of one. Frustrated, the teacher angrily pulled me around the room.

One day, at the end of October, I noticed that the children were donning funny-looking outfits for a parade around town. But . . . I didn't have one, and why were they wearing them? The teacher asked me where my costume was for the Halloween parade. Costume? Halloween? What was that? So my jacket was put on me backwards to give some semblance of something different. What I distinctly recall is the feeling of shame of being without a "real" costume as I paraded down the sidewalk with the other children. After several interactions with me and my not understanding the "normal" things a child of six should know, the teacher decided I should be tested. A test was administered. Years later I learned that it was determined that I was retarded.

In our interview, Valorie continued:

One day we came home and Mother was gone. My aunt said, She went back, she couldn't take it anymore—meaning back to the mental institution. We were even told that when we came home from school, our mother would start shaking because she couldn't deal with us.

GINGER RHODES: Did you feel that it was your fault? That you'd run your mother off?

VALORIE BUTLER: I felt that we must have been awful somehow. Now I realize she couldn't cope with three energetic children. I felt that guilt as a child.

My aunt had my mother sign a paper, a notarized paper, that she would willingly give us up. I'm not sure how willingly my mother did this—she was institutionalized for the rest of her life. But from then on we stayed with my aunt and uncle. As our guardians, they received our Social Security checks. It really began to be more abusive about a year later.

We interviewed Michael Davies, the editor, in his apartment within walking distance of the press where he works. A sound system dominated the living room of the bare apartment, as if Michael found refuge in music from any familiar clutter of home:

MICHAEL DAVIES: My father really was like Willy Loman in Arthur Miller's *Death of a Salesman*. He was a traveling salesman from 1959 to about 1971, the most difficult years that I recall for the family. By the end of his time with the company, he'd turned fifty and had been squeezed into a smaller and smaller territory to make room for the young bucks. As the job became tougher to take, his bouts of drinking seemed more frequent and more violent. So, even though the family had finally reached relative financial security, we still suffered. Especially my mom. He beat her a lot.

RICHARD RHODES: Did he beat up on you kids too?

MICHAEL DAVIES: He fought with my older brother, Chuck. Fistfights. Stuff like that. Tried to run Chuck over with his car once.

We all thought when our father died that finally, you know, finally we would be free. We thought that especially about Mom. My sisters

Michael Davies

and I tried to push her to see: "He's gone and you're no longer tied to him." The last couple of years of his life especially, she was a twenty-four-hour nurse for him because he was in extremely poor health. The last year of his life he was on oxygen all the time. He walked around the house connected to an oxygen tank.

RICHARD RHODES: He had emphysema?

MICHAEL DAVIES: He'd been a heavy smoker, heavy drinker. And he had a bad heart caused by rheumatic fever as a child. I think that colored a lot of what came later in his life. So we to varying degrees pushed her to seize this opportunity to have a real life, like Pinocchio becoming a real person. Happy ending. Because she'd been his prisoner nearly all her life. Even so, when something that has so defined your life suddenly is not there, you don't quite know what to do. Doesn't matter what a jerk he was. You're scared. Terrified. Like the parolee who can't make it on the outside.

Well, it wasn't difficult for me. I thought, wow, this is great. I'm glad that he's gone. He was a terrible man. At the funeral, I remember sitting next to my sister and she was crying a lot and my younger brother was crying a lot. I remember I was surprised at how much grief there seemed to be. Naive on my part. A lot of that grief was more for the people themselves than for my father. But I didn't cry. I don't even recall much in the way of twinges. I felt some anger, I think. But, bottom line, I was glad it was over, I was glad he was out of the way. Gone.

For me he was a combination of brutality, fear, and darkness. He was extraordinarily afraid of everything. I'll never forget his last words to me, a few months before he died. I'd gone down for a visit, reluctantly, and he'd gotten upset because I was trying to balance spending time with him with spending time with my mom. He always hogged the show. My mom always felt left out because he had to be the center of attention. I remember he was confined to the bed. He was in bad shape, and I'd gone in to say good-bye. It was a very awkward, tense moment. His last words to me were, Be sure to give your mother the license plate number of your car. That baffled me, so I asked him, Why do you want me to do that? And he said, Well, in case there was an accident that was so terrible that your body could not be identified, they would have the plate number to go by. That's so in keeping with the kind of person he was. He was constantly afraid of the outside world.

Before her mother's mental illness deteriorated into brutal fixation, Anne O'Neil recalls a time in early childhood of relative peace:

ANNE O'NEIL: Up until I was seven we lived in a very large, gracious older house, set on beautiful grounds. There were six of us then—Pat, Mary, Leo, myself, Tom, and Mike. My father was a chiropractor; he had a successful practice in Wisconsin, which in itself was extraordinary because chiropractic was not legal in Wisconsin in those days. My father

Anne O'Neil

had been sent there by B. J. Palmer, one of the founders of chiropractic, because he had this charismatic gift with people, and Palmer felt that my father could help to legitimize chiropractic in Wisconsin.

I remember this beautiful sweep of lawn and huge oak trees, and a hill rolling down to a ravine in the back. It overlooked a canal which used to carry logs to the paper mill which was across the canal—we could smell the smell of the pulp but we couldn't see the mill. It was a very green place. Our home was a little—I wouldn't say ramshackle—but used. It didn't have a pristine feel to it like other houses that I saw nearby. I can't remember a time when I couldn't look around and see how things could be made more beautiful. My favorite things were wandering in the woods and picking flowers and swinging on this huge swing. We had a twelve-foot-high swing that my father had hung on a huge oak tree and I used to swing on it and my father would swing me.

Louise Hill's writing often veers from comedy to darkness in the space of a single speech. Her childhood, she remembers, veered wildly as well:

LOUISE HILL: I grew up in the Boston area. We were extremely poor. When you're a child and you're poor, you don't necessarily realize that you're different than anybody else. Now, in adulthood, I see some of those childhood experiences of poverty as very rich and very fun. For example, I never had fresh bread until I went away to college. I was sent every day to the bakery at the end of the day to get the day-old stuff. I was brought up on hard rolls. I was shocked that bread was supposed to be soft. These things now amuse me in maturity. I believed that we had no hot water. My mother corrected me shortly before she died. We did have hot water, she said, but my grandmother, who lived in the same house, didn't want to use the hot water because it cost money. I do remember that we would heat up the hot water for a bath on a stove. But there was never enough hot water, so we would go to public baths— to the Dover Street Baths. This now I see as great fun in our life.

RICHARD RHODES: Did you not see it that way then?

LOUISE HILL: I did. It was an adventure. My sister recently said to me, You know, we had a very rich life. We didn't lead a sequestered life. We didn't have a car; early on, we couldn't afford a car. It didn't seem like a shameful thing, it wasn't painful. We had to take public transportation and it would take five or six changes on a street car and buses to get to the Dover Street Baths. This was an adventure. We saw the entire city of Boston as we went by. It was great.

We lived in a three-decker house. My grandmother lived on the top floor. She was a tyrant. My grandfather was meek—or, not meek, he just stole away to be away from her—but she was quite a tyrant. On the middle floor lived my aunt with her husband and two children in a very happy marriage which I was very jealous of, because that didn't go on in my own house. We lived on the bottom floor. We were supposed to be disadvantaged because the first floor had the least light. In a three-decker, the thing was to live on the top floor where there was the most light—you were closest to the heavens and to God. But actually, the people that lived on the bottom floor were the people that were the least disadvantaged. I thought it was quite dandy, because we were nearest to the street.

When we would go to the baths—we were a family of all women—we went to the women's baths. My grandmother, my aunt, my mother, myself, my sister, and my aunt's two children, a girl and a boy, the only boy in the family. We disguised him in a kerchief and a dress until he was thirteen years old. He's now a very well-known periodontist in the Boston area and how he has suffered this indignity I have no idea. I guess what I'm trying to say is that because we were poor there was a positive side to our family life, a tremendous sense of adventure and of humor. My mother, who was extremely unhappy in her marriage, who was a very angry woman, and my aunt, both had a terrific sense of humor.

More bleakly, occupational therapist Anna Lee Traynor remembers a New Jersey childhood oppressed with violence and neglect:

ANNA LEE TRAYNOR: I lost the opportunity to be a child by the age of ten, when my half brother was born. That's when I became the sole responsible party to take care of an infant, and that included feedings, household care, and everything else. To that point, I had been a good student. My school records show declining grades that go back up when I moved out of there.

It was oppressive growing up. It was oppressive. Medical neglect was a significant part of life. There was battering, there were sexual connotations. But the neglect has its own element of devastation. From age seven on, there were times I needed acute medical attention and my mother and my stepfather did not give it to me. I broke my arm when I was seven, and a month later—my arm was blown up and I couldn't write—a nun at school wrote a note asking, Could you take her to a doctor? That was serious abuse.

Anna Lee Traynor

My mother had a miscarriage because of a beating from my stepfather.
I heard the fighting and I tried to intrude by knocking on the bedroom
door. I was about eight years old. My mother was seven months pregnant.
They told me to shut up and go to bed. Later my uncle came into my
room and was getting me dressed. I can see him right now. He said,
Mommy got sick and has to go to the hospital. I can close my eyes and
still see the furled sheets, the spotted blood in the furled sheets and my
mother's clothing ripped. The baby died a day later. I remember the
coffin, they picked out a white coffin.

That affected me in ways that I'm only now seeing. To have seen a
loss of life caused by these two people, in a home that's supposed to
provide you safety . . .

I remember very methodically, very contemplatively setting up three
bottles of nail polish. [*She suppresses nervous laughter.*] I shouldn't laugh.
It's not funny. It was very methodical, very contemplative for an eight-
year-old. There were three bottles of nail polish on a long bureau. I can
see the drawers. I kept thinking, drink them really fast like cowboys do

at the bar on TV. I kept the tops on the nail polish, but thought, if I drink them down really fast, one, two, three, like they take the shots of whiskey, I can kill myself. I was going to parochial school and I thought, if I kill myself, it's a mortal sin and I'm going to go to hell. I didn't want to go to hell, so that stopped me. That's the only thing that stopped me. I didn't know why I wanted to kill myself. It's not me. I never, ever contemplated suicide. I stopped myself and just went through the motions.

Recently I went to a hypnotherapist, to try to recover more of these memories. He asked me what I might want to remember. I told him that one particular memory seemed so out-of-the-ordinary for my personality, to want to kill myself. So I went back and the biggest connection had to do with the death of that baby. I felt such despair that that child was lost that I thought of killing myself. She was my sister too. I remember my stepfather with this white plastic statue of the Madonna, like you get at those patio places so you can put them outside. He filled it with sand and that was her marker. I went to that cemetery recently and found that grave. I hadn't been there in thirty years. All the beautiful and expensive stone carvings in that cemetery—gravestones—and that white plastic piece-of-garbage statue. An unmarked grave.

Divorce led Skye Smith's mother home to Oklahoma, where Skye's grandparents took control:

SKYE SMITH: My parents married way too young. My father was a fighter pilot, a top-gun aviator, in the Air Force. This was all very phallic and romantic to my mother, this woman who was growing up in Oklahoma. She was dying to get away from home. He buzzed his top-gun plane over the main street of the town, to impress her, and almost got court-martialed. He was a bit of a character, still is. So he just swept her off her feet at nineteen. She went to Germany with him and got pregnant on her honeymoon with me.

She had no business marrying somebody she scarcely knew, running off like that, getting pregnant. But I give her credit, that was her attempt to get out, to escape in a way that she could. It backfired on her, because he's an alcoholic and very violent when he's drunk. He's tried to kill my brother when he was drunk. I guess my mother spent a lot of nights out of the apartment, afraid of him. The marriage wasn't working out and what you did then to glue it together was have another baby, so she had another baby. By that time my father was out of the service and got a job with American Airlines and decided to move to Los Angeles. When I was two and my brother was not even born yet—I don't know a lot of the details here, it doesn't get talked about—he basically told my mother, I'll buy you a ticket anywhere you want to go, but you're not going with me to L.A. So she naturally went back with her parents in Stearns, Oklahoma. I think the last thing they wanted was kids, especially me, who looked exactly like my dad and had his temperament. They were opposed to the marriage to begin with. I represented everything that had gone wrong. My mother said that I caused the marriage to dissolve because he didn't want children.

RICHARD RHODES: Was this an immaculate conception?

SKYE SMITH: Yeah, right. My brother, though, *was* the immaculate conception. He didn't look like dad and my grandparents got him at birth, so he was perfect and theirs. I remember at two years old feeling very depressed, very separate, very unwanted, because I *was*. That's really the truth. Then my mother basically dumped us on her parents. She abdicated her parental role and reverted to being their child, because you're not going to live with my grandparents and be an adult. They're the adults. They're in control. So she went off to work every day and my brother and I stayed with my grandparents. I lost two parents by the age of two, in a sense. We never talked about Dad, Dad was just gone. I was connected to this man, he was exciting and fun. But now he's gone and all of a sudden I've got these dour people in this awful place.

We lived in the top of the movie theater. It was like a warehouse. There was no yard, no outdoors, no children, just work. At age two, I cleaned the aisles of the theater, up and down, picked up trash. We just worked all day: no play, my grandparents never went on vacation, never took a day off, it was a seven-day-a-week business. We had matinees, evening shows, ordering and stocking to do. In the summer they ran a drive-in too.

My uncle ran the movie theater for four or five years. But that was the expectation, you do what's required. You cannot have a life. You do what the family system needs. You can't be an individual. When I was six, my mother didn't want to move with them to Arizona. In the meantime, she's harboring this fantasy that the fighter pilot is going to come back and get us. That's why she's not pressing him for any support money or anything. Of course, he's not going to come back, he was in L.A., having a great life. Are you kidding? Come back to Stearns and these gloomy people? Forget it.

We went out to visit. I had just turned six and my brother was four. This was to be a reconciliation trip. But Dad forgot to get us at the airport. We waited in LAX for about two hours. We had planned to stay with him, but he had a woman living with him, so he took us to the beach and he dumped us, literally. He ran off; two hours later my brother is turning blue, it's May, it's very cold. My mother found a ride for us somewhere, we stayed in a hotel. I coughed all night I was so upset and I was punished for that, I was whipped for that, for coughing all night. The tension was so terrible. I guess on that trip she came to terms with the fact that there was no reconciliation, that the idea was a fantasy.

So she married this awful man that she'd been dating a couple of years in Stearns. He was the unmarried bank teller. I guess he was the only eligible one, such as he was. He was still living with his parents at the time and on the rebound she married him, probably the week before my grandparents moved to Arizona. They refused to go to the wedding. They boycotted that because they didn't approve. So that was my new stepfather. They took off, another big loss. Now we're family, but I don't like this mother very well and I can't stand the stepfather, for good reason. But that soon fell apart. He couldn't hold a job; we went to Tulsa and then we moved to Kansas City.

My family didn't like to interact with other families. In my family there were no friends. I didn't know any other children until I went to

Skye Smith

first grade—there wasn't even a kindergarten in that town. When you're being abused at home, it's one thing if you can go out with your friends and say, My dad hits me and it feels terrible and I hate him. You can run it past other children. But when there's no one to talk to . . .

RICHARD RHODES: Why the isolation?

SKYE SMITH: I think my family was afraid of getting close with people and developing intimate relationships. They like to feel that they are the lords of the town and that way they can be powerful and in control. They have to control everyone's lives they encounter. There can't be much social interaction with that attitude. You have to brainwash your child so that everyone stays together and the children take care of the parents ultimately.

RICHARD RHODES: Your family had power in the town?

SKYE SMITH: [*Laughing*] In the town of Stearns, Oklahoma? No. It's interesting. I have the view that they're huge people, huge, huge people. But it's like in *The Wizard of Oz,* you peek behind the curtain and there are these scared little people. They ran the movie theater in town, big deal. But growing up, I thought they were the lords. My uncle was the mayor. The mayor of the town of Stearns, Oklahoma? [*Laughing again*] But why did they choose those little systems? So they could be big and powerful.

Barbara Hamilton entered her stepson Dan Hamilton's life before she worked through her own childhood abuse:

DAN HAMILTON: I don't know my own mother. She left when I was six months old. There was a stepmother who died when I was four, and then Barbara was my second stepmother. She had her doors closed, and I had my doors closed.

GINGER RHODES: Emotionally, you mean?

DAN HAMILTON: Yes. When I was eighteen and first in New York, for example, at acting school, I had a relationship with a woman who then became pregnant. I knew I wasn't ready for family and children, partly due to being young, partly because I understood I wasn't going to be making any money anytime soon, and partly because of my family and all of its connotations. My image of myself at that point was certainly the loner. I wanted to be as alone and romantic as I could be. So I said, No, I cannot be your husband, and I will not take the responsibility for raising this child. And she went back to California, where she had come from, and put the child up for adoption. I knew it existed, I knew the child had been born, but I closed that door and moved on with my life.

California businesswoman Karen Seal, like many of the survivors we interviewed, had been waiting to speak, and plunged into her story as soon as we to set up our tape recorder:

KAREN SEAL: You're welcome to use my full name. I have no reason to protect anybody. Both my parents are dead, I've told both sides of the family what happened to me, and I don't care who knows. I was born August 8, 1944. My parents were both working-class. Both had eighth-grade educations. My mother came from probably the poorest family in her small town in Idaho, and my father was a carnival worker. He had jumped railroad cars during the Great Depression. They were married in 1940. *His* father pulled him out of school every single fall to work the harvest; so he was sixteen in the eighth grade and he finally just gave up. They were very bright people, they just had really disadvantaged backgrounds.

As best I could tell, my grandfather on my father's side was an acting-out sex addict. He would go to the barn and nail a calf if my grandmother wouldn't do what he wanted her to do. He would fondle her breasts in front of her children. He would moan and complain to the children about "Mamma won't give me any." So my father was raised around that. My grandfather was approached by the police when he was about seventy-three for hassling a thirteen-year-old girl. He also apparently got a lot with my grandmother—they had eleven children, five boys and six girls. She didn't have many options, but one day she packed up the oldest five or six kids and left. She didn't know where in the world to go and went back home. My father was the firstborn son of the eleven kids. Three of the younger ones behind him were very active alcoholics. My father was very, very controlled and rigid and didn't drink. He probably was a dry drunk. There was a lot of unhappiness in that family. On my mother's side, she was one of eight, fifth-born I believe, just a lost-in-the-shuffle daughter. My analysis is that about half of them are rageaholics and the other half are pacifists, and my mother was one of the pacifists. They were tenant farmers. She lived her life in denial, and clearly she denied what was going on with my sister and me. I was my father's main target most of my young years.

My father was always the Pied Piper around our neighborhood. He was so charming. I don't know how many kids he damaged. I know when I was eight, one of my cousins told me that he had approached her. I never

Karen Seal

told my mother. My recollection for many, many years was that he would want to have me touch him, fondle him, kiss him. He didn't really do much to me that I can remember until I was about twelve, when I was already old enough to have pubic hair and had begun menstruating. When I came home from school and he was there alone, it always scared the shit out of me. Anytime I was alone around him just really scared me. One day when I was twelve, I walked in, he was alone, and my heart was just beating: Oh, God, Dad's here alone. He asked me to get up on the counter, take off my panties, and spread my legs so he could look. I finally said, I don't like this. And he said, Oh, okay. Then I got really guilty about why I hadn't said no a long time before. My therapist thought that he probably was tired of me—he was a pedophile, a true, unadulterated pedophile. He also acted out with women. He was always at my mom, talking about sex, grabbing my mother's ass and whatever. He was really obsessed.

RICHARD RHODES: So his inspection that day confirmed that you were no longer a child.

KAREN SEAL: Yeah, what the heck, she's boring, right? I don't think there was ever intercourse, but I'm not sure.

My reaction to my father's molestation was to become a super good girl, a real prude. I dated my first husband three and a half years and we never had intercourse, and he was nearly seven years older. I was fifteen and he was twenty-one when we started dating, which was stupid. I married at nineteen, the first time. That lasted fourteen months. I wasn't sure I was a virgin, but I didn't know. I had so much memory loss about my childhood. I didn't remember my dad having intercourse with me. My hymen was clearly intact and the first time I had intercourse was difficult. I had thought the molestation began when I was about four or five. Later, under hypnosis, I had a recollection of being a baby and thinking my father's penis was a bottle. I also could see my hands with the little indented knuckles—you know how a baby's knuckles look, there were little dimples—and I had my hand on his penis thinking it was a bottle.

I didn't tell anybody about the molestation until I came to San Diego, when I was twenty-seven. I was hired by Grossmont College. I met a woman, an older woman, who became a sort of surrogate mom—she was one of my students even though she was twenty years older than I. One of my uncles, my mother's older brother Jerry, was also living here and this woman knew him. My higher self, or my soul or something, said, Tell her, because she'll tell Jerry, who will get the secret blown off this bullshit. So I told her, she told Jerry, he told my mother, and my mother was so angry with me: "How could you tell her that?" I thought, Jesus! So that was the only way it ever got confronted, and it never was directly from me to her.

GINGER RHODES: What kind of a relationship did you have with your father as an adult?

KAREN SEAL: It was quite cordial. Until Jerry passed the word, I thought I'd fooled my mom, I'd kept their marriage together. Because that was part of what I'm sure he threatened me with—"If you tell your mother, there's going to be a divorce and you're going to be on welfare, your mother can't earn a living and where'll you kids go?" I know that's the kind of stuff he told me. So I was probably feeling pretty proud of myself that I could tolerate his abuse and had kept the family together. It's a power trip. Plus, he was much more appreciative of my intelligence and charm and such than he was of hers. So we had a decent relationship.

But his second wife was a compulsive gambler. He had taken a cash settlement from his pension and when she finally convinced him to put her name on it, she gambled it away. He wound up at age sixty-six just about flat broke. So he went to Texas and bought a piece-of-poop kind of a house and hated it. He really wanted to come back to California. I needed a manager for a trailer park I was operating. I told him, I'll let you come back here—the only time I ever mentioned this to him, ever— I told him, I'll let you come back provided you never touch a child, because if you do touch a child, I'll throw your ass in jail. And he said, Oh, honey, I can't do that anymore. Besides, he said, that was no big deal. That was his response.

I was with both my parents, to the bitter end, as they breathed their last breath, and neither of them ever expressed any remorse.

David Ray, the Oklahoma-born poet, wrote extensively about his childhood in an essay for the Contemporary Authors Autobiography Series, *"Prolegomena to an Autobiography":*

DAVID RAY: Most of the time, my father seemed to have nothing to give us but his anger, which erupted violently. My memories of him are inseparable from my later efforts to find explanations. Yet I see him as trying very hard to establish a home. He must have been trapped by poverty and early loss. And since I came on the scene in the Depression— the day Amelia Earhart flew the Atlantic in May of 1932—and knew my grandfather Ray only in hard times, I was surprised not long ago to discover a portrait of my father's parents in the late twenties when they had been relatively prosperous. They are rather elegantly dressed, standing before their new touring car. Nineteen twenty-nine had wiped out what prosperity they had. . . .

The day my father left for good was one I have pondered repeatedly

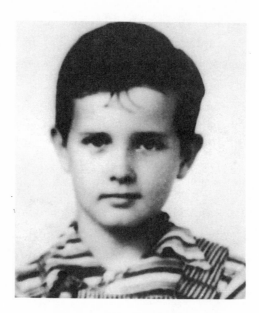

David Ray

over the years, trying to make sense of it, writing it out again and again. It must have been 1939, for I was in the second grade in Tulsa, where we had moved into a yellow two-story apartment building near the farmers' market area. After school in the still-sweltering heat of late summer, my mother would send me across vacant lots to fetch root beer from the drugstore soda fountain, carrying a milk bottle to be filled. The pharmacist would lean over his marble counter, handing down the milk bottle filled with bubbling root beer. But on the last of those afternoons he looked down at me oddly, and I saw that tucked between the bottle and his thumb was a folded note meant for my mother. I sensed instinctively that the note was from my father and that he was leaving us. He had chosen to leave a note at the soda fountain rather than face my mother. In effect, he had left me the dirty work. My mother was crushed, of course, and I felt my inadequacy in trying to comfort her. And my spasmodic attempts over the years to communicate with my father were never more productive than that afternoon. He was always mysterious and always rejecting, unable to give. He has been a void in my life, a great emptiness. The words of his note were unforgettable: "I got a ride on a watermelon truck, so am heading West."

That was not the last abandonment in David's life. Of a later period of childhood, his essay reports:

DAVID RAY: This time we had run out of foster homes, so we were made wards of the court and placed in the Children's Home, an institution in Tulsa for orphans and "dependent" children—a U-shaped brick building where girls slept in one dormitory wing and boys another. The fenced playground was segregated by sexes (segregation by race had already been attended to); friends and siblings communicated by touching through a wire-net fence (and were whipped by the matrons when caught); official visits were confined to a half-hour's play period in the front yard after dinner.

In poems as clear-eyed as a hungry child, David has reported how the neglect and abuse he experienced in childhood felt:

Captives

The day Sis and I were taken
to the orphanage in the back seat
of a social worker's car

we looked through the rolled-up window
as if at another world—
the one being left, unreachable.

We touched that window—I on my side,
she on hers, under the useless
straps for a hand to grab.

Suddenly a boy on a bike appeared
by the roadside—my friend Johnny,
with his pet monkey on his back.

He glumly stared at us, then waved,
and I could not understand for years
why Johnny could ride that bike

and play with that monkey
which he most of the time kept chained
in a tree while Sis and I

were being taken away
as captives to a place beyond
the town. There by the road

Johnny reared up on his bike,
balanced on its back wheel,
then returned to earth

and rode beside the car,
dropping back like a dog
outrun. Our days as playmates

were over—stealing those pennies
his parents kept in a pickle jar
under the kitchen sink,

crawling on hands and knees
through tunnels and culverts,
kidnapping a coyote pup

out of his nest. Even then,
looking back at my friend,
I knew that the place we were going

would be as bad as we feared, and worse.
And yet the black iron gates opened
as if by magic and the car

rolled through with a bounce
over a hump, and the pretense was made
that we were being rescued.

My sister was led off to one wing
of the building, I to another.
When I pass such places now

that I too am one of the grownups,
I cannot even slow to bless
those children inside, still captive.

And I cannot be fooled by kindness.
Love is not quick to grow
in the simmering crucible of doubt

and I know that survival is everything
and nothing—that the matrons
and guards on that vast estate

did not have as much of our fates
in their hands as they thought,
as they threatened. We need not

have feared them half so much,
nor wept through the night.
They had no electric chair

in the basement, no rope
that would hold
our scrawny necks.

And they are dead by now
like the big bad wolf.
And the pigs are dancing.

In our interview, in his home in Kansas City, Missouri, David told us:

DAVID RAY: The orphanage was called the Children's Home. I think it's no longer there, on the west side of Tulsa. One of the tough things for me was the segregation. The boys and the girls were kept in opposite wings and there was a fence between the playgrounds. That was tough. I would lie there at night crying and wondering why my mother wouldn't come on visiting days most of the time. She very rarely came on Sunday. I was really feeling abandoned and then she showed up with one of her boyfriends and said she was taking us back to live with her. This is the pattern as I see it that I'm stuck with, this emotional roller-coaster of rescue—here's an opportunity, here's rescue, and then some kind of disillusionment or new betrayal.

We were there only a few months. It would be interesting to check that but I think we were only there five or six months. I'm not sure because a lot of things were so intense that they seemed longer. But I think in actual fact it probably wasn't very long. With the foster homes, we were always moving, always a different school. The first five grades, I think we were in at least seven different schools.

David carries his story forward to adolescence in his "Prolegomena to an Autobiography." Seeming rescue then led to further abuse:

When I was fifteen, yet another arrangement was made for my care. I had, it seems, caught the attention of a visitor to our church-basement Boy Scout meetings. When he learned that I had asthma badly and that the doctor had recommended a dry climate, he came forward with an offer to give me a home on his Arizona ranch. My mother gave her permission, and I left for Arizona with this wealthy man, just back from infantry service in World War II. By that time, my stepfather was regularly threatening suicide and my mother, unable to deal with him, sent my sister to talk him out of his gun. I witnessed this scene on several occasions, enraged and powerless.

In Arizona, my physical health improved remarkably—with an unbelievable weight and height gain, even in the first month away from Oklahoma. But this new arrangement had its price too. Though the wealthy man who took me to Arizona offered to adopt me and make me his heir if I would only prove my Honesty and Loyalty and Obedience (all terms he used as if capped) by doing everything he told me to, his generosity exacted the price of both physical and mental abuse, for he engaged in a form of brainwashing—insisting on my telling him my every thought. And though he never acknowledged himself as a homosexual and in fact reacted violently at the suggestion that he might be, the cost for refusing to sleep with him was both physical assault and humiliation.

3

"Murder of the Body or the Soul"

Despite the many differences in their backgrounds, the survivors we interviewed reported strikingly parallel experiences of abuse. Do abusers learn their brutal trade at some secret school? Dysfunctional families, torturers, governments that rule by terror, all evolve similar techniques for abusing human beings, and there is nothing in the worst reports out of Nazi Germany or the Argentina of the "dirty war" that hasn't been duplicated at more intimate scale somewhere within a family. The unanswered question is whether the family is the secret school of abuse, the crucible where even Hitler and Stalin learned their cruelties. The brutalities our survivors report, small and large, give cause to believe it may be.

Louise Hill's family woke early in its triple-decker row house in Boston:

LOUISE HILL: Another bad thing was to be sick or stay in bed late. You could not be sick. It was like the army. Six o'clock in the morning, everybody up, rise and shine! Maybe it was the immigrant sensibility— You'd better go out there and grab the day. To this day I can't sleep in. I think sleeping to eight o'clock in the morning is sleeping in. But the larger problem is being ill. You weren't allowed to be ill. If you were sick, my mother would say, It's in your head. You're not *sick,* you just *get out of bed.* This abuse, this maltreatment, this poor treatment, this degrading treatment, really continued into adulthood.

When you're over sixteen you couldn't have the physical abuse, but I didn't understand until recently that this mental abuse, this verbal abuse, continued into adulthood—I didn't understand what damage it did. At one point, I was pregnant with my third child and my other children were two and three. I was only twenty-four. My husband was in the army—he was a doctor—and couldn't come home in time for my delivery. So I had to come back to my mother's home and be there, which is a difficult position for anybody.

I had one week before delivery and I was sleeping on the sofa bed in the little study she had. I must have been frightened or depressed, because

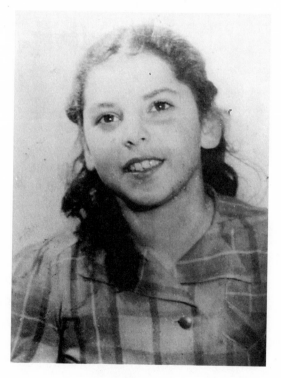

Louise Hill

I felt sick. I just felt sick to my stomach. The gynecologist said it was probably—I'd come from a long distance—maybe it was jet lag, maybe it was the pregnancy. But I remember begging my mother not to go to work that week, begging her to please stay home with me. I was frightened to stay home alone. It was too much for me. Now, I knew she needed the money and it was very important. But I said, Please, just one day. She said, No, I have to go to work.

No matter how important money was to her, I find that very cruel, it was a terrible abandonment. Another instance that left one of the worst impressions on me, as much as anything in childhood. In between the sense of humor and adventure that was going on in childhood there was a constant reign of terror. The scenes that you remember—bleeding and no one wanting to come to your rescue, yelling at you, *What's the matter with you, don't you have any friends?* But what continued into adulthood had just such an effect.

I was twenty-one when I was pregnant with my first child. My husband was an intern at that time and we could only afford this very horrible apartment that was at the back of an apartment building and had rodents and so forth. It was really unpleasant. I went to the hospital to deliver my baby and my husband brought me back to the apartment but he had to go back to work because he was on duty that weekend. Now I wonder why he didn't exchange, but that's another story for another day. Today, we're talking about parents and abandonment and abuse. My mother was to come over to help me because I couldn't afford help. So there I was, a young girl with my first baby, alone in this rather dreadful apartment, and my mother came over with my sister, who was then in high school, nine years' difference between us. My mother helped me out for a couple of hours and then it started to get dark. And my mother said now she had to go home to her own house with my sister because my sister had homework to do. I remember getting on my hands and knees and crying and begging her to stay. I said, *Please, Ma, please, Ma, please stay. I don't want to stay alone.* She said, There's nothing I can do, I have to go.

I will tell you, that's about one of the worst moments I ever had in my whole life.

Menninger Clinic psychotherapist Susan Voorhees explored with us the distinction she tries to help parents draw between physical punishment and abuse; to us as to Susan, the line often seemed invisible:

SUSAN VOORHEES: When does abuse become abuse? I think there are two main determinants. One is when the person *experiences* the behavior as abusive. The other is when the behavior has a negative impact on the person's capacity to function. For instance, with emotional behavior, when a kid is constantly called names or put down or belittled and that begins to have impact on her capacity to learn, or to grow, or to get on with her life, then it's abuse.

We all say things we wish we hadn't said to our kids, but most people are either able to apologize and back off from that negative statement, or to realize that that wasn't the right thing to say. And then somehow to do something to repair the mistake, or maybe it isn't the important part of their relationship with the kid. A child may get used to a parent talking about their "damn toys all over the place," and know in the context of the relationship that that's the way mommy or daddy talks. Not that they don't like the kid's toys or they don't like the kid for having the toys. There's more to the relationship, so the statement may not be an abusive statement. Whereas in another situation, where there isn't an emotional fabric to the relationship, where there is a coldness or an aloofness or a distance, and that's what the child hears—"your damn toys are always on the floor"—that becomes then a statement about the child, because the toys belong to the child. So that's a differentiation.

In terms of physical abuse, what's a swat on the butt and what's abuse? Well, there are some real camps here. There are a lot of people who don't believe in physical punishment or physical discipline in any way. Other people say it's okay. For me, one clear definer is: There should never be a mark left on a child. If you hit a child hard enough to leave any kind of mark, you've hit too hard. Now, I don't personally believe in hitting, so I don't like any form of physical punishment. But it's very hard to say to some parents, You can't hit your child, because some parents can't *not* do that and some children can't respond except to some direct method.

But there's a real difference between swatting a baby on the butt that's covered with diapers and hitting a child on the leg or the arm or the head. That's the other distinction. What a parent may call "physical discipline"—where on the child's body was it administered and with what? You should never need an implement, you should never need to hit a kid on the head. And is the punishment appropriate to the crime that the child has committed? If a two-year-old has a potty accident, is it really appropriate to burn her with a cigarette? No.

In his essay "Prolegomena to an Autobiography," David Ray writes:

DAVID RAY: In this orphanage where . . . non-orphans were at the bottom of the pecking order, the matrons were as spiteful as witches in a fairy tale. I remember being beaten in the basement by one of them for "sassing," and whipped more than once for fighting with Donald, an archenemy; we fought each other in the boys' playground by running toward each other with lowered heads. In [*his poem*] "Donald's Apple," I describe my jealousy of his regular Sunday visits from his only living relative, his fat grandmother, who brought him an apple, symbol of her love and her poverty, all she could afford. Through the long afternoon visiting hours on Sundays I remember vainly waiting for my name to be called. There was a very special form of humiliation involved in being one of those who continued to sit on the dormitory floor or foolishly searched the driveway from the bathroom window after the names of all those who had visitors had been called out. At last one was left with no companions but the rejected and despised. Those who had any spunk left made up excuses for those who had forgotten them or disappeared from their lives.

At the lower end of the spectrum of violence, neglect shades into abuse, Menninger teaching therapist Alice Brand Bartlett told us:

ALICE BRAND BARTLETT: I include all types of abuse—emotional abuse, sexual abuse, and physical abuse—when I teach. There are also people who just can't parent. They're too busy and absent. There is not enough of a relationship for the child to hold on to. That's emotional deprivation, but certainly it's also abuse.

RICHARD RHODES: That raises the question of where you draw the line. When does the level of punishment that many Americans have assumed to be "normal" become child abuse? If you really don't believe that children should be hit, then spanking is abuse, isn't it? Or am I stretching the point?

ALICE BRAND BARTLETT: I'll stretch it even farther: If you think of the way many men are raised in society—not to be able to express their feelings, proving their manhood through aggression and sexuality—then isn't society creating abusers by the way it socializes men?

✤

LOUISE HILL: I can't think of any positive reinforcement at all. It makes me very sad to say that. I weigh things enough to understand the good things that went on. But I cannot remember any positive reinforcement until I announced that I was going to marry a doctor. I do believe that was the first positive reinforcement that I had. Marrying a doctor was a good thing.

John Wood and Celia Golden remember halters and restraints:

JOHN WOOD: I was haltered as a child, a halter and leash. Which most people assume is innocent. It is not innocent. It is absolutely child abuse. It's the same as a child being taken by the wrist, like this [*demonstrating a severe grip*]. If you want to know what that feels like, have somebody do it to you, grab you by the wrist. See, if the two hands—the parent's and the child's—clasp, there's interaction. If it's one hand gripping, it gets the child to understand, unmistakably and perfectly clearly, that they have no soul, that they're not a human, they're a thing. It's the same with the halter.

RICHARD RHODES: Maybe the halter even more because it says—

JOHN WOOD: Doggy. Yeah. An animal.

✦

CELIA GOLDEN: The winters get cold where I grew up. I remember one day when I was in high school that it was fourteen degrees below zero. But when we were small children my mother would put my brother and me outside and then lock the door and we weren't supposed to cry. I can remember my older sister coming home for lunch and my mom would decide my brother and I could come in. Sometimes it would just be me out there and then I could come in and eat. But I'd have to go back outside when my sister went back to school. So I had all this time by myself or just with my brother. I remember my mother tying my brother and me to the fence in the summer. I learned how to untie the rope and would push my brother over this picket fence. But she caught us and then put this dog collar around me. So we learned about how to live within her rules.

I have clear memories of my mother tying my arms and hands down to the high chair, and tying down my legs so I couldn't kick. She wrapped a tea towel around my neck, tying me back. I remember it being too tight to swallow. You start gagging on food, it goes up your nose and you can't breathe and you're choking. You can't even cry. I remember my mouth being cut and her hitting me in the face, poking my head and my face with a fork.

✦

LOUISE HILL: When my sister was born I started to wet the bed. Now, we don't have to be a rocket scientist to figure that out. I was nine years old. But my mother would ridicule me for wetting the bed and she would drag the mattress to the back porch to air it out, and then she would make fun of me. She would say, Now it's out there for all the people to see. The whole family would mock me. They'd say a word to me in

Yiddish—*pisher,* a very derogatory word which means someone who pees in their bed. When my mother was in the hospital with a ruptured disk, the whole family would say, See, Louise, you did that because your mother had to drag that heavy mattress.

The punishments Valorie Butler's aunt inflicted extended beyond standing on the stairs:

VALORIE BUTLER: Long hair was a big deal to me when I was a teenager. My sisters and I were very skinny, and I felt like the long hair helped out. You know, teenagers and their self-esteem. One day I trimmed my bangs. I was not supposed to do that—my aunt was to do it, not me. Actually, I snipped a little piece here and a little piece there and that was about it. To this day I do not know which one of my sisters told on me. My aunt's punishment was to cut my hair off. It was just really ugly. She cut my long hair above the ears on the sides. That was really humiliating.

❖

DAVID RAY: Verbal abuse is terribly destructive, no matter how casually rendered. Ridicule was always such hell in childhood. One time, when I was staying with my Aunt Edris and Uncle Henry, I was going on about Superman. Uncle Henry resented our being around. I said, I'm Superman, and he said, Well, I know about the soup, but I don't know about the man. It just crushed me. He used to throw firecrackers at me. When we would drive across a bridge, he'd say, Let's throw David off. All very, very funny and not funny at all.

❖

LOUISE HILL: As a child I was extremely lively, very outspoken and got bored easily. Those are still my character traits, and I see now that they're part of who I am. My mother would say, very deprecatingly, You always need a three-ring circus. As though it was a bad thing. Now I can say I do need a three-ring circus and in fact my life *is* a three-ring circus. So that everything that I was seemed an affront in that particular household.

She would say, You and your big mouth. That was the biggest problem in the house—You and your big mouth, your big mouth. She was always washing out my mouth with soap and water.

RICHARD RHODES: Literally?

LOUISE HILL: Literally with soap and water. I don't know what I could have said. I certainly didn't know words like *fuck* or *shit*. Having a big mouth was when I answered her back. When she said something and I gave my own opinion, that was having a big mouth. There was a list of things in my house that were bad. They contributed towards being a Bad Girl. And for being a Bad Girl you either got beat up by my mother or you were screamed at and ridiculed. One of them was for having a big mouth. Another one was for telling stories. She said, If you don't stop making up those stories, Louise, you're going to get punished. Well, I probably was an exaggerator. Probably if I saw a cat I might have said I saw ten cats, because it made a better story. And now I make my living telling stories.

❖

JOHN WOOD: I went to Danbury State College, before it became Western Connecticut State College. My ancestors went to Yale and Harvard and Princeton and Dartmouth. All the Ivy colleges. I'm pissed off that I was denied that. I was never encouraged to do anything. I was called "silly little boy," "stupid little boy."

GINGER RHODES: By your mother?

JOHN WOOD: My mother and father both. My father called me "stupid little boy." My mother said, Don't be silly, you can't do that.

❖

LOUISE HILL: I lost my coat once. We were very poor and I had a new spring coat. I took it to the movies with me, to the Oriental movie—stars on the ceiling, by the way. We would change seats back and forth when we got into junior high because we were trying to attract certain boys. The girls would change seats to be near the boys and in all this changing of seats I lost my coat. When the movie was over I couldn't find it. I was so terrified, so terrified of my mother's anger, so scared.

I told her I lost the coat and I remember the screaming and the yelling and the shouting. Then I did a little creative storytelling. I said, Well, a lot of people lost their coats that day.

So even when I was grown, even when I was forty-five, fifty years old, when I would say, Oh, but everybody, everybody does that nowadays, Mother, she would say, Oh, sure, like everybody lost their coat.

I still get terrified when I lose something. In fact, my husband has just given me a beautiful ring with a sapphire in it for our fifteenth wedding anniversary and yesterday I was walking and discovered that the new stone had fallen out. I was panicked. I came to my office, a grown woman, chair of a university department, and I had to close the door and started to cry and empty out my bag, called a friend to help me find it. I called my husband. He said, It's all right, it's all right. He said, The ring is insured, it's only a ring, we'll find the stone. We'll have another stone. Very fortunately I found it in my bag, but I was panicked. [*To herself:*] It's all right, it's all right if you lost the coat. You don't have to say that everybody lost it. It's not your fault. You didn't do anything bad.

[*Looking up:*] It's something I have to keep repeating.

Editor Michael Davies found a way to limit his father's escalation to violence by giving him the company his drunken loneliness craved:

MICHAEL DAVIES: My father and my older brother, Chuck, got into fistfights.

RICHARD RHODES: Was your brother trying to protect your mother?

MICHAEL DAVIES: He may have sometimes. I don't remember enough to recall. He ran away once or twice.

RICHARD RHODES: Did your father hit you?

MICHAEL DAVIES: I don't remember much. When it came my turn to interact with my father, I don't know why exactly, but we would talk. I mean, he would sit me down at the kitchen table. I would be at one end, he would be at the other. He'd have a drink and he'd have a cigarette pack, and he would be smoking. And, he had this kind of unfocused, bleary, suspicious look in his eye. And he would start grilling me. I guess it was when I got into my early teens. He kept looking for a way to get me into a physical fight. And, maybe because of what I had seen happening to my brother, and also because of my disposition, I refused to play into that. I'd seen so much conflict growing up that what I wanted most of all was peace. [A long pause] Which was hard to come by. At an early age, I think that what I wanted most was for it to stop.

On the bright side, later—this was mainly in my teens—when I would sit down, we would start at ten or eleven o'clock at night and we would go until about five in the morning. That meant he wasn't beating up on my mother.

RICHARD RHODES: You'd sit up all night with him.

MICHAEL DAVIES: Yeah. It was like trying to close a conversation with somebody you don't want to talk to—they don't quit. My clue that the conversation was going to continue was every time he lit another cigarette, that meant at least another ten minutes that we would have to talk. I got to where I really just wanted to hide the cigarettes. The older I got the more intense it got.

❖

LOUISE HILL: It wasn't just my mother. It was her whole family. Her family was all very hard-edged, very bitter, not very warm. Anybody to this day that's hard-edged like that, I have such trouble with because it reminds me of them. There was abuse from the whole family. My uncle would yell at me—You bad girl, you no-good girl, bad girl. I was the fault of everything. There wasn't anything that I did that was right.

Skye Smith gives voice to her childhood experience in ironic private poems:

Shame on You

Shame on you
you ugly bore
to think you're great;
expect much more

than serves you right
for all you did
to wreck your home—
your mother's bid

to have a life
all of her own
with her crown prince
all hers alone.

You entered life
and ruined the nest
your mother sought
and gave her best.

So shame on you
I hope you dwell
on what you did
to ruin that belle.

✦

MICHAEL DAVIES: I would be upstairs. It was like the Emergency programs when people in trouble call 911, trying to get help, explaining
what's happening to them, that's being recorded—but while the 911
people are trying to make some sense out of the call and get help to
wherever the location is, in the meantime these terrible things happen.
Someone gets killed or knifed or something. That's the kind of helplessness I felt as a child listening to my mother pleading with my father not
to hit her or to hurt her. Suddenly there would be a stillness in the middle
of all that pleading and then there would be this huge, repeated scream.

I just remember feeling terrified, and ashamed because I couldn't help. I kept praying that it would end. I wanted to call the cops, kill him, run away, disappear. But we'd been taught to be terrified of the outside world. I mean, where are we going to go? The world was supposed to be a terrible place. We felt there was no place to go. And also, we didn't want anybody to know. Too much shame. We couldn't ask for help because if we asked for help people would know what was going on.

Once, when I was in my teens and he was on another one of his rampages—this was in the middle of the day, he'd started early on a Saturday—I came in and he had his own mother down on the floor. He grabbed her hair and he was shoving her down and grabbing her. My mom was trying to get him to stop—everybody was trying to get him to stop. I just blew up and I shouted over and over again, *Leave her alone, leave her alone,* and he suddenly realized that I was shouting at him, and like a bull who's just seen a red flag, all of a sudden, he took off after me. In a lumbering fashion, he was overweight. I just ran out of the house and ran over to a park, climbed up in a tree and just stayed there until it got dark and my sisters came looking for me.

❧

DAVID RAY: My mother was with violent men. A series of them. Some of my earliest memories are of my father beating his mule and the mule running away one day. I think there was something in me that thought, he's going to get mad enough, he's going to do the same thing to me. So when he was whipping me with his razor strap, I must have been absolutely terrified.

There's real guilt as well. Like, not protecting my sister. She went through a lot.

I was twelve months older. We both wound up abused as teenagers. But I left. I left with my so-called benefactor. I still feel guilty that I didn't stay and protect my sister. In actual fact, if I had—this never occurred to me until a psychologist suggested it, many years later—I would have been killed. My stepfather probably would have killed me. Because he was totally infatuated with my sister starting when she was about twelve. Before I left, it had progressed to the point where he was waving a pistol around almost daily and threatening to kill himself. My mother couldn't deal with it, so she would send my sister to talk him out of the gun. I would watch these scenes, and you can imagine how tempted a kid is to interfere—to argue. Well, all I would have had to do was to step into that. After I went to Arizona, this thing played itself out, and he did kill himself. He killed himself in front of my mother and sister.

✤

CELIA GOLDEN: We were each abused in different ways and to different degrees in my family. I was the most severely abused. My younger brother was the most physically abused by my father, until he was about eleven.

Ralph Kessler, the retired proofreader, recalls his stepfather's violence escalating—a regression usually inevitable when no one intervenes:

RALPH KESSLER: Early in 1932 we moved to Jersey City, New Jersey, near the embroidery mills. My stepfather was an embroidery designer. The living room of our apartment was converted to a beauty parlor. My mother learned the beautician's trade before her marriage as an ace in the hole to her occupation of waitressing.

He made perfumed business cards advertising their beauty parlor and I was instructed to give them out from house to house, knocking on doors and if no one was home to slip them under the door or to put them in the mailbox. While doing this, I was met by some older youths who stopped me, examined the cards, smelled them, and then promptly took them away from me—all of them.

I came home and told my stepfather what had happened. He then took the belt out of his pants and began hitting me across my legs, and the pain was greater because I could not understand what I had done wrong. . . .

We moved in spring 1933 to Emerson, New Jersey, a small town in Bergen County where my parents had bought a nightclub which they

Ralph Kessler (with his older uncle)

named "Gypsy Sonia's." Prohibition was ending and they probably thought that this business would be profitable. They hired Russian musicians and entertainers. My mother sang and emceed. They went bankrupt that summer.

I no longer remember why I was beaten by him but I just remember being taken down to the basement to be whipped. Now he ordered me to drop my pants and the beatings were harder. Our home was a business and I suppose taking me down to the basement was meant to spare the other people from the sounds of my screaming. I remember once after a beating crawling into our dog kennel and hugging our dog and my stepfather laughing at me for it.

That summer, I went with other kids to a swimming hole nearby where we all jumped in naked. Suddenly, the other kids pointed to my backside, full of strap marks. I never went swimming again. The same thing happened in school physical training class. The other kids and the teacher saw my whipping marks at gym.

Violence isolated them, Alexa Donath and Barbara Hamilton report:

ALEXA DONATH: One of my earliest memories—I really do remember it—was in nursery school in temple. I don't remember what happened, but I remember I was hurt. I have this in my head just like a movie playing. The teacher kept saying, What's wrong, what's wrong, what's wrong, and I wouldn't tell her. This first time, I think she called me into the rabbi's office because I was so upset. I remember that memory. I remember being in eighth grade and having blood marks all up and down my arm. My mother had very long nails. It was winter, so my arms were covered up. I remember looking around at all the other kids and thinking, I'm different from anybody else in this class. I'm different and they don't know it.

❖

BARBARA HAMILTON: The emotional essence of incest is to feel oneself becoming spoiled to the core and powerless to stop it. I don't know how you spent your childhood, but I spent my childhood feeling guilty, dirty, and ashamed.

❖

SKYE SMITH: There were very rigid but expanding rules. One time I was in fourth grade, I guess my stepfather needed to hit me. I was reading Ann Landers. Oh, that's transgressible, that's a whipping right there, you're not supposed to read Ann Landers. But I didn't know that. One time I was in the middle of an art project and he said, Come here, and I said, Just a minute, and I got whipped for that. Because, Don't you ever say "just a minute"—that's a new rule. The rules changed. It was a fixed game here, you weren't going to win.

I remember once when I was three, I wouldn't eat canned beets. My mother yanked me out of the chair and threw me into the bathroom on the linoleum floor. I hit my head on the tub. Followed by a beating with a belt, a major beating. Then I was told, Get back to the table and eat those beets *now*. You *will* eat those beets. That was dinner—constant, joyless, somber, serious.

❖

ALEXA DONATH: My mother would hit, scream, beat me with her high-heeled shoes, with hangers. Oh yeah, she was creative.

RICHARD RHODES: Did she give you reasons for beating you?

ALEXA DONATH: My father was away five days out of the week. She would often say, I have to do this all alone, I have to do this all alone.

❖

LOUISE HILL: I can't remember much before the age of five or six, truly. But I do remember from early on that my mother was always putting me down. I recently said to some friends, Well, she wasn't physically abusive all the time. I didn't get beat every day.

I can't tell you how many times I was beat up. We lived in a railroad-track apartment, which means one room after the other, and she would chase me. I would keep backing away and the furthest room back was my own back bedroom. I finally backed myself into my bedroom, then against the furthest window and then there was no place to go. And she would slap me. How often it happened I can't tell you except that it happened many times. I do remember being beat up, my face bloodied, sitting outside on the back stairs—we had a front stairs and a back stairs—and bleeding and crying and going upstairs to ask my aunt or my grandmother for some solace. They said, You're a bad girl, you're aggravating your mother. So I had no ally in the family. I wondered so much what it was that I did that was so bad. I'm still trying to figure out what I did that was so bad.

RICHARD RHODES: When you say you were bloody, that sounds like more than slapping.

LOUISE HILL: Punching me with her fists, pulling my hair, pulling my hair, pulling my hair, pulling my hair, punching me again and again and again and again.

❖

DAVID RAY: In Arizona I fell in love with this girl, Ann. It was very intense. My Arizona savior would let me take the car and go out on a date. But then he would grill me about what happened. So we would go out and have a perfectly wonderful evening, and then he would be waiting up to hear the car arrive. One time, he started grilling me, What did you do, where did you go? We had gone to this movie: What was the movie about? Where did you drive? What did you do? You kissed her, didn't you? You French-kissed her, didn't you? You felt her tits, didn't you? No. So I start lying, to protect this intimacy that had been very beautiful. Now mind you, by this time, I think he had his belt in his hand, and he said, Come on. Here it is, the middle of the night, we go out to the car. *Get in.* He's furious. *Get in.* Incidentally, he had these Lugers around, he had a lot of guns around. So I had to drive, redo the evening. He had checked the odometer even before he had started confronting me. So I drove to the movie theater and drove up this little mountain outside Tucson where there's a parking lot, a lover's heights. Well, he wound up beating the shit out of me where I had been with the girl two or three hours earlier. And the threat—If you ever try to lie to me again . . . I don't know if he actually said, I'll kill you, but the threat was there. Try to keep anything normal alive under those circumstances.

Abusers escalate their violence in pursuit of control, too panicked or seduced to realize that violence alone can never bring victims under complete control, short of death:

VALORIE BUTLER: We didn't start standing on the stairs until we moved to a different house. Before, we might have to go to bed after supper for fighting over a washcloth or whatever. But this house had an upstairs and a downstairs. That's when the standing on the stairs started. Weeks of punishment. It was like you were never done with it. Something else would come up to add on. The punishments were way too long and too unfair for the crime, so to speak.

I guess the relationship between my aunt and uncle is what escalated my aunt's fury. She could just be absolutely a monster over triviality. Our crimes weren't even anything quote "right or wrong."

You had no freedoms. We weren't free to *be*. They squashed our innermost person. Like I was artistic, and those things were taken away.

GINGER RHODES: "Those things" meaning art supplies?

VALORIE BUTLER: Yes. I should have . . . [*She begins crying.*] I can always boo hoo.

GINGER RHODES: We cry.

VALORIE BUTLER: I'm not comfortable with it, though.

GINGER RHODES: It took me a long time to learn how to cry again.

VALORIE BUTLER: The things she did to us were just ungodly. A girl-friend of mine in school wanted me to call her mother and let her know that she was going to stay after. She didn't have a dime to make the call. I thought, no big deal, I'll ask permission to call her. But when I got home, my aunt and uncle were out. Just my siblings were there. The phone was off the hook. That is what they did to keep people from calling. They lived in a fearful world. They would say, People are nothing but trouble. That was how they perceived the world. They didn't do too many social things. They would take the phone off the hook just to keep people from calling, just to block them out.

So I'm thinking, I see the phone off the hook and I need to call this girl's mother. If she's not called, the girl's going to be in trouble, and this is my best friend in school. So I thought, I'll call her and then put the phone back off the hook, no big deal. Well, my sisters are saying you better not do that. We all ratted on one another because we wanted to be on my aunt's good side. The morale was destroyed between us, to be in her good graces and to get a privilege. Get you off the step, maybe, instead of staying the fourteen hours—after a few hours you might get off the step. So anyway, when they got home my uncle immediately asked me to go to the store with him. When I came back, this enraged woman was at the door and she grabbed me by the hair and just dragged me across the floor by the hair and just literally beat me. For using the phone.

❖

CELIA GOLDEN: I have this memory of my mother calling me in to give me a bath. My younger sister was already in the bathtub. That wasn't unusual; my sister often had my mother's attention or was treated with special care. I always thought that there's hope that maybe my mother will someday want me, maybe I'll feel special, like maybe the worm has turned. Which is a great analogy, because that's my symbol for my mother. I have a real phobia about worms. Nothing scares me as much as worms. It's always been that way.

My mom would get this look on her face. I can't put words to it, but I remember that look. It was her crazy mode, the beware mode. I remember her turning my sister so that her back was to me, so she couldn't see what my mother was doing. Then I remember my mother getting my sister out and putting her to bed. I was sitting there real anxious, knowing that nothing good was going to come out of it. I was cold, and I was being ignored, yet I knew I couldn't do anything.

I remember her doing stuff to me in the tub and then taking me into a bedroom and laying me on the floor. My whole image of myself is like looking down at me, but it's more like I'm a shell. I wrote this piece about a dead bird that's my analogy for that whole thing, where it was as though I didn't exist. I'm no more real than the tile on the floor. I don't have any feeling or consciousness and it's like I remember seeing my mother's eyes and I'm gone. The analogy with the dead bird is that the dead bird doesn't feel anything when the maggots are eating it. Worms. *Sssssss*—worms are silent.

◈

JOHN WOOD: Apparently, the abuse started when I was an infant and the reason I say that is one of the pictures that I've had in my brain forever—I can't overstate the importance of saying that I have pictures in my mind. Sometimes I have a picture of a person or a thing or whatever and the word won't come for a while, I fumble for words. So I have a picture in my mind that I've had for many, many years of a little baby boy on its back with an erection and a hand flicking the erection, the erect penis. I used to think why did that come into my head, you know, what the hell is that all about? I used to wonder. Now I know, that's me, preverbal me.

RICHARD RHODES: And that flicking hand?

JOHN WOOD: I don't know. It could be a nanny. It could be my mother. It could be my fa— it could be anybody. I don't know. My mother had thick, ugly hands, so, it could be her. It could be anybody. It's a hand as big as my adult hand, so it could be my father, could be anybody. I don't know. That'll come to me sometime.

RICHARD RHODES: It sounds like the physical embodiment of the phrase "sex reared its ugly head."

JOHN WOOD: Yeah, it does.

California businesswoman Karen Seal's experience with her father's mo-lestation demonstrates a commonplace of sexual abuse: that the abuser knows his behavior is criminal:

KAREN SEAL: As far as I can remember, my father never tried to stim-ulate me. I wasn't beaten and I wasn't raped. There was never intercourse. He probably didn't know a woman could respond or he didn't give a rat's ass. I feel so fortunate, because I know so many women and men who were abused as children by being stimulated to orgasm by some adult, and then they hate their own bodies for responding. I feel so much gratitude that he didn't do anything like that to me, so far as I know. In fact, I'm really pretty certain of that, because when I first had an orgasm, I wondered what the hell was going on. I didn't even know it could occur, I hadn't even read about it. I think I would have remembered that feeling.

So my reaction to my father's molestation was just disgust, and revulsion, and fear. I remember that his penis was so big, you know, a little bitty girl, it just looked huge. My brother's was small and pink and didn't have hair, but his, oh, it was just scary, it was so scary.

RICHARD RHODES: Disgust and revulsion because you sensed that this was wrong?

KAREN SEAL: Absolutely, and I know the reason I knew it was wrong—because he told me from the very beginning, This is our secret, don't tell anybody. A kid can pick that up. Shameless, he was completely shameless.

❖

JOHN WOOD: The first thing I remembered about my mother's sexual abuse was a seduction. I was nine years old and my father had a heart attack. I came in from the pool and went upstairs. My mother was in her bedroom, my room was on the right. It was late afternoon. She called me into her room, and she was sitting on a chaise longue, sitting on the arm of the chair, naked. I had my bathing suit on when I went into her room and she pulled me up to her like this and put her hands in my—boy, it's hard to relive it—put her hands in my bathing suit and pushed my bathing suit down and of course I had an instant erection. She just pulled me into her, manipulated my penis into her vagina. That's really all I remember of it.

❖

SKYE SMITH: When I was sixteen, my mother forced me to go on a business trip with my stepfather. I never really understood why she wanted me to go with him on this overnight business trip. In the car he does the birds-and-bees lecture, I guess as a warm-up. I was really still so naive, I didn't know what he was leading up to. That night we have dinner out and we never went out to dinner, so it was kind of a big deal. When we got to our room, he gets in bed with me, two hundred miles from our house on a business trip. He was clearly intending to rape me. He started fondling me and I remember being just sickened, just sick inside. I thought, this isn't supposed to work out this way, this is wrong. I started feeling my rage, my full sixteen years of rage, and whatever he sensed from me, he got off of me. I would have killed him, no question. When you get that much bottled-up hatred and rage, somebody is going to get hurt. Then I got to live with him for two more years, no eye contact and never, never referring to this incident, just burying it.

RICHARD RHODES: You never having eye contact or he never having eye contact?

SKYE SMITH: The two of us not. Well, how would I know? I never looked at him, couldn't stand him.

RICHARD RHODES: Was that to avoid dealing with him?

SKYE SMITH: Yeah, he was so repulsive to me, so absolutely repulsive.

RICHARD RHODES: It wasn't shame or guilt?

SKYE SMITH: Probably some of that too, it's complicated. Why did he do that? Was there something about me? From that point on he began calling me a bitch, a whore, and a slut. He was always asking if I was a virgin. I was a high school junior, and he wanted me to break up with my boyfriend, Dave—"You've got to break up with Dave"—constantly. I guess he wanted me and was jealous. It was sick. It was disgusting.

Many survivors report attempts by their abusers to control their bodily functions:

RALPH KESSLER: My first memory of my stepfather, Irving, was the first night when he told me that I had to move my bowels before I went to bed because it was healthier that way. I tried and tried and nothing. I told him. He said to go back and stay on the toilet until I did. I suffered trying, like no suffering of that kind, but nothing came out. I so much wanted to please my new father and I strained my body to the point that I still can remember it. Just as one cannot forbid natural functions, one cannot command them. Eventually I was allowed to go to bed suffering his displeasure.

In later years my mother told me that, observing how he treated me, she decided that he was "a little peculiar" and took precautions not to have a child with him. I thought silently: You protected yourself but not me.

✤

VALORIE BUTLER: When we stood on the stairs, we just basically did without water unless it was at mealtime. We had to ask permission to go to the bathroom. Of course, then she felt like we were asking just to sit down. We called our body functions number one and number two, so she'd ask which you had to do. One time in particular I really had to go, and when I did ask it wasn't just to sit down. It was probably just a couple times a day, I imagine, with not much water anyway. So this particular time she said, I don't want you to flush the toilet. She was going to check to make sure I went. Well, I had to go, but when I got in there I really got uptight. This is kind of graphic, but I just strained for all I was worth and I got this very little teeny ball out, no bigger than a marble. I told myself, okay, I did it, at least I did it, so I go back on the steps and she goes in there and checks, and she says, Is that all you had to do? She went into a rage about it. I was thinking in my little rebellious mind, well, do I have to do a certain amount for it to qualify?

✤

ANNE O'NEIL: Mother decided that Dad needed help in the office. She said that his girls—that is to say, the women who worked in his office—were robbing him blind, they were cheating him, so she had to go down there and organize things. First she worked as a receptionist, then she started administering colonics [*deep colonic lavage*]. Once she started working on the colonics, we got colonics. Can you imagine a person who spent eight hours a day giving people colonics? Then another four giving her children colonics?

RICHARD RHODES: I was struck, in the manuscript you sent me, with your description of the colonic irrigator itself. [*Anne's description: "The apparatus consisted of a wall-hung source for fresh water and a sewage link-up. To its speculum or business end were attached two black rubber hoses, one for conducting the water in and another for conducting waste back out. These hoses connected to a framework with glass tubes for viewing discharged waste. With Mother the treatment went on indefinitely. She prowled the crawl spaces of our minds and bodies until both were "clean." As exorcist she commanded: "Satan! Begone!" Or: "I'm going to drive those devils out of your system!"*] It made it possible for her to monitor what you had eaten, by looking at the residue.

ANNE O'NEIL: At least that's what I thought. She'd watch for a peanut, peas, whatever.

RICHARD RHODES: And in this bizarre way, could read your mind.

ANNE O'NEIL: It *was* a way of reading my mind.

RICHARD RHODES: At least you felt that she could tell if you cheated on her food discipline.

ANNE O'NEIL: Yes. Anyway, she told us that she could read our minds. I believed that she could read my mind with or without a colonic. But it was worth our lives to go against her in any way. You know—by thinking what she didn't want us to think or by feeling what she didn't want us to feel.

RICHARD RHODES: Was she inflicting pain to inflict pain or was she doing what narcissists often do, not being aware of you as a human being, using you for her purposes?

ANNE O'NEIL: She always had a purpose, a higher purpose, in everything she did. Mother was a *true believer* in the ultimate sense. She just had these visions of what was right, and fixed beliefs that could not be impacted in any way.

RICHARD RHODES: Isn't it Yeats—"But Love has pitched his mansion in / The place of excrement"? Religion so often reeks of the most elemental focus on bodily process; it's often such a deliberate and desperate attempt to escape from the body. She linked them right there, in Yeats's place. She was doing God's work with the colonic.

ANNE O'NEIL: That's right. It was either about driving out Satan or about being perfect. One of her favorite admonitions was "Be ye perfect, as your Heavenly Father is perfect."

RICHARD RHODES: Driving out demons is biblical in itself.

GINGER RHODES: Beating you and shouting, *Satan! Begone!*

ANNE O'NEIL: D. P. Schreiber, whose memoirs were the subject of one of Freud's case histories, has a very powerful description of how you bring the child into line, into submission. I can tell you how it was with Mother. She required first, admitting the offense she suspected you'd committed; second, apologizing; third, taking the punishment, the beating; fourth, thanking for the beating—"Thank you, dear Mother, for loving me enough to discipline me"—fifth, not showing any residual physical manifestation whatsoever of what you have just experienced. No crying, nothing. You have to cry during the beating and then afterwards you may not cry at all or show any lingering response such as sobbing or shortness of breath. Rigorously applied, this practice leads to what Schreiber calls "soul murder."

GINGER RHODES: I'll live forever with the story of your parents getting rid of your little sister's stuffed animals.

ANNE O'NEIL: Yes. My sister suffered from an extreme and painful disability. She was in school only about a third of the time. Her stuffed animals were her friends, her only friends. They were her imaginative life. She had stories, her animals were all people.

GINGER RHODES: That was her world, they murdered her.

ANNE O'NEIL: Or at least they nearly murdered her creative life. Through a complete lack of appreciation and understanding. Imaginative play is a major survival skill. My sister had found one area where she could be free and inventive—where she could write her own script, so to speak. And my parents robbed her of all the characters she had invented. My mother did not view the pursuit of happiness as an inalienable right. My father did, but he colluded with her against it.

Mother threw away all of my older sister's books also; she threw them all in the furnace, with my sister standing by, dissolved in tears.

RICHARD RHODES: And she replaced your dolls with plaster saints.

ANNE O'NEIL: All, you see, in the name of religion. All in the name of goodness . . .

One of the greatest losses in a childhood like ours is the loss of trust.

Richard described to filmmaker David Doepel his stepmother's efforts to control his bodily functions:

DAVID DOEPEL: How would you describe yourself when you were ten?

RICHARD RHODES: A woman I knew as a child sent me some photographs from the time just before my father remarried. I cherish them because one of them shows me facing the camera looking goofy, making a great face for the camera. Most of the photographs I have from that time are conventional poses and unrevealing, but my clowning in that photograph tells me that I was a normal child, that I was a happy child, that I liked to play—which is what I remember from that time.

It got more complicated during the two and a half years with my stepmother. Yet I was happy at least part of the time. In the summer especially, when I had a bicycle and could get away all day, even though I might have to make my lunch out of a garbage can. That was not inherently awful. If I found something to eat, I had food and I went on about my life. The world was as curious and fascinating then as it is for me now. It was a happy, creative time even though it was framed by violence. But the violence escalated.

Richard Rhodes

Ginger Rhodes

When I was researching *A Hole in the World,* I went out to Idaho to visit my brother Stanley. We sat down and tape-recorded the memories we shared. At one point in the discussion I asked him, Do you remember the time when we were in the basement and you had wrung out a mop in the wrong direction? (That was one of the crazy rules we were supposed to learn—you wring a mop one way, not another; if you did it the wrong way, there was a beating.) Do you remember, I said to my brother, when she was about to hit you with the mop and there was a bolt shaft sticking out of the mop head and I was standing there so afraid that it would hit you in the neck and somehow paralyze you? I was standing there, I said to him, trying to make myself invisible—which I vividly remember trying to do.

Stanley looked at me strangely. No, no, he said, *she hit you* with the mop.

He's older than I am, so I think his memory is the more trustworthy. Which means I rewrote the story.

We moved, at the end of the first year with my stepmother, to a storefront. It didn't have a bathtub. My stepmother kicked us out winter and summer so that she could bathe luxuriously in a washtub with water heated on the stove, but she found it inconvenient for us to bathe, so we simply didn't from one month to the next. We stank; our clothes were rotting on our bodies. There were great black patches of dirt under my arms and on my neck, in my groin, on my feet. In school, in the fourth grade, a boy who I thought was a friend of mine got a group together during recess and tore off my shirt and threw me down on the playground. I was horrified. It's easily the single most monstrous moment I remember from that time. Beatings certainly weren't pleasant, but at least they didn't involve a friend betraying me. By his betrayal I was exposed to the other children in my class, including a little girl I had a crush on. That was truly a time when I remember pretending I was invisible. Curling up in a fetal ball on the playground and just pretending I was invisible. I went inside and refused to go out to recess anymore. The violence my stepmother visited upon us divided us off in that way from the normal world.

In that second year of our captivity, I started going to a community center after school. That in itself was a step away from fear. It was very difficult to do that, given the shyness that I felt—to join with other people that way. At the community center, I learned to make papier-mâché roses. I fantasized that if I could make a beautiful bouquet of roses to take home to my stepmother, then maybe she would see that I was a loving child and might love me, and then all these horrors would stop. I made a bouquet and took it home and her response was truly diabolic. Her response was, Well, if you want to show me you love me with these roses, what a lovely thing to have learned, why don't we add those to the kit of things that we're selling after school—you can start manufacturing them. After that, for months, I manufactured these goddamn roses by the dozens and she sent me out to sell them door to door. I felt truly sabotaged.

I wish everyone who deals with abused children could understand how quickly you split, how quickly part of you becomes cold and calculating. Perhaps I should say "pragmatic" rather than cold and calculating, because it's really in the interest of survival. One calculates one's effects. You learn to calculate your effects even though they may be well meant and they are well meant. But even in the midst of normal expression, another side appears that's calculating. That split is probably the most difficult part of the experience to grow out of, to get beyond. You learn to be contemptuous—calculating and very, very cold. It goes with the other pathology that appears, which is enormous self-pity. Self-pity, I suppose, that tries to make up for the abuser's *lack* of pity.

One particular torture my stepmother installed was denying me the use of the bathroom from the time I went to bed, presumably nine o'clock, until the next morning. There was only one bathroom in the house and to get to it I had to go through her and my father's bedroom. From her point of view, according to an interview she gave a social worker later, when our custody came into question, I was spying on their sex life. Although that may well be true, since I was a precocious child, the fact is I was ten years old and needed to empty my bladder at night. If privacy was an issue, she could have provided me with a chamber pot. At one point I tried peeing out the back window—my brother and I slept on an enclosed sleeping porch at the back of the house—but it was a noisy window and my father heard the noise and got up to find out what was wrong.

So for more than a year, I simply lay in bed pinching my penis and clamping my muscles until they cramped and went into spasm. I remember feeling such terrible desperation. I was in a double bind. There was the possibility of being caught if I urinated out the window and there was the other terrible discomfort of not being allowed to urinate. For a long time, I couldn't see any way out. That was torture, if torture is helplessness before physical pain. I'd lie there in the dark awake and hurting and there was no one to turn to. I'd ask myself, Who in the universe will come to my aid? And of course, nobody did. Certainly not my father. Eventually, I realized I could use empty Mason jars to store my urine at night, but even then I was so fearful of being heard that I waited until I couldn't stand the cramping any longer before I relieved myself, so the torture went on for several years.

In all these ways, my stepmother progressively narrowed the margins of our lives—my life and my brother's. Food was reduced, freedom of motion was reduced, and finally the one thing that I most cherished, which was reading, was denied. Toward the end, she decided that because of some infraction of her rules we would spend the time after school until bedtime sitting in this very small room we lived in, not allowed to read, not allowed to listen to the radio, staring at the wall. That means she thought carefully how to hurt us most, how to hit us where we lived. Had we continued on that course, she would finally have reduced our space in the world to nothing—to death, to murder of the body or the soul.

4

"My Mother Was Very Angry"

Within families, one parent usually abuses while the other stands by. Although there is some evidence that child abuse is more often perpetrated by stepparents, we found no such alleviating distinction among the people we interviewed.

Therapist Susan Voorhees talked to us at the end of a long day in her office strewn with toys:

SUSAN VOORHEES: Parenting is a terrible assault on a parent's narcissism. Here's this child who's supposed to be your gift to the world and the perfect extension of you—but faultless, of course. And you're the only one who has produced this perfect child; everybody else's child is less perfect than your perfect child. Then the little kid has the audacity to begin to develop her own sense of self. She shows you that, no, she isn't you in perfection. She's herself. And, oh boy, she may even have some traits of your spouse or some relative that you don't like. And maybe she doesn't believe that everything you do is just the most wonderful thing in the whole world. Maybe she needs to stand in opposition to you regardless of what she thinks of you, even though that opposition isn't a personal attack but simply what development tells her she has to do. Unfortunately, some people are better than others at rebounding from that kind of narcissistic injury.

Writer Louise Hill's primary abuser was clearly her mother:

LOUISE HILL: My mother was born in Russia but came here at the age of three. She must have had some affinity for language. We had a poetry collection in the house—*101 Famous Poems*—and that was hers. So was *The Rubaiyát of Omar Khayyám,* a green leather book with gold pages, inscribed to my mother by some young man I never met. [*Reciting:*] "A Book of Verses underneath the Bough, / A Jug of Wine, a Loaf of Bread—and Thou," so forth and so on. My mother would often say, Well, I could have married him. So I think she had other fantasies, other desires, other wishes for another time. She didn't get quite the life that she wanted.

RICHARD RHODES: She was a victim too.

LOUISE HILL: Oh, she was a terrific victim.

RICHARD RHODES: She couldn't go out on her own and improve her life.

LOUISE HILL: No, she couldn't. She was also a victim of the anger of her own mother, who ridiculed my mother for her choice in husbands. So she was victimized quite a bit. There's no question in my mind that she was a very, very unhappy woman. She told me so. I'm a very unhappy woman, she told me. That doesn't excuse her. It helps me understand, but she abused me and took it out on me. I think it's a miracle that I've survived to have the life I've had.

My father died at the end of my freshman year in college. That left my mother widowed with my sister, who was nine years old. My mother had me tell my sister—I will never forget this—that our father had died.

But when my sister was born, I was displaced as an only child and that's when most of the abuse seemed to have happened, from the time that I was nine through fifteen. My sister and I slept in the same bed, but I have no memory of sleeping with her until the moment I told her that our father had died. After that, my mother was very angry because now she was abandoned. Well, that was the best thing that ever happened to her. She was ashamed to go out to work before he died because it was considered a shameful thing to have to work—it meant that her husband couldn't earn a living. But once my father died, it gave her the freedom to go out to work. In fact she did get a good job in an accounting department. She had been a bookkeeper. She was able to finally buy a car and finally do something. But she never found who she was; her whole life she never knew who she was. She always said, Be nice to this person, you don't know. Be nice to this person. Opportunistic. She really didn't know what her values were.

Proofreader Ralph Kessler's abuser was his stepfather:

RALPH KESSLER: My stepfather didn't just beat me on occasion. His mistreatment was consistent. I would come home tired after selling my papers. It was miles of walking and shouting just to make a penny. The family would eat together and then my mother and my stepfather went into the living room and I remained in the kitchen to clean up. I cleared the table, washed the dishes and pots, dried everything and put it all away, and then I had to wash the kitchen and bathroom floors. I still remember the seemingly endless hours of work every night. I got through in time to go to bed.

One morning he showed me a pencil mark that he had made on the bathroom tile. I had missed that spot as evidenced by the pencil mark. I had not done a good job. I got my whipping.

In the summer of 1933, we moved to Park Ridge, New Jersey, where we took rooms in an apartment with a widow. She had a son a bit older than I. I remember something the boy said to me once. He would never let his mother remarry, he said, because he never wanted a stepfather.

The mistreatment was consistent and not just beating. I was not allowed to listen to any kid's programs on the radio—*Jack Armstrong, Buck*

Rogers, or whatever. They had the radio on to classical music all of the time, to WQXR, and my stepfather just plain said NO to my requests. I'd go to other houses to listen to the radio, but I never liked classical music after that.

Early in 1934, we moved to Englewood, New Jersey. He was an insurance agent now and my mother worked as a part-time waitress. I was thirteen that April 9 and my mother gave me a bar mitzvah party. It was just an excuse for her to throw a party for her friends. I wasn't even there. It was a houseful of grown-ups having a good time. She gave great parties. I got some skates. I never even put them on. He punished me for some reason and forbade me to use them. I never did.

My stepfather drove a two-passenger coupe. He used to make me sit in the luggage compartment. I was terrified that the top would come down on my head as I crouched on the luggage floor. Of course there was room for me in the front. Neither of them was big and I was a child. Eventually, I stopped riding with them. I just said no and stayed home alone when they went out on Sundays. My mother would beg me to come along to enjoy a ride in the country and she couldn't understand why I wanted to stay home.

When I walked home from school and turned into Grant Street where we lived, if I saw his car in front, my heart sank. I was in for it. I would get it. On the other hand, if the car was gone, I could look forward to a pleasant afternoon with my mother. She was a kind and loving person, both sweet and gentle. A child can feel a parent's love and I always felt hers to me. I think now that she went out of her way to be extra sweet to me to try to make up for my mistreatment from her husband.

Her mother's mercurial personality confused Alexa Donath:

ALEXA DONATH: If my mother had been all bad, perhaps it wouldn't have been so difficult to understand her when I was little. But she was beautiful and funny and very crazy at times. Good crazy—it made it so weird to be with her sometimes when she was being the sort of mother my friends would have envied.

My mother slapped me with her hands, gouged me with her nails, wrenched my arms, pushed me, and used whatever was handy: high-heeled shoes, a hanger. It all hurt, but the words hurt the most. Words that hurt are powerful and ongoing. They can kill the good feelings you have about yourself. Those marks stayed.

When words and violence are used against a child, it's a type of rape—rape of the body, mind, and soul.

Although occupational therapist Anna Lee Traynor's stepfather beat her, her mother's emotional abuse was hardly less traumatic. When she decided as an adult to sue for damages, she sued them both:

ANNA LEE TRAYNOR: My mother didn't even consider me a valuable piece of *property*. I never felt wanted, and I learned eventually that I wasn't. My mother didn't want me. She was thinking of ways to get rid of me. My mother never held me, she never really told me she loved me. There was no nurturance of a tactile, verbal, or even spiritual nature. I wasn't worth anything from the beginning because I didn't serve the purpose of keeping my father with her. I think it's what stayed with me.

To hear my mother tell me that I was ugly—well, I still look in a mirror and I don't see a face. I put mascara on lashes, I put lipstick on lips, but they belong to some muted nonentity, not to a person of any outward beauty. That's how I feel. It's almost like a prediction came to pass. I feel more resentment toward my mother even though she wasn't the direct perpetrator, so to speak.

Economically, my sister and I were deprived of a lot of material things. My stepfather had them—he had the best food; she would even cut his meat. He had the best suits, the best clothing, Cadillacs. I remember certain things that I would never even repeat at this point. Someday I'll tell my children, when I'm ninety. We were deprived, unnecessarily so, and he flourished with whatever means my mother could give him. I had to worry about clothing and food.

From a very early age, I never let my stepfather near me. The skin crawls up my back now, thinking about it. Many people see me as a strong woman, but my first response if I were in a room with my stepfather would still be to run and hide. I would sit there through the depositions [*she means her lawyer's interviews with her parents, part of the discovery process in her lawsuit*], very still, very formidable, but deep down inside I wanted to be as far away from him as possible.

And my mother, I had great contempt for her, and openly so. I went through a couple of depositions with her. I hadn't seen her for twenty years. The second time, my mother, stepfather, and my sister were just chatting away. My sister supposedly was hung in a closet for days at a time and I'm thinking, you're talking to these people? But I sat there. And I said the first words I had spoken to my mother in twenty years. She was talking to my sister about how they missed seeing my sister's children. I looked at my mother and said, My children would like to see you too. I sat there very calmly at the conference table. She goes, Oh, would they, will that ever happen? I said, Oh yes, they will see you in a court of law and they will sit next to their mother.

She looked at me and her whole fraudulent affect came to light—the person she really was. She said, I told you when you became a mother someday you would understand things. I said, Yes, I do understand. I understand that you were not an acceptable mother, you provided me with a life that was totally brutal and abhorrent, and that's why you're in this room and that's what I'm going after you for. That was the first time I'd spoken to her, it was so great. My stepfather was afraid of me. And they *should* have been afraid of me.

At the dinner table, in childhood, my stepfather would sit down and as we would start to eat, he'd say, When you're done eating I'm going to take you in the other room and I'm going to beat you with a strap. Well, I really didn't have a big appetite at that point. So you associate eating with violence. I never ate without a lump in my throat, without a sensation of nausea. Sometimes he might not beat us, or he might, but either way you never ate without associating eating with violence and fear.

There was one particular beating that was decisive. My stepfather held me up against the door and kneed me in the stomach. It was all over losing a pair of cuticle scissors, which I then found. I think abdominally there was some soft tissue damage done that added to what had already been going on for years. I probably would have ended up with some kind of inflammatory bowel disease anyway, for whatever reason. My mother was talking on the phone at the time. I was sixteen years old. I looked at her like—You're letting him do this to me, you're participating by talking on the phone while he's holding me against the door, you're closing all the doors and windows? I remember trying to hide behind her at one point. She walked away: Don't think *I'm* going to protect you. That absolutely was my realization, as a semi-adult, that this is what I'm living with here and that I had to find a way not to be a part of it, to leave. I think the illness then [*she means the colitis that led to an ileostomy and ultimately nearly killed her*] just precipitated from that.

Valorie Butler's strong and hard-won religious belief enables her to look behind her aunt's violence to the unhappy woman hiding there but still to hold her accountable:

VALORIE BUTLER: When my aunt was angry with my uncle, she usually acted out her rage towards us. She picked out minuscule things that wouldn't amount to a hill of beans. It wasn't our misbehavior, it was her own rage she couldn't deal with.

The book *Forgive and Forget* helped me a lot. It talked about what forgiveness is. I always felt to forgive I needed to say it's okay. Well, it wasn't okay and it's still not okay, but I can suffer all that now. I can put my pain in this one box, and be a friend to her in another box. I'm not vulnerable to her, I don't want to make myself vulnerable to her, but I can be her friend and look at her through different eyes, in a sense.

GINGER RHODES: What do you see?

VALORIE BUTLER: I see a pained person who's very un-free herself, who has her own stuff to deal with. But the book helped me realize that she is still accountable. That means yes, this monkey is still on your back and you're not going to have peace until you deal with it. It was helpful to me to be able to say that. My healing is separate from her. Whether she opens up about it, whether she is able to deal with it or not, I can still heal separately from her. I call it seeing through Jesus's eyes. He has an unconditional love that's stronger than human love. Human love needs justice or feedback more. His is more sacrificial, I look at it that way, because He's already filled up Himself. He's not so needy. When I feel that strength I can help her or be with her. She's been suffering from a depression for about a year or so. She's looking to me for support because she knows I've suffered a depression. She's not able to deal with the past and I don't press her to do that. I used to want to throw it at her. But I don't feel that need now.

GINGER RHODES: So you are actually able to be of some help to her?

VALORIE BUTLER: Yes. At this point in my life, yes. And I feel the freedom to do it. In other words, I'm not doing it out of obligation. It's okay to go back to my past; I can think about it and say what happened is really crappy. I can be angry about it again. But it doesn't have a hold on my whole life. It's not the core of me anymore. It's on the periphery. I can own the whole of my soul. Before, I felt like I had to say, that's that, that's not important anymore. It *is* still important, but I can't go directly to my aunt and say I'm angry that you did that.

GINGER RHODES: Do you feel it when you're with her?

VALORIE BUTLER: No. Only when I'm going into it myself or thinking about it. If I were with her and thinking about the anger, I probably would feel it. It probably wouldn't be a good time to feel that. I'd rather feel it when I'm not going to feel like doing something destructive or saying something destructive. When I'm with her, in her depression, I see a needy, pitiful human being. I feel sad for her. I actually do feel pity for her. I hope that she heals.

In order to heal, though, she's going to have to go back into all of it. Go all the way past our childhood back into her own in order to really heal. But I have my doubts about her courage to do that. She has made a couple of comments about our childhood. She will say, I did the best

I could. But I won't endorse that. I have to be careful with myself because I have a natural co-dependent nature that wants to say, That's all right. I don't say that. I try not to say that. I just won't say anything. Or I will acknowledge her feelings about something. She said not too long ago that my uncle made her do these things. Now I know that's not the truth. He wasn't around much of the time, because he was alcoholic. He probably would have been strict with us as far as dating and things like that go. But she was a raging woman. I was terrified of her, her wrath was unspeakably horrible—the expressions on her face and the things she did to us physically. It was her own and she cannot own it.

As with Anna Lee Traynor, there were multiple active abusers in Skye Smith's childhood:

SKYE SMITH: My grandparents punished us physically as well. They had a big red belt, and they beat me nearly every day. Yet they were moralistic—churchgoing and all that for-your-own-good stuff. So they beat you with the belt, then you sit on the naughty chair for another hour, enraged.

There were no children in my life but my brother. Thank God for him. It was a bizarre childhood. People have these little monitors they put in their children's room to make sure they're safe? Well, we were two floors up, above the picture show, and there were long wooden stairs to fall down that you could really hurt yourself on, especially when you're two or three years old. The whole family worked the concession stand at night and left my brother and me up there alone, unattended. There were windows on this third story you could fall out of onto the brick pavement below. That was in the day of the 3-D movies—with the special glasses. I would hear people down there all the time, screaming at horror movies. I didn't know what was going on. No one at home, no adult presence, just me and my brother. They just didn't really care.

My stepfather was a bully. He carried on my grandparents' physical punishment and also did the emotional dismantling. From six to eighteen, he was my primary abuser. Horrendous abuse with him. He'd had an alcoholic father—a real shameful secret—very, very shameful.

RICHARD RHODES: It sounds as if the violence got worse when he came onto the scene.

SKYE SMITH: The violence was worse and the terror was worse. He was menacing. I think he was crazy enough and capable of killing all of us. He couldn't hold down a job, he couldn't make a living for us. He and my mother had two more kids, so they had four kids to support. He always hated my father's children because he knew my mother still loved my father. She still does. So he particularly hated that. He also hated the fact that we were smarter than he was. He retaliated by being physically abusive.

GINGER RHODES: Was he abusive toward your mother and his blood children?

SKYE SMITH: No, not his blood children, just me and my brother.

RICHARD RHODES: It's extraordinary how standard the abuse system is, from families all the way up to totalitarian societies. It's always the same—the same expanding rules, the same rigid systems.

SKYE SMITH: Yes, the dismantling of the human process. Then I had the threat of sexual abuse with him. It was always looming, always looming. He showed me naked pictures of his girlfriend from when he was in the service when I was about twelve or thirteen. I didn't want to develop physically. He took away part of me, that joy of—I can't imagine it being joyous—of development. It certainly wasn't joyous for me. When I first began menstruation, I begged my mother not to tell him. Begged her. That's all I thought about—instead of, I'm a woman now! or whatever you're supposed to think. Just don't tell him, promise you won't tell him. That was always looming.

David Ray's special horror was to have his evident savior turn out to be yet another abuser:

DAVID RAY: My mother had been told that my health was so bad that if I didn't get out of Oklahoma I would probably die. I didn't know that. She told me that years later. So this guy came to the Boy Scouts. I might as well name names: his name was John Warner. Arizona rich guy. Here's this sick kid, and this guy hears from the minister that this kid needs a place. I was a special-delivery messenger and John picks me up as I'm leaving the post office one day. All this stuff about asthma comes out and he says, Well, you can come live on my ranch in Arizona.

So we made that trip out there and the first night on the road, he starts the sexual abuse. I had just turned fifteen, but I was very undeveloped for fifteen. I gained twenty-five pounds my first month in Arizona. I think I was already in denial. I was probably scared to death with all the gun-toting that had been going on with my stepfather. Ironically enough, John was a psychologist. He was a veteran, World War II. And he told me this was a psychological experiment. A psychological experiment. He did a lot of brainwashing. The idea was that I had to tell him everything. What's more important to an adolescent than privacy? So that became a war with this guy, right from the beginning. It's really terrible to have somebody doing something to your body that you don't want. There was actually physical pain involved. For years after that, there was physical pain when I ejaculated.

The sexual abuse became a real, real big shame issue. I couldn't tell anybody. Yet I defended this guy. A friend of his asked me, Do you think John's the sort of person you should be living with? Well, this was after a couple of weeks in Arizona. I should have just spilled the beans. But I couldn't. I protected him. And at the same time, I was already fighting to get away from him. I got these jobs—motel bellhop, for example— and I rented a basement room. I got a job in a school, a private school. Playground counselor. I'd get these room-and-board arrangements and then this guy would come around and screw them up. I mean literally, come around and get me fired. I realize now that it was deliberate. I didn't know that then. But he would come around and cause trouble.

His line was always the same. I have a friend who went to high school with me out there. He tells me that John would come to him and say he didn't know how to deal with me. Because I wasn't being "obedient." He would speak in terms of shame. Like, You have no Honor. You have no Integrity. You have betrayed my Trust. You have betrayed your mother's trust. Then my mother would put pressure on me. He would go to anybody he could, and he knew, of course, as these abusers do, that the victim would keep his secret. I'm pretty sure he never feared exposure. So he got all of this pressure put on me.

Well, then I got a scholarship to the University of Chicago, and then it was war. I would get these letters from my mother, Why don't you do what John wants you to? And I would get these letters from him. Daily. Special delivery. You have betrayed my trust. You have no honor. And so forth. Literally trying to drive me to suicide.

RICHARD RHODES: It was the standard orphan's fantasy, wasn't it? A rich person who will come and take you away and save you from all that you've been through. Then you find out what the price is.

DAVID RAY: Yes. Our poverty in Oklahoma was really something. No toilet, hand-to-mouth. We were living in an old leaning house. Right after I left, they moved into a streetcar behind a tavern that my stepfather ran, where they stored the beer cases and supplies. Had I gone back to Oklahoma, that's where I would have had to live and to deal with this stepfather. Whereas in Arizona, I've got luxury. I drive. I've never had anything. Now, at fifteen, I can drive a Lincoln Continental. I'm served bourbon and ginger ale. I can smoke. I have a very nice house with antique furniture. I get letters from this guy's mother saying, Are you taking care of the cherryboard table! But there's only one catch. No privacy, being grilled all the time. I come back and say to him, I don't want to do this anymore. Is this homosexuality? I ask, because they're talking at school. . . . So I get beaten up. You see? There's just that one little catch. You see?

I go back to Oklahoma and say, I'm going to stay here. Then, of course, he would promise that there would be an end to the abuse. Well, okay, you just do the yard and I'll leave you alone, I won't touch you. Back to Arizona and it begins again.

Confusion was also Barbara Hamilton's portion, she reports in The Hidden Legacy:

BARBARA HAMILTON: I can see Dad now, running naked into the cold water and turning quickly around with a loud whoop. He joked to my brothers about the shock coming to their genitals, as he urged us all to join him. The boys seemed to be having fun. They romped around, in and out of the water, squealed and laughed. I pretended, but I couldn't enjoy it. I also couldn't reveal any hesitancy or displeasure. Our parents were trying to throw off their Victorian upbringing, and I knew that any doubts of mine would have been ridiculed.

I was receiving another sex lesson; namely, my feelings about displaying my body were different from the rest of the family's, therefore unacceptable. The best thing to do was to pretend my feelings didn't exist. It didn't feel good to be me. When we were undressed, I felt exposed and uneasy. I hated my body and wished I could disappear. From then on, I never felt safe or that I had any rights to privacy. Dad not only knew I was embarrassed—he delighted in it. He had a sort of leer, a strange grin that would appear when I knew he was going to be talking about something sexual. I believed he knew something about our bodies that we didn't. His way of watching us made his eyes glitter, and he always laughed in a knowing manner. At those times he was someone else—not my companionable father, with whom I felt close. He seemed to exude a tremendous power that made me feel helpless. I felt very lonely when we were naked. . . .

Although I can't remember what he did to me when I was very little, I do recall that I was deeply afraid of him when he was naked—even when we were with the family. I remember that I became phobically aware of my genitals, wished I could put my panties back on, and always felt vulnerable when there was no cloth covering them. I was terrified of being hurt there and anxious about their mysterious sensations. My body seemed to be sending me messages of warning, in a foreign language that I couldn't understand. . . .

Much as I dreaded his intrusions, I believed Dad when he said he was teaching me how to make love, to prepare me for marriage. "I want you to enjoy being with your husband and doing what couples are supposed to do. After you children were born, your mother hasn't wanted to very often. I don't want you to grow up that way." Since they had all the children they said they wanted, Mother's lack of interest didn't seem unreasonable to me. But I had no cause to doubt his motivation. I had never heard of a father sexually abusing his child. . . .

Dad always cautioned me not to tell anyone about what he was doing to me. Later he said, "When you are grown-up and married, you can tell your husband about it."

My inner voice asked—Why should I do that? Ohhh, I don't want to ever get married. I don't want to be a wife!

"But you must never tell anyone else," he went on. "It will always be a private matter between the three of us."

Now I know he wanted to be sure I wouldn't tell Mother. But he needn't have worried because I tried to avoid personal talks with her. Furthermore, I couldn't conceive of his doing anything wrong ever. I thought that as a participant in something that felt wrong, even though I was unwilling—I was the one who was bad. The possibility it was his "badness" didn't occur to me. His behavior was incomprehensible, so I soon drifted away from reality, assuming his guilt as my own.

It was confusing to have him woo me sexually, treat me as a confidante about Mother, and then be very intolerant of me if I disagreed with her. If she was upset, I was punished. Publicly he expected me to respect her, while his private behavior destroyed that possibility. He made our lives a lie.

As their child, I craved their approval and love, but it seemed beyond my reach. Mother's attitude was predictable. I thought she usually worried about me, didn't like me very much, and wished that I was different. But I never knew how I stood with Dad from one day to the next. Sometimes he was the warm, fun-loving father I had when I was little; at other times he seemed a harsh, cold stranger who hated the sight of me. In between I was his child-wife. . . .

One day, as I approached my bedroom, I heard a slight sound, peeked through a crack in the door and discovered my father—his hands working with something on top of the bureau. I watched in horror, too stunned and afraid of his anger to move. He was breaking my Japanese puzzle box! It had always been special to me and in some symbolic way I identified with it. Its secret compartment gave me a wonderful feeling of having one safe, private place of my own.

Because I couldn't keep my brothers out of my room, I didn't display it and had it hidden in the back of my top drawer. But Dad had found it. Piece by carved piece, he tore it apart with his bare hands until it was just a pile of wooden scraps that could never be mended and whole again.

I slipped into the bathroom down the hall before he saw me, and waited there—hardly breathing—tears flowing. After he tramped by the bathroom door and down the stairs, I rushed to my room and gathered up the broken pieces. Then I quickly wrapped them in a scarf and tucked them in the back of my bottom drawer, underneath my sweater. I couldn't throw them away.

Afterward I never mentioned what I'd seen, but watching him destroy the box was like watching him destroy me, and I was gripped by sudden fear of him. I couldn't imagine why he would do such a thing, unless he hated me very much and wanted to hurt me deeply. He succeeded. . . .

In our interview, Barbara continued:

BARBARA HAMILTON: I remember my mother had been raised in a hotel, and she had to pick up all kinds of housekeeping skills. When we got out here on the ranch there was no one to help her. She was so conscientious, she would try so hard, talk about anxiety. She would get into an absolute tailspin when people were going to come. Everybody had to pitch in and help. My father would blow her cover. When the guests would come, he'd go out on the patio, and make some kind of a joking, disparaging remark about the fact that she wasn't quite ready. He was very nonsupportive of her to us. And yet, you let one of us say anything against her or question her in any way, and he was just a Jekyll and Hyde. I mean, he just tanned us. He wouldn't allow it. But he was so disrespectful himself. Something came up about the way I used to beat up on my brothers, after we came out to the ranch and I hadn't done that for a couple of years. He asked one of them, You're bigger than Barbara now; why don't you ever go after her the way she went after you when you were little? This brother said, I always thought I would, but she's too nice now.

RICHARD RHODES: So we lost our childhoods—

BARBARA HAMILTON: Not lost. Stolen. Stolen.

RICHARD RHODES: Stolen. Exactly. It's very hard to accept.

BARBARA HAMILTON: My father was a turncoat. When I got into my teens he wasn't still molesting me, but one time when I was sick and home from school and the doctor had to come, I overheard my father in the hall saying, She always exaggerates when she's sick. Words, very derogatory words. I was really sick. I felt terrible. His betrayal left me feeling really abandoned as well. I didn't associate it with the sexual thing. It was my dad. My mom would cut me down or challenge me, but my dad had been my favorite parent. It doesn't make any sense that he should have been, but nevertheless he was, because he would seem to appreciate things that Mother seemed incapable of appreciating.

There was so much that was unanswered. If I'd had any idea, things would have been so different for my children. My father indulged any kind of sexual abuse as long as he didn't get caught. He would go out of his way to tell me things. When I was thirteen, he told me about a couple I knew—that the man was being adulterous with some other woman. It was like talking about something behind the barn; these were people I knew and cared about. Why would he do that? Why did he have this lecherous side or whatever it was? There was something about him. He would brag about what they used to do in the olden days on Halloween, try to find outhouses that had somebody in them, preferably a woman, and turn them over, upend them. He would tell us about his outhouse adventures at the table when I was growing up. He and my brothers would laugh. They thought it was so funny. Mother didn't say anything. What kind of a sick thing was that? Yet people thought he was wonderful.

RICHARD RHODES: Did he think that he could discuss all this with you because of the earlier violations, that you were somehow a partner?

BARBARA HAMILTON: I suppose. He knew I couldn't say anything. There was no way I was going to tell Mother.

RICHARD RHODES: Right. He probably couldn't talk that way with her.

BARBARA HAMILTON: No. When I was seven we had a house with a little space underneath the stairway where I used to hide from my brothers. Whatever I was doing that day, I don't know, but my father came home. I heard him, and I wanted to come out of this little cage, this little space underneath the stairs to say, Hi, Daddy. He was just home from Chicago. He was just starting to tell Mother the latest dirty joke when I appeared. I remember that joke to the word. I had no idea what he was talking about, but I knew that it was bad, because Mother said, Ed, do you have to tell me that in front of Barbara? Naturally it was just cemented to my mind, even though I didn't understand it. I think he controlled us in all kinds of ways.

One of my brothers remembered that my father would grab us while roughhousing.

GINGER RHODES: Grab you sexually?

BARBARA HAMILTON: Yes. My brothers, too. I didn't remember the grabbing. I remembered the roughhouses, and they were fun. I didn't know that he was grabbing my brothers. I thought I was the only one. He always did mine in private, so I just didn't remember when he did it during the roughhouses, but my brother did. My brother remembered that my father grabbed them too, and that he always roughhoused with his pajamas open and had an erection.

Her predatory father continued to threaten her even after she was a mother herself, Barbara writes in The Hidden Legacy:

BARBARA HAMILTON: One morning Dad dropped by. I called to him from our bedroom, where I was bathing my daughter Beth. In the corner we had a large, high table covered with oilcloth that I dressed and bathed her on. She was a few months old—calm and relaxed in the basin of water even when I washed her face. I was enjoying this pleasant interlude in a busy day, and when Dad came in he watched her a few minutes, then joined my mood, saying, "Isn't she a sweet little thing? What a happy, contented baby." I basked in motherly pride and agreement.

Our conversation drifted to her not having been a boy, when I heard him say, "You can never bring me too many little girls." The words stabbed like a knife thrust deep into my gut! They jerked me away from the innocent present, and back into our murky past. I never wanted to be reminded of his molesting me, and yet it happened so suddenly, I couldn't ignore it. . . .

Despite the evil pall of sexual abuse that permeated my childhood, inexplicably Dad was always my favorite parent, partly because I never felt that Mother liked me. But long after both were dead I discovered that she was not entirely responsible for my unease with her, which was different from my unease with him. I always sensed in her a permanently imbedded anxiety toward me along with her basic inability to understand and accept me (I can only imagine her torture when she knew Dad was molesting me and didn't know what to do about it). With him, my unease stemmed from hating what he did when we were by ourselves and fearing to be alone with him, but I always felt that he cared for me and appreciated me even in nonsexual ways—that Mother didn't. So he was my favorite parent.

But he didn't deserve to be. . . .

In our interview Barbara added:

BARBARA HAMILTON: The defense is always that he's never going to do it again and this and that. But the real message that the victim gets is, there's nobody out there to protect her. There's nobody.

Dan Hamilton, Barbara's stepson, has had to deal with her exposure in her book of an incident of sexual abuse involving her husband—his father:

DAN HAMILTON: I'm still in the process of resolving Barbara's book with my dad. He's just read it after all this time and he's furious. He feels violated. He feels nobody knows his side of the story. I wrote him a long letter saying he'd had years and years of silence and denial, and all of his children had been abused. I told him, If you're not ready to stand up and accept that, we need to move forward. And I haven't heard from him yet.

In the book, Barbara essentially lumped my dad in with her father and brothers in terms of the horror and evil of the crime. Dad's incident [*with a granddaughter, a ten-year-old*] was one night, from drinking too much. It wasn't a recurring need or pattern in him. His defense is that nothing happened, he drank too much, and he tried to comfort her because she was unhappy. No intercourse. No penetration.

He's cut me out of his life before and may do so again in his own frustration and anger. That was my one hesitation as I thought about what to say here. My initial response was, Gee, this is going to hurt Dad a lot. My wife said, Well, you have to stop worrying about that and do what you need to do for you. And that's pretty much where I am now.

It was normal, accepted discipline in our house for Dad to drive me out to a dirt road and whip me with a belt. If I did something wrong, it was reported to him when he came home. That was the threat that hung over my head. That was the means of dealing with me until I was too old to control physically. He was not a particularly angry man. He may have been angry *inside*, but his normal, day-to-day presentation of himself was much more self-contained and controlled. He did not live in a rage or in a physically violent world. But whipping with a belt was the accepted means of dealing with your son. I don't know where he learned that. My grandfather, to my knowledge, would not have punished him that way.

Dad is really trapped behind a mask of American silence. He has no skill at all at emotional communication. You'll get a long dead silence and a Hmmm.

But Dad was the weak, enabling, silent parent, not Barbara. It's strange to me that you think of him as the abuser, because of the episode in Barbara's book. That was just one moment, and it occurred long after I left home. My experience of him as a father was the silent, gutless type—

RICHARD RHODES: Then Barbara was the disciplinarian?

DAN HAMILTON: Well, Barbara was the power.

RICHARD RHODES: And angry.

DAN HAMILTON: And angry.

RICHARD RHODES: She's still angry.

DAN HAMILTON: Of course. She's very angry. But she ruled the roost, and he acquiesced on every issue, or he would get angry out of proportion to the cause. She decided what was against the rules and if I should be punished, and he carried it out, because she told him to.

Dan recalled a confrontation with a dangerously unstable guru who lived for a time with Barbara and his father:

DAN HAMILTON: In her book, there is an incident when I and my first wife visited them in California, before they had separated, and our son Josh was not quite a year old. My sisters came to me and said this man John, who was living in the house at that time, is coming on to us. The three girls were still at home at that point. I went to Barb and asked, What's going on here? She started screaming. John came out with a gun and started firing around in the house. Well, I've got a young infant under one arm, an innocent young twenty-two-year-old wife on the other who's going, Hahahahaha—so we got in the car and left. She told my dad that I was no longer welcome in the house, and he wrote a letter to that effect—that I was no longer welcome in that family. That letter stood that way for about ten years, until he left—however long it took until my dad had actually divorced. He would do whatever she wanted. She was the absolute power.

So my experience of Dad was, Would you please stand up and be the father, the man of the house? He may well have thought he was doing that by paying the bills, providing a home and clothes and so on. So my rage is against both of them. I understand, intellectually, why she was the way she was. But it's very hard to get past, Yes, but why couldn't you solve your own problems so you didn't have to dump them on us? And my father: Why were you a silent nonentity while all of this was happening? Nobody could come to you. You didn't protect anybody.

From years of observation, Anne O'Neil came to know her mother well:

ANNE O'NEIL: It's such a hard thing to talk about because we always talk in words that are linear. The words go one by one by one by one, and to get it all in one place is very hard. On the one hand, my mother was brutal and incredibly cruel. On the other hand, I don't doubt that she cared. She always told us that we could do whatever we set out to do—that we had the power within us. That's very confusing because it's grandiose, but then again, most people underutilize their abilities. So having a mother who was constantly saying this to us was a kind of encouragement, albeit mixed, since it also implied that we were never doing enough.

The only secular book I ever saw my mother read was Napoleon Hill's *Think and Grow Rich*.

Thinking positively is a way of facilitating action, but it's not a replacement for work. My mother believed that you could visualize a parking space and it would open up before you. So we were constantly being told, Now I want you all to visualize a parking place because we don't want to be going around the block twelve times, we want it to be open right before we get there. And if it didn't open up before we got there, that meant that we hadn't visualized well enough.

The first awareness I have of an enema was when I was five. They probably started earlier. My sister, Mary, told me she was eight when she started studying piano, and that means that I would have been two, and Mother used to turn Mary over the piano bench and beat her if she didn't think she was practicing seriously. There was no such thing as *playing* the piano; you *worked* the piano. I don't believe it's possible that I wouldn't have seen that, and of course anytime a child witnesses abuse, that child is being abused. There's even a kind of double abuse that happens because you feel powerless to do anything about it. So you're being abused because you're seeing the possibility, but then you're also feeling guilty because you can't do anything to stop it. For somebody like me, with such a very, very highly developed conscience, there probably was never a time when I wasn't thinking about what I could do about something. By the time I was three, I was trying to learn how to do ironing. I know that had to do with helping my mother. I know that.

One of my strongest recollections is that I had beautiful dresses to wear. They were washed and starched and ironed and I watched my mother's process, I knew how it was. She had an electric tub with a hand wringer and once the washing and wringing was done, she sometimes put bluing in the rinse. After that she starched my dresses and hung them out on the line. Then they would be taken down, sprinkled, rolled, put in the refrigerator, and finally ironed. I'm sure that I knew in my bones how much work that was. My mother gave me these dresses and I could wear more than one a day if I wanted to. I had blue-and-white striped pinafores with long sashes and white blouses with ruffles. They were luxurious. And I loved that. Thinking back on it, I realize I also knew it was too much work for my mother to have six children to deal with and to be that particular and not to be able to endure anything less than that.

Mother had Mary to help her. Because I was younger, I felt more like a little princess. My father always called me Sweetie. In recollection, at least, I was the only one who ever had a real birthday party. When I was five, everyone from my kindergarten class was invited to come to this party. I had not one but two pale blue organdy dresses to choose from, beautiful dresses. It was a full-blown, wonderful, traditional children's party with games and prizes and balloons. After that, there was never another party.

I think what happened to my mother was that she completely lost her trust in my father when he told her that they could afford both the office building and our house. It turned out that his practice dropped when he moved offices and he couldn't keep both properties. I think that destroyed her confidence in him forever. She had experienced the death of her father when she was five. She said that was when all the joy left her life. This was a repetition of that loss.

But she stopped giving me clothes even before that. She discovered that I had become, in her words, spoiled—vain and proud. Certainly I was spunky and full of a sense of my own importance. That terrified her. There was nothing that frightened her more than what she called the sin of pride. Because the sin of pride would lead you to hell. She told me explicitly that she could see that I had become vain and proud and it was her fault. So for Mother, being the kind of person she was, extraordinarily intense and intelligent and creative and determined—creative in the sense of inventive—there was nothing she would not have done to make up for her awful mistake. From that point on, she mounted a campaign to cure me of this pride. [*A long pause*] I was about six at that time.

I link that change to a visit from a Jesuit Scholastic we knew and liked—a young man studying for the priesthood. He was very charming, full of fun. I knew that he loved us and liked to play with us. He was a real hero to me. He called me Raggedy Ann, which I thought was fun, and teased us and played jokes and let us climb up on his shoulders.

I had this dance routine I did with a two-piece bathing suit, not a bikini but a two-piece bathing suit, a transparent raincoat over the top, and an umbrella. I thought it was a great new routine. I thought it would be fun to wear the swimming suit when he came over to visit. Mother didn't want me to wear the suit, but I kept begging her until she agreed. She told me to put a blouse over it. I didn't, I just marched right into the living room and sat there without a blouse on. Of course I knew very well that this was naughty. I was feisty like that.

He came in and he laughed at me. I was really hurt and then I was mad. I started pouting and fuming and stomping around and trying to get him to stop laughing at me, but he wouldn't. I went to mother and she said, Well, you got what you deserved; I told you to put a blouse on. Something closed down in me from then on. I'd had an openness before, a sense that I was fine no matter what. It closed down. Yes, it really closed down. I became far more guarded. It was the first sense I had of being ashamed of my body, which is something I've fought my whole life. It's a very great battle and it's never finished, no matter what I do, it's just there.

RICHARD RHODES: I had a feeling, when I read the version of that story in your manuscript [*the autobiographical memoir Anne is writing*], that this confrontation had a sexual component.

ANNE O'NEIL: Oh yes, definitely. I sensed it as a child. I knew that I wanted to be sexually attractive—I would say sensually attractive, because I didn't have an awareness of sex, but I did know about sensuality. That's for sure. I'm very sensual, very tactile—that was clear always with me.

RICHARD RHODES: So your mother's response had to do with more than just pride?

ANNE O'NEIL: Oh yes. It also had to do with my body, with being attractive, and with my sensuality. "Vain" was the word that she used. I knew that my mother did not want me to be attractive to men. She was terrified of sexuality. She told me she had held a pin at our genitals when as infants we reached down to touch ourselves. She was proud of how successful her aversion treatment was. She said, "Babies learn quickly. It doesn't take many times."

GINGER RHODES: Was she afraid for you and your sensuality or was she jealous of you and your sensuality?

ANNE O'NEIL: I think she was both. I think she was overwhelmed with the results of her own sexuality. She repeatedly warned us, "If you get married, you've got to take the children God sends you." I think she was afraid for me in the sense that she was terrified that somehow she had unwittingly encouraged me. How do we say it, the cows were out of the barn? But I know she was jealous, too. One time I went to my father for help when my mother was beating up on us—the only time I can remember. I told him that I needed him to stop Mother. From then on, she accused me of *always* trying to come between Dad and her. She said that I would do anything to split them. That simply wasn't true. I wanted to make things better, and I never imagined things would be better if my father wasn't there.

My mother was a rageful person and her rages were quite terrifying because there was no end. She was so inventive. There was no end once she was in a rage, she would go on and on and on.

RICHARD RHODES: Did you know when her rages were coming, or did they just explode out of the blue?

ANNE O'NEIL: They were pretty unpredictable. There were certain things that would never, ever be allowed, like talking back, like having the last word about anything, never. But at other times she would just get to the point where she couldn't stand it. The pressure that was inside her. It just erupted. For instance, seven of us would be piled into a car to visit my brother Pat at boarding school. This was a two-hundred-mile trip, which meant four hours in the car. We would be giggling and poking each other, you know how kids do. And my mother would just explode, she just couldn't stand it.

GINGER RHODES: You'd watch this rage escalate?

ANNE O'NEIL: Yes. She worked it out physically by beating us or screaming or whatever. Then, once it was worked out, so to speak, she calmed down. To feel that terror again is so painful, so sad.

Abusers seldom acknowledge their abuse. David Doepel asked Richard what had become of his stepmother:

RICHARD RHODES: The latest word I've had of her, all these many years afterward, is that she's still alive. My oldest brother, Mack, didn't grow up with us and therefore sees her simply as our father's widow and stays in touch with her. She's in her nineties now. Around a year before I wrote *A Hole in the World*—say, 1989—she told Mack, "If those boys would just say they're sorry and call me Mother, I'd die happy." Which is an incredibly revealing statement on her part. Neither one is likely to happen, so I guess she's likely to die unhappy. That's fine with me. So *we* were the reason why the marriage didn't work, we were the reason why she was angry. I don't know what to call that. Paranoia, I suppose.

She was extraordinarily volatile. She would switch instantly from normal to violent and back. How much of that was controlled it's hard to know. She, like most people who are like that, could walk to the front of her little store to deal with a customer and come back and turn it back on. But there were other times when it didn't look so controlled, when it seemed to have been a real switch in her. It could stop just as abruptly, so it was very difficult to anticipate.

Unlike many families where there's child abuse, we didn't try to appear "normal," to preserve an image that our family was normal. I don't think my stepmother really cared. She cared what other people thought. But she certainly didn't care how we appeared physically because we were dressed in the worst kind of rags—they were dirty and we were dirty. Our hair would not be cut for three months at a time and then it would be nearly shaved off and then it would grow out into a fright wig again. It was no concern of hers how we appeared. It was only a concern of hers that she not be directly accused.

Richard asked Karen Seal, the California businesswoman, if she felt emotional turmoil during the years when her father was molesting her:

KAREN SEAL: Oh God, yes. I felt stalked. I was unsafe all the time.

RICHARD RHODES: Stalked? He was lurking around the corner?

KAREN SEAL: You bet, you got it. When Mother was going to go somewhere, man, I didn't want to be left behind.

Celia Golden is the striking California blonde whose mother abused her sexually:

CELIA GOLDEN: My father was a Golden Gloves boxing champion, but we were beaten by both of our parents. There was a political agreement that my mother played the feminine role and my father played the masculine role. She could sic him on the kids, or he could come to her "defense." As if she was *our* victim. But when he wasn't around—when she didn't have a "feminine" image to protect—she could come on full force. The way I was raised, it was just not nice for women to yell. I was raised with these rules about what's feminine. So my mother did not do unfeminine behavior like raging around my father. She raged when he wasn't there. That way there was no threat to her image.

RICHARD RHODES: When he was there, he was the primary abuser?

CELIA GOLDEN: He was the primary physical abuser only if they were both present. I saw her as the height of feminine manipulation, which added to my scorn of feminine images. It's like any other sort of a crime— in order for you not to be caught, you have to have an image that's not going to betray you. If you have something to hide, you have a reason to create a persona to protect that part of you that you don't want seen. If she was to be seen as the victim rather than the perpetrator, she couldn't afford to have a witness. My father would have been an adult witness if he'd been there to observe her raging at us, but without him, it was just these kids.

Within her circle of family and friends, everyone saw her as the victim. They saw her as the weakest member of her family. The victim of us. Of my father. Of life. Everyone always wanted to protect my mother. They still do. She was the baby of her family, the youngest of eleven children.

Abusers often choose one child for a scapegoat; Celia recognizes the special conditions that may have determined her mother's choice:

CELIA GOLDEN: The circumstances around my older sister's time of birth and her first couple of years were different from mine. There were different nurturers and people taking responsibility for her. She wasn't the sole responsibility of my mother. Also, my mother had lots of witnesses and lots of people loving her. They were congratulating her for this beautiful child. Whereas, when I was born, my family had moved to a different state and my mother's father was dying of cancer. My mother had a miscarriage before she got pregnant with me. My father had just gotten back from Europe during World War II. He was a paratrooper and had been involved with the battle of Nuremburg. He'd wake up screaming. So my mother was dealing with a lot of problems and then my brother was born two weeks after my grandfather died. There weren't the witnesses and she didn't have a support system. She had never really lived with my father, so she was also adjusting to a man she didn't know. And he was a different man from the one she'd dated and married.

Celia wrote of her experience of abuse in the journal Matrix:

CELIA GOLDEN: I chose to invent a better mother than the one I had. I was so practiced in creating my own myth that when I disclosed the truth to one of my long-term friends, she responded, "I always thought your mother was supportive and had a good relationship with you. You told me your father was physically abusive toward you, but you never said a word about your mother."

Having a mother who daily admits to hating you, creates a mini-Dachau versus a home, and tells you at age eight that she wishes she'd killed you when she had the chance was not something I expected others to understand without holding me suspect. I didn't want to explain why I had nightmares when my mother visited, why I avoided being alone in her presence without another adult to safeguard me, or why I wouldn't let my daughters visit her on their own until they were eighteen. I created excuses and committed lies by omission to avoid revealing how I had experienced my mother. . . .

Women have greater access to children and their bodies than do men. They are able to repeatedly abuse a child with less opportunity of detection from other adults—particularly if the victim has not yet acquired language or developed the necessary vocabulary to describe his or her experience. When abuse takes place during the most vulnerable period of a child's early development and extends over many years, the extraordinary is made ordinary.

It was ordinary for my mother to sexually abuse me every time she "bathed" me. Even when my father was in the house and I was ten years old, my mother could claim to be checking on my bath while in reality she routinely raked her nails across my genital area while poking and pinching my orifices and genitalia with her fingers. She didn't wash other areas of my body. My crotch was the single area of interest to her.

And when my father protested her pretense of "maternal care," she continued to walk into the room while I bathed, dressed, or undressed to voyeuristically leer at my body. She did not allow me to lock my door or otherwise protect myself from her eyes for the eighteen years I lived in her house. I continue to feel vulnerable even with saleswomen when trying on clothes in store dressing rooms.

Same-gender sexual abuse compounds the unlikelihood of disclosure for reasons including its being referred to as homosexual abuse. My mother, like the overwhelming majority of men and women who sexually abuse children, is heterosexual. Her adult sexual relationships were exclusively with the opposite gender. My mother was not a woman who loved women. She didn't love. She was a sadist. . . .

During our interview with Celia, we discussed the story of Sybil, the multiple personality who was a victim of maternal sexual abuse and whose life was reported in a best-selling book and dramatized on television:

RICHARD RHODES: Did you see the television production of *Sybil?* Or read the book?

CELIA GOLDEN: I didn't read *Sybil* until about five years ago. I was just blown away. My personal feeling is that what I experienced from my mother was a lot worse, but I'm not a multiple. I've had a pretty ordinary life. I mean, I've been married too many times and that sort of thing and not everyone attempts suicide. But I had different things going on. I'm a different person. Why is it that all I've heard about *Sybil* is multiple personalities? Nobody ever told me it was about child sexual abuse. I watched that movie two years ago and it was really tough. I get really angry and there's nothing to do with the anger. There are these scenes like the mother calling Sybil into the kitchen and then purposely letting the door hit her. Well, that's exactly the kind of thing my mom would do. You know, like push me down the stairs, but it's always an accident. There's that crazy-making thing, where my mother wouldn't rage in front of my father. Sybil's mother didn't rage in front of the minister or the people on the street. Sybil was the only one who got to see it. The father saw some of it, but he didn't see.

In her Matrix *article, Celia elaborated:*

CELIA GOLDEN: Much of Sybil's experience of "mother" parallels my own. And like Sybil's, my mother was a heterosexual, conventional wife actively involved in Girl Scouts, PTA, and our church as a respected member of the community. She didn't smoke, swear, use drugs, drink alcoholically or otherwise step out of bounds in any way that would bring her private behavior into question: her public image was her camouflage. Just as more women than men hide their alcoholism, I believe more women than men successfully conceal their sexually abusive behavior. . . .

Women as well as men can replicate what they learned in childhood. Members of my mother's family certainly never suspected that she would repeat the sexual abuses perpetrated against her by a minister from the time she was four until she was sixteen years old. No one believed that she or her friend Doris, who was also sexually abused throughout her childhood and adolescence, was a threat to her own or someone else's child. Yet the last time I was raped by my mother, Doris was her accomplice. I was nine and a half years old and no longer as easily overpowered by an adult woman acting alone. . . .

Celia discussed her relationship with her mother further in our interview:

CELIA GOLDEN: My father died when my twin daughters were two weeks old and my husband and I and my daughters flew in for the funeral. I didn't want to leave my kids with anybody and I didn't want to be separated from them. But I got talked into going to the funeral service without them. I remember people not understanding why I wouldn't let anyone else change my kids' diapers. All these women just took it for granted. I couldn't say it, think it, or write it, but I knew my mother would sexually abuse my daughters if she had the opportunity. I knew that there was the chance that she would see them as being me and hurt them. She would want to hurt them if she saw them as being anything like me, and later I broke off all relations with my mother.

Years later, I did *est* training and went through this thing about my parents. You know, that it's important that I be able to have a relationship with my mother, she's my mother. So I made contact with her and she came out to California. I was working full-time, so I let my mother borrow my car and take my two daughters and my stepson, who was a month older than my daughters, to the Oakland Museum. That was just a day trip from where we lived. I felt that my daughters were old enough then—they were twelve—and there was this boy along. My mother will always put out energy when there's a stranger around. She puts out the charm to win someone over, so I thought they'd be safe. It was summer and they were wearing shorts. My daughter Jessie got to sit in front— they were always arguing who got to sit in front—and Jessie said as soon as they got into the car, my mom kept looking at her instead of paying attention to the road. Jessie said she just kept getting more and more uncomfortable because my mom wasn't paying attention to the road. Then my mother got this really strange look on her face and all of a sudden she slapped Jessie's bare leg as hard as she could and immediately started laughing. Jessie said it scared her, plus it hurt like hell. You could see the print on her leg. The other two kids were in shock, and my mom said, That didn't hurt, I was just kidding. She'd always say stuff like that— This was all a joke, there was no pain here. When they got to the museum, the kids made a pact to stay together. No one was going to be left alone with my mom, and all three sat in the backseat going back. They didn't say anything to me until she left the next day.

When they had graduated from high school, and I finally told them what my family was really like, they told me that they had never liked my mother. They said, We'd always try to be nice to her because she was your mom, but we never liked her. We used to make jokes that she looked like a witch, and we never thought of her as our grandmother. Jessie said, You could look at her eyes, Mom, and tell she was evil.

I always thought I didn't have a right to tell them and to prejudice them and that it might be different with them. I've had other adults who've met my mother who've told me that they thought she was crazy. As she's gotten older, she's lost some of her ability to keep up the public facade. It's like that evil part of her pops out where it's not supposed to. It shows up and changes her whole face. These people have said, I don't know what's going on with your mother but she's really spooky, she looked at me like she could kill me. That's validating for me to hear. I saw that as a kid and thought, nobody sees this part of her but me.

GINGER RHODES: It does sound like classic crazy behavior.

CELIA GOLDEN: I think she was certifiable, but at the same time it bothers me when they want to make my mother this rare case. My mother was in touch enough with reality to be able to know how to maintain this facade when she had to. In front of my father and most people.

Celia writes further in Matrix:

CELIA GOLDEN: I will never again use the minimizing term *molest* to describe what my mother did to me. My memories are of being bound, gagged, sadistically raped and tortured from infancy. But the narrow definition of rape I had come to accept from others was limited to forced sexual intercourse with a woman by a man. In my childhood, there had been no sexual intercourse by a man and his penis. *Webster's* definition of *molest* is not limited to the perpetrator's gender or physical features:

1. *to annoy, disturb, or persecute especially with hostile intent or injurious effect.*
2. *to make annoying sexual advances to.*

I now know that when a man shoves an object into a woman's vagina to simulate intercourse it is defined as vaginal rape. When a man shoves an object into a woman's rectum it is defined as anal rape. And I say, when a woman shoves the same object into the same orifices of a child's body, it is rape.

But as long as therapists define women's substitution of fingers and objects for penises as "emotional abuse," how are victims to name their experience for what it was? If researchers who are invested in theories that ignore, deny, rationalize and minimize the incidence and significance of female-perpetrated abuse continue to go unchallenged, how are victims of female perpetrators to understand their experience?

In our interview with Celia, Ginger asked if speaking out had affected her relations with her family:

CELIA GOLDEN: I don't use my maiden name, so there's no identification with my family. I have no contact with anyone from my childhood. I broke off all contact with my blood relatives five years ago except with one cousin who's like a mother-sister figure for me. She knows how to reach me and she has read the statements I've published. She'll have nothing to do with my mother, but she won't let anyone know that she has any contact with me.

My therapist tries to get me to experience anger towards my mother, which is difficult for me. Recently there was a news story about a little boy murdered, beaten to death. His mother was the only suspect. She was a wealthy socialite. She paid her attorney over a million dollars and got off. The jury said, She's the mother, a mother wouldn't do that.

That really pissed me off. It brought up anger I have never expressed towards my mother. I wanted to just go and choke the woman, I was so angry.

But as for my mother, I don't want to touch her. I think she's really foul. When I was four years old, we had a punching bag that looked like a clown. You would step on its flat feet and punch it and it would bounce back up. I had this image that if I could hit my mom, it would be like that clown—I wouldn't do any damage and she wouldn't make any noise. If I knew that I didn't have to feel guilty, then I'd just bash the hell out of her. I would get it out but not have to pay a price for it. No one would be mad at me.

That's as far as I can get. I can get angry at other women and other men. I can get angry at my father who, to me, was not inhuman like my mother. He had a sadistic edge, but it wasn't malicious. He was human. I felt that there was a conscience there. It's possible to be angry at him. But she's in the superhuman category.

RICHARD RHODES: Because of the lack of conscience, or simply because of the violence?

CELIA GOLDEN: It's the lack of conscience, but also that response a baby has to its environment, a sensory response. A baby has limited capability to be able to name what is happening, so my mother had this incredible God-like power.

[*She points to a doll, a waif.*]

I wasn't in communication with my mother, but one Christmas she sent me this doll. Her note said, I just had to buy her because she looks just like you—it's just the way I think of you.

This doll has one hand out, she's begging.

[*She shares photographs with us.*]

This is my favorite picture. I was a year old. You know, I had this image as a little girl that I was ugly. But I look at this picture and think, there's no reason someone couldn't have liked me.

[*Of a photo that includes her mother, she says:*]

There's a kind of coldness to her. I used to think she looked like Snow

White's stepmother. I remember when this picture was taken. My mother used to say that I couldn't remember things, but I remember this picture: the photographer, my mother holding my brother, and my dad holding me. Which was the way it would be. My mother didn't hold me. The photographer wanted her to hold me and I remember looking at my father and thinking, Aren't you going to tell him? My mother doesn't hold me; you're the only one that holds me. My mother doesn't want me in her lap.

5

"She Was In on All of It"

Children depend on their parents to protect them. A parent who stands by, passively acquiescing to abuse, is also an abuser. The violent look to bystanders for cues, and they count passivity or indifference as endorsement.

The question of why his mother acquiesced in his abuse has haunted Ralph Kessler throughout his long life:

RALPH KESSLER: What effect did my parental treatment have on my life? I think it made me an angry and unhappy person. I had and still have a burning question that I have never resolved. It is: Why did my mother allow my stepfather to beat and mistreat me and to finally send me away? I believe that one word from her—No!—would have stopped him. He adored and worshiped her. When the wolf kills a lamb, blame not the wolf because that is its nature. Blame the shepherd entrusted to guard the lamb. I blame not my stepfather, the wolf, but my mother, the shepherd. I have one regret—that I didn't get this grievance with my mother out of my system while she was alive. She died suddenly of cancer in 1960, and when she did I was in shock because now it was too late to find out whatever I could from her.

Shortly before my mother died, she told me that when she was gone, I was to see a close friend, Shura, who would have something to tell me. After my mother died, I wrote Shura and told her my feelings, which were the same then as now, and I told her that I did not want anything of my mother's. Shura gave the money, jewelry, papers, whatever, to a relative. I have no regrets.

I will always wonder why a good and kind mother, after remarrying, allowed a fiend to mistreat her child. I've lived under this permanent cloud and it will never be lifted.

Editor Michael Davies responded to a letter from Richard:

MICHAEL DAVIES: In your letter, you discussed your father's complicity. And, I realize, I've not mentioned my mother yet. She was brutalized for years by our father. Her screams form the chorus for some of my most vivid childhood memories. There's a part of me that still feels full of blame for not having been able to protect her or any of the rest of us.

Anne O'Neil remembers her father with warmth:

ANNE O'NEIL: My father was extraordinary. He was a natural leader, always the president of everything he was in without ever pushing. He never pushed. My father was just there and that was the way it was. He was a gifted athlete.

GINGER RHODES: As a child, how did you find some balance between the fierce loyalty you had for this woman and what she was doing to your body and the fierce loyalty you had for your father, this natural leader, and what he wasn't doing to protect you? What did you do with these dissonances as a ten-year-old?

ANNE O'NEIL: With children, anything is possible. That is to say, children don't know anything other than what they experience. So if you experience all of these things, you don't question it or try to make any sense out of it. It's just the way it is, and children know what they experience. So whatever goes on, it's just going on and the child is enduring and adjusting to it.

RICHARD RHODES: I was struck, when you were describing your father in your memoir, by the contrast between his openness about his profession and the secrecy of what was going on in your house.

ANNE O'NEIL: But it wasn't secret. They were blatant. My mother was blatant; my father, in the sense that he was allied with her, was blatant. She screamed and hollered and beat us with the windows open. We lived next door to the city hall. The mayor and all the social workers of our town came and went under our windows, day after day after day. My father had his chiropractic practice on the first floor. He sometimes came up and told my mother, "Pipe down—you're disturbing the patients." How many people in town knew we were being beaten?

It took me a long, long time to come to terms with what happened to my dad. It finally became clear to me that he was a very special man and he lost it. He was degraded—he was more than degraded; he was destroyed, I think, entirely. It had to be morally degrading to see his children being treated this way. If he had thought it was great, *he* would have done it, wouldn't he? He wasn't doing any of these things.

From her home in Boston, Alexa Donath wrote us:

ALEXA DONATH: No one ever had anything but good things to say about my father. When I was a little girl and visited my father's factory in Boston, many of his employees made a point of telling me that he was the nicest man they knew, and the best boss. His assistants and designers always said how unusual it was to know such a "gentleman," so honest in business. When his business failed, he refused to declare bankruptcy, because it was not the honorable thing to do. . . .

Alexa elaborated in our interview:

ALEXA DONATH: I've asked my friend, Do you understand how lucky you are? Your parents adored you. Do you know what that means to somebody like me? I have no concept of that and if my parents are reading this, they would say, What do you mean? Yes, my father would swirl us around in the ocean and call me his little tootsie. But you don't prove to somebody that you love them by watching your wife hurt your children. My father just stood aside and let it happen. He's the quintessential gentleman. Everybody adored my father. They thought he was soft-spoken, lovely. My father still says to this day, I never laid a hand on my children. It's eerie. It's eerie. He still says it. He still thinks that.

Celia Golden's father was the Golden Gloves boxer:

CELIA GOLDEN: I know that my father had to have a clue that something was really wrong. I used to defend him. When I heard other survivors talk, I'd get so pissed off at the nonperpetrating parent. Then I'd think, why are you mad at this person? And then I'd have to get mad at my dad.

RICHARD RHODES: I had the same reaction.

CELIA GOLDEN: I have to have *one* good parent, to believe that *one* of them loved me. It's a lot harder to make excuses for him than it used to be. If he were here, I'd really let him have it, I think. Maybe I'd succumb to his tears and want to make him feel good, the way I did as a kid growing up, but I think that I could get really pissed.

Well into writer Louise Hill's interview, Richard noted that she hadn't discussed her father beyond mentioning his death:

LOUISE HILL: Oh yes, my father, my dear father.

RICHARD RHODES: Was he completely absent from your childhood?

LOUISE HILL: Yes, a lot. My father was quite handsome, quite dashing. He indeed looked like Clark Gable. I indeed was passionately in love with him. I thought he was very tall until an aunt of mine recently told me, Your father, he was a short man. But he was very tall to me. I think I must have been in such pain that the few small contacts I had with him at least weren't abusive, at least weren't beating me up, at least weren't putting me down. I now realize that he was quite absent. He was working all the time and I think he stayed away from my mother a lot, because she was bitter and angry. So he wasn't home much.

He was home in the evening for dinner but I think he had a hard row to run there. He had a wife who was very unhappy with him and the marriage. A mother-in-law who despised him. A sister-in-law in the same house who hated him. And he had heart trouble early on since he was forty. They used to yell at him, *You hypochondriac*. It was very confusing for a child. I grew up with the fire department coming once a month with oxygen to try to revive him and visiting him in the hospital. If he was such a hypochondriac, how come he died of congestive heart failure at fifty-three?

But he wasn't there for me except for occasional fun, so it was like a relief. He wasn't a strong fixture, but now I see the fantasy as a child. My fondest memory of him is walking and holding his hand and going into a toy store and looking at the dolls. I realize now that he didn't *buy* me a doll, all we did was *look* at the dolls. It was that small a thing, but it was a relief from what was going here. It's like wearing a tight girdle and taking it off once a year. Once a year I got to take the girdle off—with him.

My mother made fun of him. He was very outgoing and I believe one of the reasons my mother was so abusive to me was that I reminded her of him. I'm very much like him. He was very outgoing and she made fun of it. She would say, Your father, he doesn't come home until so late, he's the mayor of the whole city of Boston. I say it to this day. I live in Greenwich Village, so I walk, and when I walk I sometimes meet people I know and say, Hi. Sometimes, when I'm in a vulnerable mood,

I'll feel like—bad girl, bad girl, who do you think you are, you're being the mayor of the whole city of Boston.

[*She leads us into her bedroom office and shows us a photograph.*]

This is interesting. I recently came across a picture of my father. He was president of two veterans' organizations. He was very much a military man. He was in the Navy, which makes me understand part of why I married the very wonderful man I'm with now. One of the reasons is that he's a navy man. He's a navy man and it's very comforting to me.

My father was in Paris in the First World War. He had a hole in his back. He told me it was a bullet hole. My mother said it was really from an infection and they had to dig something out and where the truth is I don't know and I don't care. But he did have a hole in his back. He was president of the Veterans of Foreign Wars, one of the posts in Boston, the Francis Langford Post as a matter of fact. There he is in the middle of the picture with all his medals. On occasion he would bring me to those places.

My mother made fun of him. She called him "soldier boy." Oh, there he is, soldier boy.

[*She shows us another photograph.*]

Then I found a picture of me when I was in high school. I was president of a local Jewish women's group of B'nai B'rith. The same kind of group picture as my father's, me sitting in the middle as the president with all the girls. I've hung them side by side. I take great pride in them. So I was like my father and that was a bad thing to be.

RICHARD RHODES: From your mother's point of view?

LOUISE HILL: From my mother's point of view.

GINGER RHODES: How old were you when he died?

LOUISE HILL: Oh, that was terrible. I see I'm going to have to smoke a couple of cigarettes. [*She lights a cigarette.*] It was very sad for me. When I lost my father, I think of that old song [*starting to sing*]: *I lost the sunshine and roses . . . summer the whole winter through.* My father used to sing this song. *I lost the gladness that comes with the sadness when I lost you.* [*She begins to cry.*] My father died at the end of my freshman year in college. He was my only ally, small as it was, he was my only ally and I never, never, never got over his death.

When my father died, the light went out of my life. The life went out of life. Every year, to this day, when August comes, I get very sad that he's gone and it's been forty-one years. Forty-one years I'm sad still in August because he's gone. Well, nobody loved him, except for me. Once she threw something and broke his glasses and they shattered right on his face. So that's about my father. I don't have anything more to say except I loved him and I miss him and I'm not unrealistic enough to say that he was there for me or that he was wonderful. He wasn't. I think he was terrified of her too. And I get the idea that he fooled around. I sure wish he was around now. He was the only positive thing for me, just because he wasn't beating me up and just because I liked some of the things he was about. He had a tremendous spirit about life, which my mother didn't have.

David Ray, the poet, still struggles with conflicting feelings about his mother:

DAVID RAY: I think maybe my mother was dead a long time ago to me. Although she's living and I still get close to confronting her and asking her questions about this stuff, I back off and say, Well, I'm sure she was a victim too. She couldn't have been that way if she hadn't suffered some sort of abuse in childhood. You want to forgive. That's the thing. You want to forgive. You want to be done with it. You don't want to keep stirring it up. You feel that it was all your fault in the first place. Everything that went wrong was all your fault and you don't want to be reminded still again.

GINGER RHODES: So you see her.

DAVID RAY: Well, very, very occasionally. We beg off. My wife and I have been back from a year in Australia a couple of months now and we haven't gone down and seen my mother. My sister's there, and her family. They're all very much enmeshed. It's so terrible to see it lived out with new people coming into the family and just the same old stuff.

RICHARD RHODES: Why did she encourage you to go with the chickenhawk to Arizona?

DAVID RAY: I still don't understand her denial. I can only see from the indirect evidence that she herself must have been abused as a child to tolerate it—or even, in the case of my sister, to set it up. I remember from the day her second husband came calling, her saying, Go ahead, sit on his lap. He's not going to hurt you. Well, my sister didn't want to sit on his lap. My mother didn't have an alcohol problem, but she was married to three alcoholics in a row. My father, who beat her and abandoned her. Her second husband, who killed himself. Her third, who once tried to kill her.

From Godiva

. . . But Mother, you kissed his hands and stayed on,
as trussed-up as those pigs, as helpless as I.
And if I cannot quite get even the tense of this
straight, as I lift you young and naked again

onto a mule and babble my tale through the town,
please know it is only to lift the tax on us all.
The leaden lies have weighed us down,
made hunchbacks of your children and left much debt . . .

Skye Smith's mother also stood by:

SKYE SMITH: My mother prides herself on being such a wonderful mother. And she is, on the outside. She's a wonderful mother—home-made tablecloths, homemade everything. It's just so perfect.

RICHARD RHODES: Could you talk to your mother about what was happening to you?

SKYE SMITH: No, absolutely not. She was in on all of it. She would have sided with my stepfather, and I couldn't trust her with any of my fears—of sexual abuse or anything.

RICHARD RHODES: Did you try to, or did you know you couldn't?

SKYE SMITH: I just knew. I just knew that my mother was not safe in any way. Do not open up to your mother. It will come around and slap you in the face. So my thought constantly was, Don't let them know anything about you. Nothing. They would use it against you. I always knew that about her. And it's the truth.

GINGER RHODES: Did your mother see his violence?

SKYE SMITH: Yes. One time, when I was seventeen, I came home ten minutes past midnight from a date with my boyfriend, Dave. My step-father knocked me to the floor and she was lying in bed right there watching it and didn't say a thing. She saw it many, many times. But she hit with the belt too and she used to slap me as hard as she could when I had braces on my teeth, across my face, as hard as she could. And a woman can slap. My mouth was bloody a lot. A lot of swollen lips, swollen cheeks, you know. I hoped nobody noticed. When I went back to my twentieth high-school reunion last summer, a couple of friends came up to me and said they knew something was really wrong in our house. One friend said, I used to have nightmares about your house. I thought she was talking about my stepfather. But she said, Your mother was in a recurring nightmare where she was the coldest, meanest woman. In this dream my friend would come up to my house and find nobody home, but my mother's face would be in the window. She said it was a terrifying dream.

In her memoir The Hidden Legacy, *Barbara Hamilton writes:*

BARBARA HAMILTON: One morning while I was playing outside, I found myself getting too warm. So I took off my sweater. Then I went in the house, intending to go upstairs and put it away, but paused in the front hall when I heard Mother's voice. It was coming from the living room.

". . . worried about Barbara, and I don't know what to do."

On hearing my name I had to listen for more, and tiptoed down the hall. Just before the archway leading into the living room I stopped and stood beneath the wall telephone in the corner.

"He said it would be good for her," Mother continued telling her friend. My heart began pounding.

"He said it would keep her from being nervous like me when we are in bed."

Oh, Daddy, I thought it was our secret! Why did you break it?

"When I asked if she wasn't too young to understand about foreplay, he said it was better to show her before she began to grow up; so she wouldn't get romantic about him."

What is she talking about!? Ohhh— Why did he tell her? And why is she telling her friend? Please, dear God, let me die. I don't want them to see me, ever again.

I pressed my face into the corner. My face, my face, that naked part of me I couldn't ever hide.

"Barbara has always been so difficult, as you know, so hard to handle," her voice continued. "I hoped she'd be happy in the new school. But she's worse than ever."

Oh, Mommy, you're never going to like me now. I didn't want him to do it. I knew it was bad.

Mother, pressing her friend, asked, "What do you think? I really don't know what to do about her anymore."

"Well, I think it's very wrong," her friend responded, "but I know it would be hard for you to convince him and make him change."

Mother agreed, saying, "He knows I'm upset, but he's always said I'm too serious and idealistic about sex. So I'm not sure what he'll do."

Suddenly it's like being in a falling dream. Noise is in my head, then I begin to shake all over. It stops the falling feeling, but I know now that there will be no stopping Dad. . . .

Mother never knew that I had overheard the conversation with her friend several years before. One day when she came into my room, she shut the door and I knew she was going to ask me about sex. I thought she had my friends on her mind, so I wasn't prepared to have her blurt out:

"I know that Dad showed you about your body when you were much younger. What I want to know is if you think it was a good idea. Do you think it harmed you in any way to learn all that?"

"I don't know."

"Please, try to remember. Tell me what you think about it, now that you're older."

"Mom, I really don't know."

And I hate to remember.

"I've been worried about it for a long time. I was afraid it was bad for you, but I wasn't sure. Now, I want you to tell me."

"Please—I can't talk about it."

This was the first of many similar non-discussions about the incest, as she continued to question me for the rest of her life. She was too intelligent not to recognize my distress when she pressed me. She simply chose to ignore my feelings and to badger me for the reassurance I was unable to offer.

During our interview, Barbara told us:

BARBARA HAMILTON: I went to a therapist eventually, not primarily because of the incest but because my second marriage had fallen apart. Although we did get into incest a little bit, I was very resistant to saying anything negative about my parents. I remember writing something and my therapist, who was a woman, not encouraging me. That was such a click for me because my mom had never encouraged me to write. She—my mother—would beg me to share something; I'd share it and then she'd find something wrong with it or pass it to somebody whom she respected to analyze. She did that with my writing—nothing to do with incest, just what was in my heart.

I used to write home to the family. I thought I was the only person who had ever been molested as a child. When I wrote I never mentioned it. But I wrote these letters home to Mom and Dad about their grand-children, my two older daughters. The fun and the changes, the dancing lessons and all that. When I'd go home for my two-week vacation in the summer, Mother would sort of razz me about my letters. I remember feeling as if I was struck with a sword, because she said, "I don't really believe what you write because you write so much more than you say." That was very hard to take. Very hard to take.

When I did remarry a few years later, into a family we'd known for years and years, the mother in that family accepted me just as I was. She'd always been wonderful to me. She knew my mother very well, but she didn't know anything about this dialogue I had with my mother. Yet she would make a special point of saying, I love to read what you write about the children. She's gone now. I can't tell you what a difference there was in feeling supported by this older person I respected. It was impossible not to compare that support with my mom's inability to accept me for the way I was. It was very undermining, because it meant that I had no defense against my father at all.

Rejecting her self-absorbed mother, Karen Seal told us in her immaculate condominium, she discovered she had swerved to the opposite extreme:

KAREN SEAL: I remember being around three and telling my mother about my father. And I remember her saying, I don't want to ever hear you say that again. And she didn't.

GINGER RHODES: You never approached her again?

KAREN SEAL: My sister did, because my father flashed to my niece when she was about two and a half. My niece went home and said, Mommy, I saw Grandpa's pee-pee. My sister just came unglued, and finally confronted my mother and my father. My sister said she'd throw his ass in jail. But my mother wouldn't say anything. As a matter of fact, my sister finally told her what he'd done, that he did the same molestation to my sister. Of course, my mother's reaction to my sister was: How could he do that to *me*?

RICHARD RHODES: The narcissism.

KAREN SEAL: You got it—narcissism. To my mother, it was like *we* were having an affair with her husband.

GINGER RHODES: What kind of an adult relationship did you have with your mother?

KAREN SEAL: From about that point on, I was doing a slow burn. I mean I had disdain for her. She became so neurotic in her later years. She was agoraphobic, hooked on Valium, a heavy cigarette smoker, drank a lot of coffee—she was very depressed. She wouldn't get dressed until noon, she was a nervous wreck. She was really, really neurotic. My mind said, okay, I've got these two role models: my father who is competent in the world, gregarious and charming, who had the power, or this woman who was a doormat, who sacrificed her children to stay in a sick relationship. She never worked out of the home. I had such disdain for her. In her presence I would get super-efficient, and she'd just fall apart. It was cruel, but it was revenge.

In my late twenties, I heard somebody somewhere speaking on the radio who said, No child can keep incest a secret from an aware parent. I said, Well, I did, but I also thought, oh, no, you didn't. She chose not to pay attention. And when that realization came along, I spent years seething at her. Whatever she was, I chose not to be. I was going to be a career person, I was going to be independent, and I was going to know how to handle money. She didn't even drive until she was thirty-five. Instead of actively choosing a life, I reacted: Anything she is, I ain't going to be. And in a sense, as my therapist pointed out, I wound up bonding with the aggressor. I thought, oh, gag. That's what's wrong with our lives—we don't see choices. Got to choose this or got to choose that—yuck. Moderation, what's that? I didn't see it. It's just so sad.

At another point in the interview, Karen interjected:

KAREN SEAL: Oddly enough, I'm angrier at my mother than my father. It's like, yeah, he's a psychopath, but what's your excuse? Well, she's neurotic, I guess. But as a feminist, I expect more from women. You know, mothers throughout the whole universe take care of their babies, don't they?

Karen added in a letter:

KAREN SEAL: But my heart and soul ache over the fact that she did not protect me and my sister from our father. . . . I feel so frustrated that I have such rage at *her,* when *he* was my perpetrator (I have plenty of rage at him, too, but there is a great deal toward her).

Only in middle age, Richard told David Doepel, did he finally realize that his father had acquiesced to his abuse:

RICHARD RHODES: It was, again, only in writing *A Hole in the World* in my early fifties that I began to understand that my father might have been at some fault here. When I lectured about the book, the first question someone in the audience always asked was, Where was your father? Because I didn't really explain, in the book, where my father was. I hadn't fully resolved it even then. I haven't fully resolved it now. It's hard to know what I felt at the time, but I don't remember thinking that my father was at fault. I just assumed as a ten-year-old that he was as helpless in the face of this extraordinary violence, verbal and physical, as we were. It's probably significant that the one experience of violence that I remember most vividly against him was my stepmother threatening to throw a pot of boiling water on his genitals when he was standing naked in the kitchen one morning after they had obviously been arguing all night. That of course would be enough violence to make him back off. The other experience I think I recount in the book was when she hit him in the head with a shoe and seemed to have knocked him out. Yet my father was physically a strong man and in fact he was renowned among our friends for his physical strength, so there certainly was no question that he could have overpowered my stepmother. He could have taken a spike-heeled shoe or a belt out of her hands—that's not what stopped him. He had plenty of opportunity to speak up and it's even clear from the social worker's record that he did speak up.

DAVID DOEPEL: But he never kicked her out.

RICHARD RHODES: Exactly, or took us away from it or did any of the things that one would expect a father to do. So, at the time, I didn't grasp that my father was supposed to be protecting us. He was to me a third child in this house where a very violent woman was dominating us. And finally, my brother when he was thirteen and had begun to feel "rebellious" as he describes it—had begun to realize that something had to be done—after a particularly severe beating ran away from home, spent a day thinking through what his options were, and finally simply went to the police. So it was Stanley, then, who realized he'd have to take responsibility—who realized that these two adults who were supposed to be taking care of us weren't going to take responsibility.

It didn't even occur to me to blame Dad until I thought the business through as a fifty-two-year-old. It was only then that I realized that he was the "good German." At least he stood by and allowed his sons to be beaten, to be tortured, to be starved. I don't understand how he could possibly have allowed that. How terrified he was of this woman—unless he was also implicated emotionally. Unless he was to some degree receiving secondary gain somehow. I don't know enough about my father to know what it would have been. I don't know how much he blamed us for our mother's suicide, or blamed himself. I learned something recently. Someone who worked with him wrote me and said, Your father really had an acid sense of humor. I found that absolutely extraordinary. He hadn't seemed that way to me at all. So clearly, he was a more complicated human being than I recall.

I should mention my brother's explanation for our father's behavior because it indicates how far we distanced ourselves from it. My brother told me recently he understood that my stepmother had two older brothers who were connected to the Mafia and had threatened my father that if he left her . . . I'm quite sure that's not true. It's an extraordinary fantasy. I imagine it's my brother's way of denying my father's responsibility for what happened to us.

In her unpublished memoir, Anne O'Neil writes:

ANNE O'NEIL: It was in the power of positive thinking that Dad's extremism met Mother's, but in a different way: it contributed to his inability to address the horrors around him. I never heard my father say an unkind word about anyone—a basis for the impression he gave of being a "good" man, part of his persona. I believe his lack of discernment was tantamount to not being there at all. To quote Molière: "Esteem is based on some preference: To esteem all, is to esteem no one." He gave the impression of being a man of moderation—in this he was not moderate, but wretchedly, tragically extreme: he never confronted the oppression to his children. Mother used to say: "For a time parents carry their children. Later it is the other way around." If I had opened my eyes, I could have seen precipices everywhere. The "power of positive thinking" had been prostituted: this was the powerlessness of polarized thinking.

Even in an earlier family generation, David Ray discovered the indifference that supports and fosters abuse:

DAVID RAY: My father died last year, so I have guilt toward talking about him, too. He wouldn't have known me. His wife told me that if I came for a visit as I was going to, he wouldn't have known me. He never knew me anyway. When my son Sam died, I called my father and said, Your grandson was killed and I thought you should know. He said, What was his name? Well, that wasn't the Alzheimer's yet. I think that was just indifference. There was nothing there. There were a few times when I went to visit him or I would write to him, and it was always just another rejection. I have a little story called "Hair Oil" that's about one of those trips when I went out to visit him in Long Beach. He made a big scene, offered to buy me a pair of pants, and then balked when they were too expensive. So there was just nothing there. There was nothing.

And there was this business of always trying to get something. As a young man, when I was in the hospital after a suicide attempt, I wrote to him, and I told him that I had tried to kill myself. I didn't hear from him. Long afterwards, my sister said that he had said to her, I didn't know I had a son who turned out to be a nut. [*He pauses.*] I asked for a loaf and got a stone. And yet, I still feel the guilt of my rejecting him. I mean even now, I feel like there was something I should have done to make it come out differently. I have so much guilt about my children that I think, well, he must have had that too. But I really don't think he did. I mean I think the evidence says that he didn't.

6

"They Knew All Along"

*B*eyond the immediate circle of family, abused children encounter other adults—relatives, family friends, teachers, physicians—who might intervene to protect them. But the borders around families are nearly as sacrosanct as the borders around nations, and crossing those borders requires courage. This chapter is brief because the larger community of adults failed most of the survivors we interviewed.

Alexa Donath's glamorous mother threw up a smokescreen of charm:

ALEXA DONATH: Friends who didn't really know me would come over and say, Your mother is so great, she's so funny, she's hysterical, I love her—she's a riot and she's so beautiful and I wish I had a mother like that. And I'd be dying. I would be dying. And then there were friends, really, really good friends, a few of them, who knew, and who knew what my life was like. They didn't *really* know because even as a child I wouldn't let them know too much because I was so ashamed. They knew my mother wouldn't let me do things that most kids did. But they didn't know about the beatings.

Very recently, the mother of an old friend of mine, a friend from way back in third grade, met my friend Mitchell, who is like my brother. She came into the store where he was working and they were talking about people they knew in common and she said, You ever see Alexa? And he said, Of course, I see Alexa a lot, she's a dear friend of mine. And she said, Her mother was so hard on her. And he said, Hard? She was an abusive parent, she wasn't hard. She said, You know, I knew, I knew but . . .

California businesswoman Karen Seal wrote us:

KAREN SEAL: All of my aunts and uncles deny that they had any inkling that something was going on; but how, tell me, would an infant and tiny child hide such abuse? My father did not stop until I told him to stop when I was about twelve. Where were my family members, grandparents and teachers? Unfortunately, in my case, no one noticed.

In Santa Cruz, Richard asked Celia Golden why she called her experience with her mother "Dachau":

CELIA GOLDEN: You have all these images of the Nazi concentration camps and the German people going about their lives pretending nothing's going on. That's the way child abuse feels to me. I have real mixed feelings about people who I thought cared about us and yet, how could they not have had a clue? There are specific episodes where there were incredible beatings where I don't have a memory of my screams. I have memories of my brother's screams. My brother was like a mirror for me. When you hear kids crying because they get hit or they fall or whatever, they're different cries. People cry as a natural response to some things, but we were raised that nobody was supposed to know what was going on. That's why we weren't supposed to cry, so nobody would know.

We were trained that if either of our parents was beating us, you were supposed to stand still to make it easy for them. If you did cry out, you would get hit harder, they said. If you jump around, it'll just be worse. It's like they're telling you the only way to control it is to keep everything inside and not exhibit any response. That's another parallel for me about the sort of torture that happens to political prisoners and people in the concentration camps. You finally reach a point where you can't take it anymore and your body just cries out. I have these vivid memories of that happening with my brother. Where he's behind a locked door and I can hear his silence, but I hear my father's belt. Maybe initially there's some pleading from my brother as my father's getting ready to hit him. We were always beaten in the nude or bare-bottom. You hear this belt, and then all of a sudden, it's this scream. It's going to lift the roof. I used to have flashes come. I'm going about my normal life and all of a sudden I have this flash of my brother screaming. And it pisses me off that the neighbors didn't hear—because I know they did. They just left us there. It really pisses me off that they could close their doors and windows, turn up the volume of the television, and pretend we didn't exist.

RICHARD RHODES: They have a phrase for that. They call it a "family matter."

CELIA GOLDEN: It really angers me, this country, our society, the right-to-lifers and that family-values stuff. My father would have supported the Republican Right.

RICHARD RHODES: Those people usually do.

Poet David Ray was actively encouraged to stay with the man who was abusing him sexually:

DAVID RAY: Now back to this business with John Warner, the man who "sheltered" me. It did become so painful that I did have to speak of it. The real crusher. I went to this minister, who was the guy who brought John around in the first place. Presbyterian minister in this little town. You want to guess what happened? What he said? I'm sure this is classic. He said, Well, John has a lot of problems—you have to try to be sympathetic. You have to try to understand. You know his mother is in the insane asylum. His brother was killed in the war. Why don't you try to show some concern?

They knew all along. They knew all along. It was just so much massive betrayal.

RICHARD RHODES: "They" meaning who?

DAVID RAY: All of them. I think I still have a little bit of anger about that. They knew all along. My mother said, Oh, we knew about that from the time you and John stayed in Aunt Ruth's apartment and you left something on the couch. She knew what that was. They knew all along. Here I was, going through this stuff about how I really didn't want to live with John anymore and I had to have my own place, and I had to go off to college, so what's it all about? Is it a class war? I mean like this guy's wealth had them, he talked about adopting me. He would have, I think he would have if I had, you know, agreed.

GINGER RHODES: Could he have been giving them some money?

DAVID RAY: Well, he gave them little things. I think he probably gave them dabs of money. But I think it was that authority. Here's the rich family on the hill. He had actually, physically taken this kid off their hands. I think my mother felt genuinely bad about the fact that I was sick, physically sick with asthma. So she probably just rationalized it to herself. Well, the gains are big and he's bothered about some little thing. It's very easy, just total denial. Not think about it. It solved a lot of problems for her. Yeah, she had her hands full dealing with this other thing, my step-father. . . . I think the emotional rejection had always been there anyway. When we went from relatives to one foster home after another, it was always a lousy situation. It was always a step down. We went into the Children's Home and that was another step down.

Barbara Hamilton spoke angrily of the resistance she met when she published her book The Hidden Legacy:

BARBARA HAMILTON: I don't feel sorry for myself at all. I'm finally beginning to believe Ellen Bass [*author* of The Courage to Heal]. Ellen Bass who said that survivors of incest are the strongest people she knew. I'm finally beginning to feel that, because I just wouldn't be here otherwise. I couldn't have been here because there has been so little support from the family. When I think of my own little nephews and nieces—if somebody had told me that they had been molested, how furious I would have been. Yet nobody in my family has offered one bit of understanding or compassion for my children, all of whom were molested by one person or another or several. That to me just means as far as I'm concerned that, I don't know, it doesn't feel like a family at all.

My brothers, my immediate family, haven't talked to me about any of this. They've all gotten flyers about my book. Nobody's responded. Nobody's said anything. They knew I was working on the book some time ago. They chose not to communicate after a certain point. There was a lot of pressure on the brother who was not an abuser, who was the one who was trying to be empathetic with me, not to encourage me or support me, because nobody wanted the scandal about my father to get out. I thought it was strange that an in-law would be so strong in this, not wanting their children to know about their grandfather. I haven't had any real contact with my brothers for quite a long time now.

I find, speaking informally to groups and to individuals, that older women in general don't want to talk about it. Don't want to touch the experience of incest or sexual abuse. I love talking to students, high school or college, because they're so open. I'm up in Grandma's realm anyway, and they can say anything they want to me. I'm not a peer or their teacher or anything. I always speak with mixed groups. I never stand up and make a speech or anything; I just start out encouraging their questions. I'm not used to public speaking, but the first time it happened was with a small group of people, all teachers or counselors. To see their eyes in tears, and to have young men ask very direct and troubled questions . . . I just don't get any of that kind of response, that level of response with people anywhere near my own age. They've spent a lifetime denying: Don't bother me; don't rattle my cage; I'm fine.

GINGER RHODES: They don't want to be opened up to new pain.

Interviewing Richard, filmmaker David Doepel speculated that confiding in someone outside the family must have seemed an enormous risk:

RICHARD RHODES: To turn to someone and say, Look what's happening to us? I don't remember ever doing that. I suppose that's because we were both afraid it would get back to my stepmother. Yet it seems clear to me that people understood our circumstances. There was a teacher who used to give me a dime every day at lunch to buy some milk for myself to supplement the meager lunch my stepmother allowed me to pack. So others recognized—how could they not?—we were dressed in rags, we were filthy, we smelled, we were starving. I don't know if we were bruised, I don't remember being bruised. But it was evident that something was wrong and again I think that was part of the mentality of the time. I've talked to any number of people who remember that era who say, We just used to call those kids "poor kids." Yet that's really not quite enough. That sounds a little bit like the good Germans to me.

But I understand there was no way people felt they could deal with a situation by going to the authorities, because by and large the answer of the authorities was, That's the family, that's none of your business. In fact, according to the social worker in our case, it was only because we were so evidently starved that we were removed to an institution, to the Andrew Drumm Institute. Otherwise we would have been returned to the situation we were in, which I think would have been fatal once we had publicly declared our hostility to it.

7

"Survival of the Fittest"

*S*urviving *child abuse, at least among the survivors we interviewed, often required taking charge of as much of their lives as they could claim. Along the way they had siblings to care for, to protect, and sometimes to betray. Competing for limited resources is a brutal fact of life within dysfunctional families, a necessity abusers often exploit.*

Valorie Butler was the second of three sisters whose aunt and uncle took them in after their father died and their mother was institutionalized with mental illness:

VALORIE BUTLER: My sisters and I were forced to make each other suffer. I still find that very painful.

GINGER RHODES: Your aunt played you against each other?

VALORIE BUTLER: That's really a kind of torture. My younger sister, Judy, I'm just going to mention one very painful thing for her. She was the one who wet the bed. My aunt took her to the doctor to see if there was anything physically wrong with her, and according to the doctor, he couldn't see anything wrong. So therefore, Okay, there's nothing wrong, you're getting it. So my aunt tried all kinds of things like beating Judy with a razor strap, but that didn't stop her wetting the bed. But the way they tried to get her to stop was incredible. They decided to humiliate her. They would put a diaper on her, she's in the fifth or sixth grade, and make her stand out on the porch with the cars going by. Nothing on but a diaper, that's it. The thing that was very painful for me is that I was told at school the next day to pull up her dress and show her best girlfriend that she had a diaper on. And I did it.

I have a hard time forgiving myself. Judy lives in Texas and is married, and she's a very nervous person who doesn't sleep well at night. She doesn't trust people. I think about the way we were that led us to mistrust one another and her relationship with me. She doesn't trust me, and I feel bad about it.

We would tattle on one another, too. I found that very personally hard to cope with when I was in counseling, the fact that we ratted on one another. The counselor says, You were a kid, too. I understand that, but I still feel sad about it.

[*She takes photographs from her purse.*] I brought a few pictures of my sisters to show you. The pictures are especially indicative of what my older sister was feeling. She was the one who was scarred the most. She's in a mental institution today. She's a few years older, the other sister is a year younger, and all three of us of course were scarred in different ways. My older sister was more like our mother. I'm not an expert by any means, but her emotions are just so emaciated. Her nervous system was just not strong enough to stand up to this. She feels absolutely worthless as a person and could not cope with it. In the pictures you can see the depression. It's just amazing to me that people can have these family pictures and look at them and not even pick up on the feelings. Knowing each other intimately was not something that went on in our house.

When he moved to Arizona, David Ray had to leave behind the younger sister with whom he shared mulberries. In a 1994 poem, he accuses himself of abandoning her:

Dirge for My Sister

At fifteen I abandoned my sister—
fourteen months younger—left her
to our stepfather Lee, a man
out of a nightmare, left her
to a witch of a math teacher,
who stood over the girl, mocked her,
said "You don't have your smart alec
big brother to help you now."

My sister sat at her desk,
sucked her stubby finger, cut off
when we were playing in weeds,
intent to do our good deed,
clean with rag and knife
black grease off a rodline—
one of those sliding iron bars
that wobbled on forked posts

and pulleys—spokes of vast wheels
trembling and jiggling through weeds,
up and down hills all the way
from the tin-shedded powerhouse
to oil-wells in fields, their pumps
chugging away like giant
grasshoppers suckling the earth.

Today she has long since buried
that stepfather Lee so deep
in her mind that she can recall
only his grave—sunken clods
overgrown with milkweed and thistle,
its namecard bleached and streaked

with rust, nameless now
as I saw when I paid a visit,
took a half hour to find it,
knelt and tried to forgive him
on behalf of my sister, and could not.

She has blanked out those scenes
like obscenities censored from movies.
Nor would I remind her, stir up
those seasons of hell in the Ozarks.
But she still curses
that seventh grade teacher of math
who stood over her, gloated,
reminded her yet again:
"He can't help you now, the smart alec."

And I could not, though I might
have stayed behind and got shot—
when Lee pointed the gun at her, shouted out
his final obscenities, at the last minute
spared her, then did what he had to—
grim work I swore I would finish
as I came rushing back, as intent
as Orestes on justice. And yet
there was no need, for the tyrant was dead

and on every corner of that small town
the gathered chorus chanted the truth
as if the gods had just told them
and asked them to pass the word down to the ages,
leaving out nothing, not even the last obscenity,
muttered with bloody and penultimate breath.

There are ecological niches within families as certainly as within any other
natural system. Editor Michael Davies was a peacemaker, his sister a rebel:

MICHAEL DAVIES: What's curious about my family—maybe this is true for others in this situation too—is that as a group, we're pretty good people and we have very high moral standards. We have a strong sense of justice. Some of it might be construed as self-righteousness, but most of it's not, most of it's concern for things that are right. We're all basically just pretty good-hearted people, and I think we always were. I had a rough time growing up with my sister Penny, who is closest in age to me. I was a guy who wanted nothing but less discord at home and she was always in trouble with the parents, always criticizing, always angry, always angry—so negative all the time. I couldn't understand why she was such an angry person. Well, now I understand.

Anne O'Neil's older sister filled a niche within Anne's large family that Anne eventually moved into, maintaining a semblance of order while their mother chased demons with enemas:

ANNE O'NEIL: My older sister, Mary, taught me how to pump on a swing, which I adored. Mary was really gifted with her movements and rhythm. She was a lyrical person with a lot of physical agility. She was a wonderful dancer, beautiful singer and pianist. She taught me to jump rope with all the rhymes that we used to recite. She taught me hopscotch and jacks. My sister was wonderful, she was wonderful to me. But she also was my mother's lieutenant, so she would check up on me and make sure I was sleeping when I was supposed to be sleeping and if she wasn't sure she'd lift my eyelid and make sure. Eventually, I grew very angry with my sister because I didn't think she was on my side, so to speak. In point of fact, she had become mother's lieutenant and she was doing what Mother wanted her to do, which of course she thought was the right thing to do at the time.

Skye Smith's mother bore her stepfather two children of their own, whom they chose not to abuse:

SKYE SMITH: We were a closed shop, everything wonderful and everyone happy. Just fine. We deal with it all inside the walls.

RICHARD RHODES: What happened to the other two siblings in that family? They were much younger, as you said.

SKYE SMITH: Yeah, and they had loving parents.

RICHARD RHODES: Isn't that strange? My stepmother had two normal adult children, children of her own, who were very nice. I still can't figure that out because she was such a criminal.

SKYE SMITH: It's so confusing and terrible when you're singled out and treated one way and you see these others being treated another way. I had the experience of seeing those two half brothers loved and doted on. They did everything beautifully and perfectly and were well loved and here's me again— See how bad you are? I thought that was really horrible. At least treat us all miserably. Don't just selectively say, You're bad, you're good.

Skye and her friends also spoke of the hypervigilance that abused children learn:

LYDIA DeROBERTIS: I'm dynamite in a crisis. Shut me in a room with a catastrophe and I can calm people down, because that was my childhood. That was my job and I did it very well because I knew that my survival depended on it. But there was quite a price to pay. And the reality testing was always very difficult. My mother was mentally ill and my sister is a paranoid schizophrenic. It was just impossible to predict what was going to happen on any given day. So I was always on the alert for something.

SKYE SMITH: That hypervigilant stuff is murder. I still have it too, the anxiety, and being constantly on guard.

LYDIA DeROBERTIS: Someone told me that the first dream you remember is usually indicative of your life story. The first dream I remember: I'm walking along with my mother, I must be about seven years old,

Lydia DeRobertis

and she falls into a sewer. I can't get her out and I try to run for help. Wow, I thought when I came up with that, what a life story. Now here I am in social work, trying to save other people's mothers.

✦

ANNE O'NEIL: I was fiercely, fiercely loyal to my mother. I think that that kind of loyalty and protectiveness is probably unnatural for a child. It comes because the child sees it as survival, it's worth her life. It was worth my life to somehow do something about making my mother's life better. Part of that was that she had to have my absolute, total, one-hundred-percent loyalty. She had to have it.

RICHARD RHODES: Like Stalin.

ANNE O'NEIL: Yes. The loyalty of children is so profound and so vulnerable. Alice Miller [*author of* Prisoners of Childhood] talks about that. My mother just had to have things the way she wanted them. Alice Miller says that a sensitive infant can tell when a mother is not happy, and if the infant is crying it will stop crying. I know I was that kind of infant—you know, it's obvious. It always comes down to, okay, this is the way it is, so now what? What am I going to do about it? I have these sensitivities; I'm either going to suffer with them or I can experience them and use them somehow in a way that's useful, that contributes something. That's my choice and it's also one of my greatest challenges or struggles because it's not clear to me often how to use them well.

GINGER RHODES: How did that understanding express itself when you were a child?

ANNE O'NEIL: I looked for ways to help. I was seven when I realized that I was going to have to take care of my mother. It was after we moved into the Oneida Street house [*a step down from Anne's mother's point of view, her husband's chiropractic office and their house now combined into one*]. I heard what my mother said about my father and it burned into my soul—she could no longer trust Dad. Then I knew that there was no one else she could count on. I didn't think she could count on my brothers and sisters either, or her sisters or her brother, or anyone else. I thought there was only me. Of course that's the self-centeredness of a child. But there it was and it was immediate, it was complete, it was total and I didn't know at that time what to do. For a few years I looked for ways to escape it. But eventually I decided that it was up to me and I was just going to have to.

I had been looking at other families and seeing movies about families like *Meet Me in St. Louis*. I was gathering data and figuring, aha, this is the way it's supposed to be, so now I'm going to do what I need to do. In *Meet Me in St. Louis,* I saw how beautiful those girls were—beautiful clothes, a beautiful house—and there was an order to it. So then I started doing the laundry and doing the ironing, cleaning the house. Setting the table so that when people came to a meal there was a napkin at each place and a knife, fork, and spoon, and they were in the right order.

Mother had really given up on a lot of these things. She had been meticulous at one point, but after we moved to Oneida Street she lost the structuring of those day-to-day things that contribute to a sense of refinement. We were no longer having regular meals. We didn't know if there would be dinner or not. The clothes weren't getting washed. My brothers didn't have clean socks. They were all getting athlete's foot. The house was a mess, the carpets were a disaster, and everything was just ugly. There wasn't even the possibility of refinement that I had experienced at our previous house because this house wasn't even beautiful.

I did what I could do. I could organize the closets and keep the bathrooms clean—keep cleaning the bathroom is more like it, because there was only one bathroom. We all used one bathroom, so the bathroom was a disaster. Of course, that's where she was giving the enemas, so there were always molasses splashes all over. And hair in the sink and multiple rings on the tub and a cabinet full of messy toilet articles and brushes chock-full of hair. My recollection is that every time I went into the bathroom, I cleaned the bathroom. [*She laughs.*] It's wild, just wild to think of a nine-year-old child doing all that. My brother and I took the wagon to the store three or four times a day in the summer to get the groceries. Mother didn't go to the grocery store very much anymore. I just knew that it was up to me.

I had taken over from Mary. Mary adored reading, she lived in her books. But she would get walloped, she'd get beaten—"spanked" as mother called it, but with a belt—if she didn't produce, and she got away with as much as she could. When I finally decided that it was up to me, that's not the way it was. Because of my nature, I'm a take-charge person, an action person. I wanted results.

RICHARD RHODES: You didn't just do enough to get by, you did it to do the job?

ANNE O'NEIL: I did it to get the job done. What I didn't realize was that the job was never going to get done, never.

RICHARD RHODES: Because there was too much to do? Or because your mother's standards were too high?

ANNE O'NEIL: Both. And because my own standards were too high. By now, you see, my idea was that Vincente Minnelli [*the musical-comedy director*] had it right. I was enchanted with the musicals. I loved the musicals. I loved the beauty and the color and the dancing. I was just completely swept into it. I felt it. I knew the way it was supposed to be. I think that Fred Astaire probably had a lot to do with helping our country get through the Depression because people could go into the theater and be completely swept away by this enchantment, this delight, and this seemingly natural mastery of difficulties. Nothing in the plot was that serious, it was all going to end up fine. It let you get away from the sense of oppression. I think that had a major impact on people getting through because we need a relief. I found that I experienced musicals that way. They were very important to me.

RICHARD RHODES: But in your case it wasn't the Great Depression, it was your family.

ANNE O'NEIL: Yes. It was *my* Great Depression. The difficulty was that I didn't have the ability to assess realistically what I could do and what I couldn't do. I always felt that I was failing.

GINGER RHODES: How could you be perfect?

ANNE O'NEIL: On the one hand I felt as though I was failing and on the other hand I felt as though I was succeeding. I don't know how else to put that.

RICHARD RHODES: Did you have a sense, as I did when I was compulsively drawing rockets in school, that if I got everything just right, everything would be okay?

ANNE O'NEIL: Yes, always.

RICHARD RHODES: But in your situation, of course, no matter what you did it never was okay.

ANNE O'NEIL: It could never be enough and there never was enough because, as women understand, there is no such thing as being finished with these things. They are always, always, always in process. And I developed an intense intolerance for process. It's taken me many years to accept that everything is process. I still don't sometimes do it too well.

RICHARD RHODES: Also, your mother didn't become normal, no matter how much you helped.

ANNE O'NEIL: No. She became less burdened, she became happier, she backed off, she didn't beat me anymore. She didn't use enemas as a punishment or as a way of getting devils out. But she used colonics as a way of treating me to make me healthier, so to speak. So it was different. She wasn't saying that I had devils anymore. I really succeeded in that.

GINGER RHODES: Was she happier, or was she happier with you? Did it deflect off in some other way or did it help?

ANNE O'NEIL: It helped because she didn't feel so alone and so burdened. I was successful in that.

GINGER RHODES: What a terrible burden.

ANNE O'NEIL: Yes, it was a very, very great responsibility. At the same time, my younger siblings were furious with me because they thought I had gone over to Mother's side. They remember that I was hard on them. But it makes sense that I would have been. At the same time, I was trying desperately to make things better. For them too. I remember caring very, very much. Yet my denial of some of the abuse, to my little sister especially, was very deep. Our denial was very deep about that. So when I'm talking about making things better for my mother and making things better for my family, I'm not thinking about my little sister.

GINGER RHODES: You poor child.

ANNE O'NEIL: That's right, but you see, the point I'm making is that I knew I couldn't think about it. There's a profound separation, a split, when you can't allow yourself to know what you know.

RICHARD RHODES: Which reminds me again of totalitarian societies, of all those Russians walking around talking about the workman's paradise in the midst of corruption and breakdown.

ANNE O'NEIL: Exactly. And the German people during World War II. The only explanation I can give is the intense need of the child to see the parents in a positive light. Which is a loyalty and also a survival need.

I think that citizens are that way to their country. It's that next level up, it's the way we're put together.

Out of loyalty we will do horrible things. Children will hurt themselves so much in order to take care of their family. It's the need of the child for a parent. I believe there was a tremendous amount of function, real function, in what I was doing. I learned a lot. I developed a tremendous amount of confidence. But with it came a grandiosity, the sense that I was the one who was completely in charge. It was all up to me. That kind of control doesn't have anything to do with the way things work in the real world. No, we can't have control if we're going to work with others. We can't view ourselves as being able to make everything perfect if we're going to be functional, we just can't do it. We will always, always be utterly frustrated. So that delusion, which was part of what made it possible for me to do what I did, was a habit, a mental habit. And I've attacked it over and over and over and over again.

Anna Lee Traynor in New Jersey and Skye Smith in Oklahoma both took care of favored younger brothers:

ANNA LEE TRAYNOR: My mother let me know very frequently that I was an ugly little girl, and that I was fat. My daughter is shaped just as I was, but I tell her to eat. Her metabolism is different than her brother's. Many times every day I tell my children how beautiful they are, how much I love them. They're going to school today. I write, "Mommy loves you, have a good day at school." I never got that. Never. I just had to take care of my brother. The first time I had to get up to do a four-o'clock feeding, I remember the next day I packed up my doll case and never played again, because it was no longer play. It was real life. I was just there for their needs. Then, when I became ill, I was no longer necessary.

RICHARD RHODES: When you took care of your little brother, when you kept the house clean, what were you thinking about?

Anna Lee Traynor: I wanted to make sure my brother was taken care of. Even though he was their child and didn't have the outward abuse that my sister and I did, he was the kind of child you give everything to. Really it was my protectiveness maternally to him. I used to go pick his clothes; we walked to the grocery store. I would dress him for his pictures and everything. It was to take care of him.

✦

Skye Smith: My mother worked every night from four-thirty until nine-thirty at this beautiful furniture store. She worked at this quiet tranquil place and left me, at age twelve, to care for these two kids and my brother, Bob. The children were ten and eleven years younger than I was. So basically from infancy on I raised my two half brothers. I put them to bed, diapered and bathed and all that stuff. My stepfather was selling insurance in those days. He was a menacing presence and my mother was not there to protect any of us.

Richard Rhodes: You really were relegated to the job of child care all through childhood.

Skye Smith: Yes, child care and housekeeping, it was a Cinderella thing. I remember one day in the seventh grade, reading *Jane Eyre,* and my mother shouting, Get up and vacuum that rug! Yet if I had not pulled good grades I would have been punished for that. It was a no-win situation. A constant no-win, no-win, no-win. You're never going to win, you're never going to do it right, so just be invisible, be as invisible as you can, that's the only way you'll get out of here. Don't let 'em know anything. Don't let on, just don't give anything away of yourself. A boy asked me to go steady in sixth grade—his name was Tom, he gave me a ring. It was very threatening to me, I agonized all night, but do you think I could tell anybody anything? Do you think I could discuss any of this? No, I could never discuss anything with them. I hurt myself one time very badly because I did something foolish. I was twelve years old and I fell from the back of a tricycle. I was just showing off. I took the top of my kneecap off, it was really very bad. Do you think I could tell them?

No. Go home by yourself, put Merthiolate all over it, agonize, don't sleep, but don't tell anybody because you'll be ridiculed, mercilessly, about how stupid you were to do that. Stupid you, stupid you, stupid you, so just shut up and minister to yourself, take care of yourself, and try to hide it.

If Valorie Butler and her sisters competed, Valorie also intervened directly to protect them when she could:

VALORIE BUTLER: My older sister couldn't cry either after a while. But her rage was so great that she would do things to herself. She couldn't hurt anyone else but she would claw her face. Some really ungodly things were done to us. I was terrified of my aunt, but on one particular occasion I just rushed forth and said, What are you doing? This was when my older sister, Kathy, was doing math problems and she was slow in math. My aunt felt she was being stubborn. Kathy could be stubborn in her own silent way, expressing her anger that way because she couldn't do it outwardly. So my aunt gave her ten seconds to add each set of numbers in her head. By the time my aunt counted out loud to ten, if Kathy couldn't do it, my aunt would stick her with a needle. That was when I came in. I said, What are you doing? My aunt said, Do you want me to stick you too? But she never did it after that. I learned in hindsight that my aunt was very much afraid too. The fact that I confronted her intimidated her, even though I was a kid. It was rare that we would ever do that, but my aunt didn't stick my sister with a needle again.

❖

MICHAEL DAVIES: My sole objective was to keep the—what's the word I'm looking for, not fatalities—

RICHARD RHODES: Casualties?

MICHAEL DAVIES: Casualties. To try to keep the casualties to a minimum, keep the violence to a minimum, by channeling my dad's temptation towards violence into these long discussions. I've never talked too much about it. Of course, my sisters were listening in. Everybody was sort of waiting to see what would happen. My father might throw something, not quite at me. And he loved to walk up into my face and take his meaty fist and put it right there. Under your chin. Like a gun. You know, you don't need to use violence if you can suggest that you are prepared to use it. Mutually assured destruction. Why I was the way I was I'm not entirely sure, but what I tried to do was keep the peace. By 1961 I was the eldest child in the house, because my older brother went away to college. So he was gone much of the time. And I was next in line and then my younger siblings and then my mom.

GINGER RHODES: So you would sit down at night and try to make sure that loaded gun didn't go off.

MICHAEL DAVIES: Yes, basically. There wasn't any other choice. There really wasn't any other choice. It was either going to be me there or someone else would be there and I didn't want it to be me, but I didn't want it to be my mom.

Richard's older brother Stanley protected him, a responsibility with which Skye Smith identified:

SKYE SMITH: When I read *A Hole in the World,* I relived life with my stepfather. That's what it was like for me: being in this system where you don't think you're going to make it out alive. You really, really don't and it's so unfair and so abusive and unjust. I identified with [*Richard's*] older brother. You're lucky you had him. He was your shield. I was my brother's shield and the cost is really high when that's your job. What is that spirit? Where does it come from? Why was I so brave? That's what I want to know.

RICHARD RHODES: How did you protect your brother?

SKYE SMITH: I would physically intervene when he was getting rammed up against the wall or thrown downstairs, whatever. I would step in, literally, and say, You leave my brother alone—and stand up to my stepfather. All I cared about was that Bob was safe. I didn't care if the man killed me. I thought he would.

RICHARD RHODES: You were really redirecting his violence to you.

SKYE SMITH: Absolutely. That's how I saw myself, as Bob's protector, his bodyguard. That was why I was there, to make sure that Bob was safe.

GINGER RHODES: Your brother had been a protected child before your stepfather entered the picture.

SKYE SMITH: Yes, he was the angel of my grandparents. It was quite a shock for him. Quite terrible.

GINGER RHODES: Do you think that's what made you want to protect him?

SKYE SMITH: Thinking he was angelic and wonderful? Yeah, I just thought Bob was perfect and I was horrible and I deserved what I got.

RICHARD RHODES: I wonder how much your taking care of your brother was your way of surviving.

SKYE SMITH: Oh, I think so. That's why I thank God I had Bob in my life.

RICHARD RHODES: Someone wrote to me, Well, you know, Stanley needed you too. It's more than a one-way street.

SKYE SMITH: That's why I've done everything I can, even now, to have a relationship with Bob. No matter what, I will have to find a way to work it through. I will continue to work on it. I can't not have Bob in my life.

RICHARD RHODES: I wrote a novel about the Donner Party, the pioneers who got trapped in the Sierra Nevada snow on their way to California in 1846. The women outsurvived the men in that group two to one. The reason, so far as I could tell, was that they had children to take care of. They were able to say: Whatever we have to do, even eat the dead to survive, we will. Whereas the men tended to quit taking care of themselves, quit eating, lie around smoking, and die of starvation, just like the people in the concentration camps who gave up, the ones the others called *Muselmänner.*

SKYE SMITH: No, you're absolutely right. Thank God for Bob.

I've had a real hard time with my brother. He came out to visit me about five months after I started therapy, saw my doctor and asked when I was going to reconcile with our parents. That was uppermost in his mind. He didn't understand. Yet he said all the right things. We talked about childhood. He agreed, yes, that was bad, this was tough. But he would go right back into the system. He would even leave his children with my mother and stepfather. He found a place for them in his life. That was okay, but I couldn't. So we would go long periods without writing. But I love him so intensely. You know how bound you are with your brother when you go through that. It was very confusing and painful for me. Finally I said, Okay, I agree to disagree with you on this. I want you in my life still, but I can't tell you I think it's okay for you to leave the kids with those people. So we agreed not to discuss my mother at all. I was there recently, and I did not see my mother. I did see my brother. It was a little rocky; it took several days for it to feel okay. It doesn't feel like it did, but how can it when he's in the system and I'm out of the system? I don't think it's ever going to be okay.

RICHARD RHODES: Wasn't he always in between, getting significant rewards from your parents and grandparents?

SKYE SMITH: Right, so the system works for Bob. I don't know why it can't work for me. Why can't it be okay for me?

RICHARD RHODES: You still want to be connected to your family? It sounds as if you do.

SKYE SMITH: To Bob.

*But the stresses of abusive childhood often divide siblings, and reconciling
with them as adults can be difficult:*

ANNE O'NEIL: Eventually my husband and I moved out to California.
By that time, I had worked very hard on communication. I had taken
communication courses and read everything I could put my hands on.
So then I thought I could make another effort to reconnect with my
brothers and sisters. We were in California and so were Leo, Tom, Mike,
and Babe and my mother. I didn't put any energy into reconciling with
my mother. But I worked very hard to bring my siblings together in a
variety of ways and share with them, talk and listen to what they had to
say. I had totally dropped my anger toward all of them. By that time I
had enough sense of what I had experienced to understand that we had
all suffered grievously. I love and admire all my siblings, so the hostilities
that remain are very painful to me.

RICHARD RHODES: Did you initiate the reunions?

ANNE O'NEIL: I did. I initiated them. They hadn't really been getting
together very much. There was constant tension—covert anger and hostility, sometimes overt, often based in childhood memories of domination
and abuse of each other.

RICHARD RHODES: Do they find it hard to acknowledge now that
there was less than perfection in that childhood?

ANNE O'NEIL: Not anymore. No one claims we had a great childhood.
But some of us still don't want to think about it or talk about it. I still
see a lot of reluctance to face what happened and the price we have each
paid for it.

*Writer Louise Hill sees differences between herself and her sister because of
the different circumstances of their childhood:*

LOUISE HILL: My sister grew up in much better financial circumstances than I, which was part of the problem. My mother extremely favored my sister, who was much more like my mother physically. Nice gal. I would say not as generous as I am. She would agree. I was generous in spirit. She paid her own price. She danced to my mother's tune. She once said to me, At least you know who you are. But I still don't know who I am, my sister said, because I dance to Mother's tune. So we all pay our price in a way.

I was a well-behaved kid. I was awfully well-behaved. I wanted to please my mother. She died with me wanting to please her. I kept coming back to the door, knocking, knocking, knocking—Will this do it? Will that do it? Will this do it? Will that do it? Of course, nothing ever did.

GINGER RHODES: It wasn't about you.

LOUISE HILL: No. I do know that now.

Karen Seal also found little reward in trying to please her parents to the end of their lives:

KAREN SEAL: My mother died of lung cancer from smoking; my father died of a heart attack from being overweight and smoking. My dad was only about five-seven and weighed about one-eighty-five. He had little legs, little arms, and a big tum. I was with both my parents as they died. My dad had a heart attack and I said later, God, why did I have to be there to see this? But I get fixated on fixing them. And my recovery is to remember that I can't do it.

✤

MICHAEL DAVIES: So, basically, I'd written that part of my life off. I felt good to have escaped. It was—there were good things about it. I can remember good things about it, but the family stuff so colored every aspect of living at that time that there was really nothing left there for me to go back to anyway. So I didn't and I felt great about that. But as it turned out, I felt that way about the family too. I cared about my siblings, but they reminded me too much of what I'd grown up with. So I didn't make an effort to really stay in touch as much as I feel I should have. I think my siblings thought that maybe I just wanted to be left alone. So nobody really pushed, not among my siblings, but of course my parents were always hurt by my not wanting to go back and visit. That's still an issue right now because my mom thinks I blame her. But I don't. It's just that when our father died, I thought finally, you know, finally we would be free.

Richard told David Doepel:

RICHARD RHODES: Solving the problem of relieving myself at night when the only toilet in the house was forbidden, I felt it was only I who could find a way through it. Perhaps not change it but survive it. I'd have to do it. No one else would do it for me; my father wouldn't, no one else would. Later, when we moved to the storefront, my brother started helping me. I take that to be a loving act, but it was also a pragmatic act. There was no place to hide the jars in the crowded little room we shared. So he had to help, or put himself at risk. He was happy to do so—well, perhaps not so happy to do so—willing to do so. We worked together when it was necessary to work together and we increasingly went our own way otherwise. We were exploring fantastic ways to solve this problem: the rockets I drew, my compulsive reading of pulp science fiction, my brother's exploration of the storm sewers under the city where he imagined himself to be Jean Valjean in *Les Misérables*. We had moved beyond the possibility of any practical solution to our problems and we were beginning to try to readjust our brains appropriately—which is a pretty good description of mental illness.

In her unpublished memoir, Anne O'Neil writes:

ANNE O'NEIL: As I absorbed the desperation Mother had expressed, I decided I would take care of her from then on with no idea that my brothers and sister would separately arrive at similar conclusions. We knew rivalry, not collaboration. Ironically, Dad was a gifted athlete who had reveled in the fun of teamwork and become masterful in applying it to building his practice and his position in our town. But the culture of survival that prevailed at home was ruled by Mother. Absolute control became a matter of life and death and pulling together impossible: we knew survival of the fittest, hang the cost, kid eat kid. We still are that way sometimes, yet we somehow beat the odds: we continued to care. My heart broke for Mother. It broke for Dad. And I longed for goodness for all of us.

8

"A Drop of Kindness"

*W*e expected the people we interviewed to report major interventions into their lives to account for their survival. Some were lucky enough eventually to be shielded from their abusers or removed, but more often we heard of small gifts of attention, brief moments of contact that they saved up as children and lived on like scraps of food cherished against starvation. We came to understand that no one should turn aside from an abused child for fear they can't give such a child enough help to make a difference: even a small intervention can save a life.

Richard asked Karen Seal a question we asked all the people we interviewed: What helped you survive?

KAREN SEAL: I think it was the faith that some people continuously showed in me, that I had worth. I kind of bastardized it by thinking it was because of what I did. That and just grim determination. I was a gutsy little kid, I really was. There were three kids: my sister capitulated, my brother spaced out, and I confronted. Except with regard to the sexual abuse, I was always confronting my father or my mother. I just would stand up to them. Who helped? I had an aunt and an uncle on my mother's side, and an uncle on my father's side, who really showed me a lot of attention. I had a teacher, and this is maybe another connection to being twelve, who was really a great influence on me. I remember her telling my mother when we had an open house, This girl has got to go to college. My mother looked at her like, I don't see how. It was just not in my mother's experience at all. That teacher was my little idol, a little bitty lady.

Valorie Butler's uncle sent mixed messages, but sometimes he found the courage to intervene:

VALORIE BUTLER: We were punished for the most trivial things. My aunt had a son whom she idolized very much. He was about a year old at the time and there was a diaper folded in a really tight little neat square in the kitchen. She said, Who did this? We were mostly defensive all the time. You know, somebody's going to be in trouble, so we all said, I didn't do it, I didn't do it.

Who knows why, but I believe, looking back, her asking was probably just idle curiosity. When everyone said "I didn't do it" she just went into a rage. Then they decided that we all would be beaten—my uncle was involved with this one too. He was a barber and had a razor strap. We were beaten with his razor strap and put on the steps for days. No one ever found out who folded that diaper. I think no one even knew who folded it. I can be folding something and talking to someone. You know how you fold and talk. Someone was folding and talking and not even aware. She didn't understand that. She was full of her own rage.

My uncle would collude with her on a lot of things, would go along with it. But once in a while, it was almost like he tried to break out. One time, out of the clear blue sky, we were standing on the steps and he said, I want you all to come down here and watch TV. We said, Wow, we get to watch. So we sat down and watched this particular show.

GINGER RHODES: Was she there?

VALORIE BUTLER: I believe she was, but it wasn't a direct confrontation. Maybe she was angry in the other room. There's another scene that's really more vivid. My younger sister, Judy, and I were both on the steps and crying because it was very hot. We didn't have air-conditioning until later years—we just had a fan. On the stairs in that area it was very hot. This was an upstairs area that had no insulation. It was like an attic, with a slanted roof. We were hot and crying because we didn't have water. My aunt let us have a little bit of water, but it didn't satisfy us of course. Then she went outside and my uncle said, I want you both to come down here and get a glass of water.

The love of an aunt and uncle gave Anna Lee Traynor a model to set against her parents' abuse:

GINGER RHODES: How did you know that your treatment at their hands was wrong?

ANNA LEE TRAYNOR: I understood it was wrong because I had an aunt and uncle who had provided me love through whatever channels they could. I lived with them for a time with my mother there, in the same household. So I had an exposure to what natural love was, what real protection and caring was. I had such a good relationship with my uncle that even his own daughter, who is nine years older than I, would say that her father just adored me. I could play with him, let him touch me as I touch and play with my own children.

GINGER RHODES: How did your aunt and uncle deal with the abuse?

ANNA LEE TRAYNOR: It's almost like they knew. My mother took us away one time because my aunt and uncle were acting too protective and my stepfather said to move us away. So they took us to live in this hovel in Newark, just to get away from them. But my aunt and uncle would bring food and clothing every week. They knew it and—I don't want to say they accepted it, but they were passive to it, because what could they legally do? They would have lost us altogether. It was a toss-up between being able to still spend time with us and providing us with that extended protection.

I'm still very close to them. My aunt is my children's grandmother—that's Nanny. My uncle's been dead about eleven years, but I'll tell you, he never leaves me. He is why I have a healthy attitude about men. I work well with men, I have a respect for men as a separate gender. I don't feel that animosity towards men or a discomfiture or a need to compete with men. I don't look for a father, because deep down inside of me I did have a healthy relationship with someone.

As Barbara Hamilton writes in The Hidden Legacy, *a family house-keeper gave her solace:*

BARBARA HAMILTON: Polly was our housekeeper and my personal ally. She was always on my side and I knew it, even though she didn't say anything to countermand my parents. Sometimes during a fracas with my brothers, while Mother was scolding me, Polly managed to look me in the eye and let me feel her support. I knew I could trust her. She would never let me down or betray me in any way.

When she took me home with her on weekends now and then, she gave me a break from the ongoing struggle of being with the family. We didn't discuss my situation; she just gave me happy times with her friends—one of whom was my age.

In our interview, Barbara elaborated:

BARBARA HAMILTON: I didn't have a Stanley [*meaning Richard's brother*], but we did have a maid, and she used to take me home on weekends sometimes. We never discussed what was happening. I was sure she'd throw me out in the street if she knew, I thought I was such a bad kid. I didn't want her to know anything about that. She couldn't rescue me, this was in the early Thirties, but she could take me home once in a while. And she could catch my eye when I was getting the dickens for something about my brothers. I remember being punished because I had hurt my little brothers or whatever I was doing to vent my anger, and she made eye contact. She never said anything about my parents being unfair, or said that if my brothers were being bratty, you had a right to strike back. She never would have done that. But her eye contact was really super. It was like the only person in my corner.

RICHARD RHODES: That's another common theme that we've been finding, that people remember even brief interventions of help along the way, remember them for the rest of their lives.

BARBARA HAMILTON: You do, you do.

GINGER RHODES: A very crucial part of surviving is those interventions because there's something to hold on to and maybe also a standard to judge the rest against. There's someone who thinks I'm all right or who thinks that there's something wrong with the situation rather than with me.

BARBARA HAMILTON: My mother-in-law, second mother-in-law, the one whom I had known all my life, and who seemed to accept me so much, was that for me. We went back there for a short visit, years later, and she took me out to lunch. I don't know how she arranged for the children, but she wanted to take me out to lunch by myself. I don't remember what we ate, but I'll never forget her saying to me, Barb, I've known you since you were a child, but I don't think of you as a child or the young woman who's married to my son. She said, You're just my friend. To think that— You're just my friend. That was so wonderful.

Ginger asked Skye Smith and her friends how they broke the cycle of abuse:

SKYE SMITH: That's the question of the century.

LYDIA DeROBERTIS: When I look back on my childhood and see how painful and isolated it was, I think what saved me was another family. I just became very close friends with a classmate when I was ten years old and from that moment on, I basically lived with these people. They lived about two blocks away and I was there every night for dinner. The incredible part, when I think about it now, is they just took me in. I'm still friends with Denise, a thirty-year relationship. Every time I see her family I say, You don't know how you saved my life. I don't even know how much they really did save my life. That I think was the single most important relationship for me. It was the thing that really got me through.

SKYE SMITH: You brought a twinkle to someone's eye.

LYDIA DeROBERTIS: When I wasn't there for dinner, they would say, Where's Lydia? When I think about it now, it's incredible. They were great.

But intervention has its perils, Valorie Butler found:

VALORIE BUTLER: I had the impression as a child that it's no use, you're stuck here, there's no way out. That was my understanding as a child.

RICHARD RHODES: You were staying with your father's brother and his wife?

VALORIE BUTLER: Right. Another aunt and uncle took us away for a week just to have some fun and they weren't aware of what was going on and we told them. But what happened was kind of destructive. I'm sure this aunt didn't realize what she caused, but she decided to go back to the aunt and confront her about it, unbeknownst to us. When we went back home, we were put in the lion's mouth. Our aunt was full of wrath, and they were going to get rid of us. We were told we were unfaithful. I was eleven or twelve at the time.

David Ray sometimes felt that seeking help was humiliating:

DAVID RAY: It wasn't fun, it was a desperate thing. It was this business of getting a little crumb here and a little crumb there. I would stay with my aunt and I would say, Why, at Grandpa's we can eat all the tomatoes we want to. Or I would say, At Aunt Peg's they're real nice to us and we can have bananas. It wasn't true. These were all miserable situations. But I would play these people off against one another. Get a little bit of affirmation here and a little bit there. The kindness of strangers becomes very important. Because you're not getting stuff from the people you ought to get it from. I could sit here and list—like the little, she must have been ninety, the frail librarian of the little one-room library over the firehouse in Nowata. She actually had some books and actually was kindly and attentive. I could read *Oliver Twist* if I wanted to. I spent some time there. Anybody. I mean you get so you're stealing smiles. You're grabbing kind words. Anything. I could remember a compliment for years. It wouldn't even have to be directed at me. I could be jealous of somebody else's compliment.

Alexa Donath mentioned a gentle grandmother. When Richard asked Alexa if her grandmother knew that she was being abused, she described an intervention by example:

ALEXA DONATH: She would live with us every summer; we had a beach house south of Boston. My mother grew up in Philadelphia and her mother would stay with us all summer long. That was the respite; that was the time when my mother was a human being most of the time. She was so good to her mother. She supported her mother before and after she was married.

RICHARD RHODES: Was she happier at those times or was it only that she controlled herself?

ALEXA DONATH: She controlled herself.

RICHARD RHODES: She didn't want her mother to see that behavior.

ALEXA DONATH: That's right, absolutely.

Books and reading helped many of the people we interviewed, including Valorie Butler:

VALORIE BUTLER: I love to read. I read all the time. In fact, I was in trouble in elementary school for sitting and reading instead of doing my schoolwork. Reading is probably one of my salvistic things.

Louise Hill described her first marriage to a physician as a time when she submerged herself in suburban life. Richard asked her how she then broke through to writing—how her creativity emerged:

LOUISE HILL: I've been trying to trace that. Let me go back and tell a story from my childhood. We didn't have any money. The first free library came to our neighborhood and it came to the next street and I've written a story about that. Every Saturday morning there was a story lady who would tell stories, and if you could guess the number she was thinking you could get the book that she'd been reading. But mainly the books were free. So I lived in that library and of course my mother was very anxious to get rid of me anyway. She was very anxious to get me out of the house. When I discovered the library, the first books I went to were biographies of musicians. The first one I read was Mozart and then I read Beethoven, then I read Bach. Now I realize—because I'm a composer too and compose music—that I was interested in creativity, that I loved books. And that's when I learned to love them.

We had very few books in our house. One was *Point Counter Point*. I don't know why we had Aldous Huxley's book but my father was always quoting from it and my mother claimed that he was a liar and had never actually read it. Another book was my mother's *101 Famous Poems*. On each page there was an oval with a portrait of the poet. And poets were women as well as men. Edna St. Vincent Millay, a *woman,* wrote poetry! I can recite every poem in that book, all hundred and one. I read it until it fell apart. Of course it had Edgar Allan Poe and it had Kipling's *If*— my father's favorite poem.

So I was in love with books. I did my homework in my mother's and father's bedroom, which was adjacent to mine, and which actually was the room designed to be the dining room. But it was their bedroom. My mother had a vanity table and that was my desk. It was right next to a window. My desk was always quite a mess. One day my mother got so angry that I was making a mess out of her bedroom, so angry with all the books, that she opened up the window and threw the books out the window. It was cold—winter—and I remember that feeling of going around outside in that yard and picking up those books and bringing them in. [*She indicates the bookshelves around her apartment.*] You see these bookshelves—there are ten others all over the place, filled with books. I can't tell you that I've read all of them. I've read most of them. To this day I love books. My night table is piled with books, books I may read, books I'm going to read, books I'm going to reread.

From books and reading, by extension teachers and school. Ginger asked Michael Davies if there had been anyone he could turn to, anyone he could trust:

MICHAEL DAVIES: Not in the family. I had friends. I find it remarkable that I had any friends back then. I had fun too as a kid. I loved sports and most of my friends, we played ball together—depending what the season was, we played that kind of ball. I guess that the sense of self-worth I acquired came through doing well in school. There was structure there. And a kind of safety.

RICHARD RHODES: You got along with teachers and they liked you? That was very important to me.

MICHAEL DAVIES: Maybe I was looking for some teacher to be the parent my dad never was.

❖

SKYE SMITH: I was a good student and so I got self-esteem in school. Unfortunately, I didn't have kindergarten, so I had to wait until I was six and a half to start school, pretty late. And when I was sixteen, my relationship with my boyfriend's family was crucial. They were my salvation, my safe place. I'm positive that saved me.

RICHARD RHODES: People you could turn to?

SKYE SMITH: Yes. In fact, I just went to their other son's—my former boyfriend's brother's—wedding. I've kept in close touch with them.

Even physical beauty could make a difference; it did for Celia Golden and Alexa Donath:

CELIA GOLDEN: Some of us have strengths that other people didn't need to develop. As flaky as I might seem to some people, I don't feel like a flake. I don't feel weak. I know how to ask for help and have always had people care about me, love me. I was an attractive kid, and people responded. People do that, they respond to someone who's attractive. You could take another kid that's got a great personality and brain, but people respond to that exterior first. I think that helped teachers take an interest in me. You walk by a cute kid and you pat her head, Oh, what a pretty little kid.

⊕

ALEXA DONATH: I sent my parents my master's thesis in the mail. Isn't that stupid? They probably never read it, but there's still this little person inside me saying, See, I'm really smart.

I was the pretty girl that everybody wanted to be friends with. I pleased everybody. I was a great friend and loyal to the point of craziness. I didn't believe that I had anything deep down; basically I thought I was just looks. You can't tell now, but fifty pounds ago, before my health problems came along, I was really beautiful. I had long, long hair. Pretty people get a lot of stuff in this society. You get to go places and do things, you get to meet people, you get to date rich people. It's an accident of birth. In my experience with not having it now, I understand the difference. It gives you an entry, so you take it for granted. I'm passable now, but I was considered beautiful then. That's one of the things that helped me get through my childhood. Everyone wanted to be with me. I chose bad boyfriends, people who didn't think a lot of me or people who worshiped me and only wanted me on their arm—like my father. I didn't choose anybody who really loved me for me.

But I survived by being with people I didn't have to lie to. People who knew my mother was crazy, who made fun of her along with me. But they still didn't know the pain behind it. By then I was a teenager and she was no longer hurting me physically. She couldn't possibly. But I was still under her roof. That's what was weird because what I was like, what most people thought I was like, I wasn't like at all.

GINGER RHODES: Children who make it through childhoods like that are masters at deception. They can present themselves any way they need to be.

ALEXA DONATH: Absolutely. This is me. I'm exactly what you see right now. Always. I talk to people in stores. I talk to the man on the street. I'm really out there. That was my way of surviving; that was how I got through it. I've always reached out. I was in fact my mother's daughter, and in a way I inherited her gift for being with people. That's unusual for a child. Something in me knew that I should do that and I could do it.

If I'm going to say anything good about myself, I have to say this. I know this was very unusual, but I told everybody what was being done to me, I tried to tell whoever would listen. As a child and as an adult, all the time. My mother nicknamed me "Big Mouth" because I was telling stuff—that's why my mother didn't want me to go sleep over in anyone else's house. That's why the mother said, That mother was awfully hard on those girls. Everybody gets to sleep over with friends, unless you don't want them to tell, unless there's some secret. If you don't want them out of your sight that long, there's something going on. My friend's mother knew that, my Brownie leader knew. There were people who knew. I told people, but they wouldn't listen. They'd say, Yes, yes, yes.

GINGER RHODES: How did you feel when people wouldn't listen?

ALEXA DONATH: It was the Fifties, it was the Sixties. I was born in '51. Those things didn't happen then, and they especially didn't happen to the woman who drove the blue Cadillac and looked like Lana Turner.

RICHARD RHODES: There are subtle class distinctions in people's perceptions of child abuse.

ALEXA DONATH: My mother said, Am I a whore?—Look where you live, look at all your clothes. Well, Father was in the clothing business. If he was a butcher we would have eaten meat every night.

Interventions gave Karen Seal the courage to resist her father's molestation:

RICHARD RHODES: I'm curious about the timing of your finally finding the strength to tell your father to stop. Does it connect to anything else at that particular point in time? Have you thought about why?

KAREN SEAL: I had a series of people who took a shine to me. I was such a pleaser, such a good little girl and such a good student, so I had teachers and aunts and uncles who took an interest in me. At that time I don't know of anything special except I had begun to earn money babysitting, and I was getting more praise from neighbors about what a responsible kid I was. I think it was also the first time I can consciously remember him having any interest in my body. But I think that his turning on to my body is probably the thing that made a difference. I'm glad you asked that; I'd never thought of that before.

A visitor at school singled out Valorie Butler, a brief contact she has never forgotten:

VALORIE BUTLER: Art was a sensitive thing to me. I'm still trying to be that artist, it's all coming back.

GINGER RHODES: Your aunt didn't let you express that?

VALORIE BUTLER: She would not allow me to develop it in school. I got praise for my art, because I was skilled at it, and I liked that praise because it was something positive. A man named Dick Mansfield, a traveling policeman who did chalk drawings for safety programs, gave a demonstration. I remember specifically I was in the sixth grade and here I was all excited about these chalk drawings. After the class—we had several classes come to our classroom to see his program—afterwards he was drawing something, he kept drawing, drawing, and he was drawing me. I thought that was neat. He gave me the drawing to take home. My aunt told me to put it in the trash. Chalk smears things, she told me.

Dick Mansfield asked me that day to send him a photograph, because, he said, I want to do a much better drawing and send it to you. I never did send him one. I thought, what's the use? Living in a world of no freedom. What's the use?

John Wood found help from a teacher he threatened:

JOHN WOOD: When I was fourteen, a freshman in high school, I pulled a knife on a teacher. He instantly took it away from me and I got thrown out of the school. His name was John Plouffe and I remember him very clearly. I was then sent away to a Quaker School up in Poughkeepsie, still there and still taking rejects. I stayed out all night with a girl there, so I got thrown out of that one. So they sent me to Peekskill Military Academy— "That will straighten him out." Every day, even today, when I make my bed, the goddamn commandant is right there saying, Hey, that's not straight. I ran away from there at Thanksgiving time. I had to give up that idea, I couldn't make it on my own. So I came back home and John Plouffe, the guy I pulled a knife on, helped me. He and his wife tutored me for the rest of that year. They essentially gave me passing grades. They helped, they listened, and I talked to them. I enjoyed being over at their house. I used to go over to their house to get tutored. They didn't come down here, I went over there. So that was good. So they were there for me, both of them, really. John and Mary Plouffe. Believe me, there are gangs and gangs of people from that time in my life whose names I don't recall.

❖

VALORIE BUTLER: I do think back to the special people I love. My sixth-grade teacher, Mrs. Carrick, is eighty-seven years old and just as vibrant as can be. She treated us like a grandmother. Accidentally in class one time I called her Grandma. I was very embarrassed, but that was what I was feeling about her, this nice grandma person. I called her up recently and went out to see her and had a nice visit with her. Those people are little beacons of light along the way. We're not aware of it necessarily at the time, but as our healing comes in, we can look back and see that.

❖

LOUISE HILL: So how did I become interested in writing and how did I triumph over this? Well—

RICHARD RHODES: Let me preface this, Louise, by noticing that you evidently became those things that your mother said were bad. You became creative, open, and expressive and someone who couldn't be punished. It's as if she was describing to you exactly those things that you needed to be a whole human being. And those are the things she didn't want you to be. When did they become your goal?

LOUISE HILL: I didn't want to be her. I didn't want her life. I didn't want a life where I was scrubbing floors, where I was angry, where I had no friends, no outside life, no travel. I wanted all the things that didn't exist in that house.

When did the change come? In junior high I began to write poetry and it was published in the school yearbook. But the change came in high school. Before high school, I announced that I wanted to go to Girls' Latin School, which was a college-track school, and I was admitted. Remember, I was killed if I got anything less than an A. If I got an A-minus I was yelled at: *Why couldn't you get an A?* But my mother said, did I think I was crazy, going to Girls' Latin School—I wasn't going to go to college, so why did I think I needed to go to Girls' Latin? My father had no opinion in this, by the way. I don't remember him being present in any of these discussions. I had to go to this other school, which was a very mediocre school. In fact, it was a very big inner-city school, in Roxbury. What would now be called racially diverse. Most of the students were taking commercial courses and a very small portion of the students went to college. There were only two tiny college sections.

So I took a commercial course because it was expected that I would be a secretary. That was expected to be a good thing to do. Then the breakthrough came.

(I'd already noticed, before high school, that our town was divided into the poor and the rich. It would change from street to street and the street right next to ours—our street was rows and rows of three-decker houses—on the very next street there were brick houses. In those brick houses, single houses, lived girls who were much wealthier. Now, those families were on the move. By the time we got to high school most of those families had moved out to greener pastures, to the suburbs of Brookline, Newton, to really beautiful houses. Those girls had beautiful clothes and they all shopped at Best & Co. I had never set foot in Best & Co. It's out of business now, but I thought that the halls there must indeed be lined with gold, as was Bonwit Teller. And I was very surprised when I finally went in there and found out it was quite an ordinary store. But I longed to be like those girls. To have pretty cashmere sweaters. How poor were we? This was not funny when I was growing up, but I see the humor now: we were so poor that my mother made my underpants. She made them from leftover dresses, whatever was left over. But imagine the humiliation. This was nobody's abuse, it was just a fact of life. In the sixth grade one day, the elastic broke on my bloomers. The dress they'd been made from had a Chinese pattern. It was an orange silk pattern with black pagodas on it. The elastic broke and the bloomers fell to my feet. All my friends were around and I was quite embarrassed. I never had real underpants till I went to college.)

So. The breakthrough. High school. I had a teacher for English named Miss Sophia Palm. She was quite extraordinary. I had her for English in my junior year. We were supposed to write short stories. I started to write my short stories and one after another they got published in the school literary magazine. Miss Palm called me in one day after school. She said, Louise, you're such a writer, why aren't you going to college? I said, Oh, we can't afford for me to go to college, I have to support my family. My father was not working much, so it was just expected that I would support the family. I would get this great job as an executive secretary, not just a regular secretary. So Miss Palm said, This is silly, you must go to college, there are scholarships. I'm going to call your parents in.

I wasn't there when my parents came in, but I'm sure it wasn't my father who went. It was my mother. Miss Palm told me that my mother said it was ridiculous and I couldn't go to college. My mother was very angry at me. I was a betrayer, having this teacher call her.

At the same time, I was president of a group of girls, the B'nai B'rith girls, and there was a brother group. We had clubs in those days with our own jackets, silk jackets with our names on them, the name of the club on the back. Indian names—Iroquois and so forth. Ours were religious clubs, they had to do with helping Israel. Because I was president, I had a lot of interaction with the boys' group. The boys in this particular group were an extraordinary group of guys. Anybody who had any money had gotten out of that neighborhood, so only the poor, striving kids were left. All these boys, without exception, went to Boston Latin School. One of the finest public schools in the country and a preparatory school for college. It was a well-known fact that if you went to Boston Latin School you went straight to Harvard. And if you couldn't get into Harvard you went to Yale, Princeton, or Dartmouth.

I became very friendly with these boys. And I dated every single one of them. I can tell you honestly, I don't think that I gave a hoot and a holler about any of them physically. I think the reason I dated them was for their minds and to this day the sexiest thing to me about a man is his mind. I notice that I've fallen in love with men who are brilliant. So I used to hang out with these guys. At Boston Latin School they would prep these boys for the SATs. We had none of that where I went. These boys prepped me.

In my junior year, Miss Palm convinced me that I should go to college and promised to help me to find a way with scholarships. I said, I can't do that, it's my junior year and I've taken no college courses—I have one year left. She said, You'll go to summer school and make up for all the college courses. I said, I can't do that, I have to work. I was working in a hospital, which was my grandmother's idea—in order to meet a doctor. (Which, by the way, I did, so the idea worked.) I said, I have to work. Well, said Miss Palm, why can't you work at the hospital at night, find a night job?

So between my junior and senior year I went to summer school and took chemistry, biology, and mathematics. And this is the question I ask you. How come I had the guts to do that? That was the work that broke me out of there. But I was so miserable at home and so beaten up that it was either get out or die. And I wanted to get out more than anything else in the world. I also at that time knew I was a pretty good writer from these short stories. And I dreamt about being a writer. To me it was a dream and the only model that I had was *Little Women*. I would read that book over and over again. How Jo had the guts to be a writer and be unconventional.

So somehow or other I had the courage, but it was also given to me by these young men. We used to get pinned in those days. I was pinned to one of the guys. Who did those men become? One of them is chief of medicine at Columbia Presbyterian Hospital. Another one is president of Saks Fifth Avenue. Another one is the head of the sociology department at Brandeis. They have all become illustrious. They've become writers and doctors and lawyers and chemists and explorers and economists. So I was with the right group.

Of course my parents were furious with me. That's when my mother got really angry because how dare I do this, do something else than the dream that she had for me?

At any rate, I worked nights and weekends at the Beth Israel Hospital and Miss Palm helped me. She showed me the books where they had fellowships and grants. I applied to three colleges in the Boston area. I applied to Simmons, which was a school for women, to Harvard and to Tufts. Nowadays when kids are applying to college, you think of the parents sitting with them going over the applications. Not at my house. But I applied and I got into Harvard, I got into Simmons, I got into Tufts. I ended up going to Tufts because they gave me the most money.

The organization that helped me most through college was the Women's Scholarship Association. Their mission was to help young women go to college. My father died at the end of my freshman year and I was terrified. My mother wanted me to stop college and come home and help earn a living and take care of my sister. I refused to do that. I was terrified to go home and I went to Women's Scholarship and appealed to them. During my freshman year in college I commuted and they gave me enough to commute. But Tufts was then a live-in school and I was feeling like a real have-not. But I knew then that I had to get out of that house once and for all or I would drown forever. I asked Women's Scholarship for money to live at school. They gave it to me. They had never done that before and they've never done it since. I was the only young woman they ever gave money to live and I moved into school. To finish that piece of the story, when I graduated from college I became very active in the organization, to help other women go to college. Seven years ago they named a scholarship in my honor. It's for young women going into the arts.

A nun trained as a counselor helped Anne O'Neil begin the long work of remaking her life:

ANNE O'NEIL: Where it stops, where it stopped for me, was where I decided that it couldn't all be the way Mother wanted it. I had to have been twenty-one years old, I was in the convent by then, I was very depressed, I was not functioning well, I was losing it. I was losing my verve, and I had a wise superior who saw this. I don't know what my other superiors thought, but this one must have known that there was something missing within me. For one thing, she knew I was intelligent and I wasn't really doing that well in school. She said she wanted to see me. We would get together in the beginning for an hour, three times a week. She had a degree in educational psychology. We talked, and it was there that she told me that my Mother was wrong.

It was the first time I told anyone anything that my mother had said to me. Specifically, in this instance, it was that if God really loves you, then you belong in a religious life. My superior said, just plain and simple, that my mother was very wrong to have said that. I could accept that—that my mother's statement was very wrong. I could endure that sense of disloyalty. It wasn't too bad, you know, that I had disclosed that. That was the first time I had heard *anyone* say that Mother was wrong about *anything*. And that was the start.

Ralph Kessler found alleviation in a cause, though he came to regret its theory and practice:

RALPH KESSLER: Who and what helped me to survive? Believe it or not, it was a cause. I forgot about myself and my troubles and became involved in the world's. In short, I became a Communist, and early in 1936, I joined the Young Communist League (YCL). I was as active as it was possible to be. I had a *Daily Worker* and *Jewish Freiheit* route. I sold *New Masses* on Times Square. I passed out leaflets, went to meetings, and lived the cause. Instantly I had friends.

How did I happen to join the Communists? A vacuum will always be filled. I needed something as I had no parent or adult supervision. I could easily have turned to crime, liquor, drugs, or whatever if I had fallen in with the right person. As it was, I met Communists and I was ready. Being Jewish, I felt intensely the sting of the German treatment of the Jews, and at the same time, wasn't the greatest enemy of the Nazis the Communists?

Since I wanted to believe, the absurdities of Communist theory were no problem any more than Christian theology or any revealed "truth" would be a problem to someone who was receptive to it. How I shed the Communist ideology is another story. It occurred in stages.

At first, I held that the American Party was wrong but Russia was right. Then that Russia was wrong but Marxism was right. The last stage, when I dropped Marxism, occurred when I confronted Marxism's essential point: that the condition of working people under capitalism worsens. If it didn't, you wouldn't need the Marxist alternative. Well, I finally believed my senses. The condition of the working people in the advanced capitalist countries has not gotten worse—it has gotten better, thus bankrupting Marxism's validity.

At the time that I joined the Young Communist League in February 1936, I was not yet fifteen years old. I could read a book a day. I was intensely curious about the world. Once I joined the Communists I instantly lost my curiosity and no longer wanted to know everything because now I knew the truth. I read Communist literature and whatever else could be related to the cause. I instantly dropped comics and sports sections because they were the poison that the capitalists fed the workers to take their minds off their troubles. I only wanted to read material that would make me a better Communist.

The Communist cause saved me from perhaps personal disintegration or whatever, but I paid for it. I stopped learning and growing and only after I shed every vestige of Marxism did I read and study and learn again.

A sister who taught Celia Golden to touch and to speak alleviated the torture of her childhood isolation:

CELIA GOLDEN: My mother projected all the things she hated in herself onto me, and everything that she wanted to be onto my younger sister. I became the receptacle for those things she couldn't acknowledge openly about herself. I was sent by the devil. I was crazy.

RICHARD RHODES: She said these things to you?

CELIA GOLDEN: Yes. My earliest memory is being afraid of my mother. I have early memories of being in a crib. My mother tied me in my crib so I couldn't move and basically stuck me in a back room. I remember that gagging was one of her things. She kept the blinds pulled and pretty much tried to forget that I existed. I think that she wanted me to just die. Sometimes she actively did things to try to make that happen. My earliest memories are of lying there, cold and wet and hungry, not being able to move and fighting against that restraint. Fighting against the bars and feeling really small in that dark room. That was my normal environment.

My other sister was three years older than me. I remember her sneaking into the bedroom and walking over to my crib. There's a sadistic edge about this, it's like I'm a trapped animal, but there's another side. I would see her looking at me. She would reach through the bars and touch me. I remember that, her touching my arms and my hands and my face and telling me who she was. Her name was Carol and she would try to get me to say her name. I remember the frustration of hearing what she was saying and trying to repeat it, but I couldn't make what came out match. And I couldn't get her to understand that I understood. I eventually was able to say, *Cawo,* and she understood. She was so excited. I remember her going to tell my mother. Then I heard Carol crying out in the hall; I heard Mom hitting her and warning her not to come in the room.

I have a baby book my mom kept, where she recorded things like Baby's first words. She thought I was retarded because I didn't talk until I was two and a half. She also thought I was crazy, but first believed I was just retarded. When I was around four, other people started noticing things that I could do and told her I was gifted, artistically and musically gifted. I think my sister was important in that ability. Also my father.

It was like I was his firstborn child. He was the one who would get up in the night and walk the floor with me. He would sing his war songs and hold me and read the newspaper. I think this was another contributing factor to my mother hating me. He didn't respond to my older sister the same way. He wasn't there during the pregnancy, the delivery, and the first two years of her life. But he was there when my mother was pregnant with me. So I was getting attention that my mother didn't get, and that my older sister didn't get. He gave me a lot of affection and attention that people assume comes from a woman. Naturally not from men, naturally. I can remember wanting my dad to read to me. I also have an awareness that he believed that I was retarded, like my mom said.

It's weird, because I know that I didn't have a vocabulary to match my understanding, but I understood so many things. I understood that they all thought there was something wrong with my mind, that I was stupid. My dad starting picking up that I would repeat words. He was excited and would play these games of seeing how many words did I know. He told my mom, She can read, she understands. Did you see the movie *My Left Foot*? It was a similar kind of thing. I think when someone believes in a kid, the kid performs for them.

I did that for teachers. When the teachers were blown away at stuff I did, I thought, yeah, I'll do more for you. Then they signed me up for music lessons and my mom got this idea that I was the brain. I was going to be the one who put the family on the map with scholarships—be a valedictorian and make my family shine. Which I thought was really stupid. I really didn't want to participate in that, be used that way. But I was lucky that I had my father in that way.

✛

VALORIE BUTLER: My uncle would go by while we were standing on the steps and with everything quiet, he would do this loud pop-clap. Of course we'd jump, and then you'd get the feeling, ooohh, I might fall back off the steps, you know, because we're facing towards the steps. Or he would take these plastic Easter eggs and bounce them off the back of our head. I started laughing when I told my counselor that, and she just had on a stone face. That was not funny, it was humiliating.

The one thing that I did kind of like, though, was when he would sit at the bottom of the steps. I believe he did this out of guilt feelings. His conscience was bothering him. I believe it bothered him that we were on the steps, but he couldn't face that and deal with it. But he would get these spoons and make music—sing these old ditties. I would cackle to myself a little bit on the steps. I believe he did it to entertain us.

RICHARD RHODES: He played the spoons?

VALORIE BUTLER: He played the spoons. He would sing us a little song, "Momma don't allow no cows around here." He would go on about Momma don't allow no cows around here, then he'd say, "I don't care what Momma don't allow, I'm going to allow these cows up here anyhow." Then he would make animal sounds. He'd moo just like a cow, and then he'd go on to another animal, and he'd make that animal sound—it sounded just like the animal. I thought that was really entertaining, and to this day I mimic animals. I like animals a lot anyway, and with little kids, I will make animal sounds. Of course a lot of people do that anyway, but I think I did adopt that from him.

RICHARD RHODES: The lyrics of that song—it's a song of rebellion against his wife about the cows, you girls.

VALORIE BUTLER: Yeah, Momma don't allow, Momma don't allow, she's the boss.

RICHARD RHODES: But he's going to—

VALORIE BUTLER: But he's going to do it anyhow. He was pretty good at it, slapping those spoons against his knee, playing those spoons.

Celia Golden intervened in turn, even as a child, when her mother baby-sat other children:

CELIA GOLDEN: My mother did baby-sitting for hire. She's one of those women who goes to church every Sunday, takes kids to Sunday school. She's in the PTA, teaches Girl Scouts, volunteers for cupcakes at school, and all that shit. So isn't she the perfect person to watch your kids? My mother did not like kids who talked. She preferred them young. There were two little sisters; one of them was preverbal, but the other was a couple years older and did the talking for her little sister. She went home and reported stuff. After that, my mom would only take babies up to a certain age. I saw what she did with those kids but those mothers were convinced that my mother was a great woman.

The way my mother's house was arranged, she would put the crib in a corner in the living room, which put it at the farthest end of the house. We weren't allowed to go into the living room. If the baby woke up and cried to be fed, it didn't matter, it got a bottle at a certain time. If it dropped its bottle, you didn't pick it up. Tough shit, you know. If it's wet, it's not time to change it. It doesn't matter what's going on with that kid, you were not to respond to it in any way. If my mother was outside, I could sneak in and pick up the bottle. If my mother went to get groceries or to the neighbors, I could pick the baby up. I would do the same kind of thing that I learned from my sister. Make contact. My therapist said that was a real gift from my sister, because if you don't learn empathy, you have nothing to give. I got empathy from my father and my sister.

But thirty minutes before those mothers would come to pick up their kids, it was time to change the sheets on the bed, wash the kid and put clean clothes on it. She was sitting there holding this baby and playing with it when the mother walked in.

✤

SKYE SMITH: My doctor asked me, in one of our first interviews, What is your fondest memory of your mother? Instantly I had this wonderful memory of my mother. We had an organ in our house. When I was home sick from school she would play the organ for me. That's my fondest memory of my mother. In bed in another room while listening to a funeral organ—nice, cozy, soft. I thought that was so sweet. Isn't that sweet?

RICHARD RHODES: That's a variation on being upstairs with the movie theater down below.

SKYE SMITH: That was creepy. Those 3-D glasses—you put them on and you see these things on the screen you don't see without. I would sneak down sometimes, because I was terrified. The only person who was really nice was Morton, this chubby old man who lived with his mother—who knows what his psychological profile was. He was the movie ticket taker. He had a little seat and he would let me sit on his lap and take tickets with him sometimes. I thought I was special then. I got to sit on a lap. We had no touching in our house, except hitting—no touching, no lap-sitting, no hugging, no nothing, just hitting. He let me sit on his lap, and I was special.

The Menninger Clinic's Susan Voorhees and Alice Brand Bartlett, both widely experienced with the consequences of child abuse, find the complexities of survival and loss too complicated to define:

GINGER RHODES: In your experience, how do kids survive? I know there's not one answer, but there must be some similarities, some common factors in why some kids do and some don't. How do they make it through?

SUSAN VOORHEES: I don't know. [*The three of us laugh.*]

GINGER RHODES: For instance, we hear from people we've been talking to that they had something to hold on to, that there was an intervention. They had a favorite teacher, or someone who walked by and fluffed their hair occasionally and told them they were a cute kid.

SUSAN VOORHEES: Even if that person didn't even remember that child and never thought of what he or she did as an intervention, for the children there's some good something that they've been able to encapsulate and internalize and that has sustained them through the growing-up years.

GINGER RHODES: Why aren't other kids able to get that?

SUSAN VOORHEES: You know, I'm not sure. I think it might be availability, it might be a question of timing—that at the right moment the right person comes along. It may be that during a moment when a child's defenses are down, a teacher comes by and says, Well, you did a nice job today. Or the lady in the corner grocery who sells bread always remembers their name. Maybe it's that kind of fate—a timing factor. Some kids may just be stronger temperamentally.

RICHARD RHODES: More robust.

SUSAN VOORHEES: Yes, and so they aren't so cowed by the abuse that they experience. They're still able to accept something from somebody else.

❖

GINGER RHODES: Finally some people have had enough abuse and they walk out.

ALICE BRAND BARTLETT: Some people somehow have the resilience. Maybe because there's been a teacher or a friend's parent. They've had something good, some place that allows them to leave an abuser, to think that there might be something better. A drop of kindness that they hold on to. But other people can't do it. I don't know what, in terms of temperament, makes the difference. There are studies of temperament indicating that people come into the world with different endowments, so there's some biological component that allows some kids to engage and not be so shy and to pull something from somebody. And some kids can't do it.

With great passion, David Ray celebrates the love his Aunt Edris gave him—and returns it in a poem worthy of comparison to the work of Walt Whitman.

Hymn to Aunt Edris

That I did love thee . . . O,'tis true! . . .
Why, I will see thee in Philippi then. . . .
Now I have taken heart thou vanishest.
Ill spirit, I would hold more talk with thee. . . .

Shakespeare, *Julius Caesar*

Old katydids in the West Tulsa night!
Refineries burning off their oil in fiery pools.
Uncle Henry holding a picket sign in wind that whipped him.
At night, on his shoulder, holding hair, I stooped
through the doorway of the soup kitchen
where we bent over a long table, eating soup,
a family of hundreds, and went back for more.
Tell me again where my father's supposed to be.
Aunt Edris, your great swinging breasts
were pendulum of time too I see now, but then

this small boy wished to press his cheeks

against you, and couldn't tell you,

and you were young, though I didn't know it

then, laughing that Henry's toes were cold.

Your bed sounded warm, through that curtain

that hung between us. On the floor

we children threw cockroaches from us,

the only ones who loved our bodies,

and heard your giggles, tickles, guessed

at your rolling movements, tried to ape them

on our own flat bodies. But you turned

into a dolphin in the night, swam

as we could not, bore Henry

through the tossing waves, then wept.

More whys and wherefores to puzzle us!

The smell of your biscuits woke us

and you put us on the ice-cold table while

we watched you move in flannel about those warped

linoleum floors. The oven had a handle

made of coiled and gleaming wires.

Only for you would I run those errands

through ditches to bring back butter

that was not butter, had no color;

and later Henry left the picket lines

and his face became something that we always feared.

He threatened to throw us off

the bridge. Fourth of July he threw

firecrackers at us, had the dog chase us

round and round the house, under clotheslines.

Unwanted. So be it. But you I still want.

And dear woman find in the face of my own beloved

whose face is round as a biscuit, like yours,

and smiling, for she won't mistreat me.

Take me again, Edris, out to the outhouse,

In the rain, stepping from plank to plank.
It's our house, of cracked and rotting wood.
The lightning shows your face up close.
You hold me in your arms, and step lightly,
shaking, avoiding spiders, and the years.

9

"A Very Dangerous Way to Go"

Survivors of child abuse struggle with the complex consequences of their experience. The men and women we interviewed described both negative and positive effects on their lives; this chapter offers their testimony to the negative effects.

Richard asked Menninger therapist Alice Brand Bartlett about what she called "repetition of the abuse":

RICHARD RHODES: I've sometimes wondered, certainly with myself, if finding a parallel situation as an adult—in my case, marrying someone who was abusive in much the same way my stepmother was abusive, except that in my former wife's case alcohol was involved—wasn't an attempt to make the scenario come out right this time.

ALICE BRAND BARTLETT: There are many possibilities, yes. Consciously you want to be loved, but unconsciously you want to make it right.

RICHARD RHODES: To fix it.

GINGER RHODES: You keep replaying it so that perhaps this time the abuser will stop, it will work out.

ALICE BRAND BARTLETT: Exactly. To call it a repetition of the abuse is a misnomer. For that to be the case, Richard, to take your example, you'd have to be the abuser. Internally, though, it's experienced as a repetition of an abusive relationship, repeated from childhood.

Celia Golden remembers feeling drawn as a child to repeating her mother's sadistic play—but also feeling horrified:

CELIA GOLDEN: My mother baby-sat one of her friend Doris's granddaughters for a couple of weeks. The little girl was about two and a half. I was nine and a half at the time. This was after Doris and my mother together had raped me. She was a pretty little girl, really sweet. I was left alone with her—everyone else in my family had gone off someplace. I ended up having this stuff come up, feeling like my mother. I saw this little girl, just beginning to talk, helpless, dependent on me, no one else around, and I started playing sadistic games with her. I would hand her a doll, she'd reach for it, and then I'd pull it back and hit her. Then I'd hand it to her again and she wouldn't go for it. I'd coax her, so she'd take it and then I'd hit her. It was that sort of sadism where the kid didn't know what was up or down. There was nothing she could do right, there was no way she could second-guess me. Then I went from hitting her hands to hitting her face, to pulling her pants down and hitting her bottom. I would just keep hitting her bottom nonstop. I would realize what I was doing and stop, but then those feelings would come up again. It's just like having a physical appetite for food. I got real scared because I couldn't stop. I kept repeating it. The little girl was doing everything I'd been taught to do. She wouldn't cry when I told her not to cry. If I told her to cry, she'd let it out. She'd stop it immediately when I told her to stop it. She was like a little robot. I got really scared about what had happened.

When my family came back, every time that little girl had to go to the bathroom, I took her to the bathroom. She was at our house for several more days. I had learned from my mother how to make sure that nobody saw what I had done to this kid. Even though I didn't sexually abuse her by definition, it was a sexual experience for me. A week later her mother discovered she had a totally black-and-blue butt and called my mother. I understood from what my mother was saying on her end of the line that they were trying to figure out if my mom did it or someone else in our house. I freaked out and started crying and screamed, It was me, it was me, I did it, I did it. My mother covered up the phone, told me to shut up, got back on the phone, and said she had to go.

I was in hysterics. I hated myself with all the anger I couldn't direct at my mother or father. I felt I should go to prison, be put away, that there was something really seriously wrong with me. I didn't trust myself with kids. It's the only time my mother has ever protected me. I know now it was her secret. I couldn't handle seeing anybody in Doris's family, I felt so ashamed. There's always been self-hatred, but I went around for years feeling like the perpetrator. That was one of the last things I was able to talk to my therapist about. I feel like it's really important to talk about because I know there are a lot of us who have had the same experience. We have found that we have the capacity to be like the perpetrator. And yet, my therapist says it's different: "You could own it. You knew it was you. You didn't blame the little girl. You've always known it wasn't her, it had nothing to do with her." And that's a difference.

RICHARD RHODES: But it's the obsessive quality of the pleasure one takes from it that I think leaves one feeling so threatened about it. So threatened in your case that you thought you should go to jail, which is a place where you might be safe from your own impulses.

CELIA GOLDEN: I understand what that power was like for my mother or any other woman.

I think that kids who are abused need special attention to help them not be perpetrators and that as prospective parents, they need to have some safe place where they can talk about it. People would try to brush it off with me. I would say that I have a horrible temper, that I can get so angry I could kill somebody. Since I was a young girl, I've had the fear that I was capable of killing somebody. I probably had that much rage when I was real young. But people would say, You—I've never even seen you angry. Most people think I'm soft-spoken. Yes, I am soft-spoken and yes, I don't get angry a lot, but I have tremendous rage in me. I think it's too bad that people want to believe, Okay, now she's married, she's got a nice house and kids. You know, where's the damage? To believe that kids are resilient, that they can take anything.

John Wood is the Connecticut antique dealer:

JOHN WOOD: If you grow up in slums, if you grow up with child abuse, if you grow up with being abused as a child, you assume that the world is abusive, and the only way to get along in the world is to be abusive.

In her book The Hidden Legacy, *Barbara Hamilton reports an unsettling incident from her childhood:*

BARBARA HAMILTON: We had a young Sealyham dog that my uncle had given us, who quickly became part of the family. We all loved Pat and he seemed fond of each of us, without a favorite. One day I carried him up to my room, locked the door, and laid him on his side on the gray carpet. I then began to masturbate him. Although I had seen dogs mate, I didn't associate this with mating. I knew what to do with my fingers to make him climax. He didn't resist and I knew that he enjoyed it. I remember thinking that I didn't want anyone to know what I was doing, but that he liked it, so it must be a little bit okay. I knew that pretty soon "gooey stuff" would come out and that it wouldn't be urine. When it did, I was satisfied that everything happened the way I expected it to.

After the "research" was over that day, I had no desire to repeat it. I knew that Mother would be horrified if she knew about it, and I suddenly felt guilty and deeply ashamed of what I had done. But I felt safe because

Pat couldn't tell on me. Whenever I remembered the incident, though, I felt like a dirty, bad girl and hated myself. . . .

In our interview, Barbara added:

BARBARA HAMILTON: I don't remember everything by any means, but I never forgot something that happened when I was seven—masturbating the family dog. I used to think, years ago, that that was the first time anything happened. It took a lot of therapy and a lot of working through to realize it wasn't and to put things together. I wouldn't have been like that [*she means without previous experience of sexual manipulation*]. There's no way. When I asked my second therapist about masturbating that dog in my room, I just thought it was because I was bad. I said, How would I know, how would I know? And she said, Yes, how would you know what to expect?

It's amazing how we grow up protecting our abusers.

✦

JOHN WOOD: One of the things that's pretty much gone from my memory is my stay in jail.

RICHARD RHODES: How old were you?

JOHN WOOD: Eighteen.

RICHARD RHODES: You really started being rebellious and acting out when you hit adolescence, didn't you? A lot of the anger came out.

JOHN WOOD: Oh, yeah, boy, when that testosterone really got going, I was getting in trouble a lot.

GINGER RHODES: Were you an angry kid? Did you feel that angry?

JOHN WOOD: You bet. I went to jail for burglary, which was reduced to breaking and entering. I was hanging out with a guy who was adopted named Chuck Palmer, who had been in reform school. Chuck and I hit it off right away. And one time, Chuck came over to our house with another guy and they had a whole bunch of tools and stuff in the back of the car. I said, Geez, where'd you get that? They said, Come on, we'll show you. So I went with them. They had cleaned out a house very much like yours here, summer digs. The guy was a collector really, collected stuff, tools, anything. They had really cleaned out the house. This was the third night that they had gone in, and so I participated in that to some degree. I got scared the next day and threw all the stuff away. A couple of days later, the cops showed up. New Year's Day the cops showed up. Packed me off to jail.

RICHARD RHODES: How long?

JOHN WOOD: One hundred seven days. I was in the slammer for forty-seven days before trial. Allegedly my parents' lawyer advised them to leave me in the slammer because that would count. I got a year, suspended after sixty days. I believe at this point, at least to the best of my knowledge, I was spared being raped in jail.

John wrote us:

JOHN WOOD: The fear is about loss of control. The fear that talking about the abuse is the same as reliving it. And we'll be out of control all over again. So the only way to be safe is to maintain control. Control. *The* big C. Cancer is a mosquito bite by comparison. Control is the most insidious, widespread, longstanding, and virulent killer the world has ever known. Control is the reason that man makes death. . . .

My mind was filled with short-circuits (dyslexia), my soul was murdered, my body was raped and whipped, my hopes were dashed, my dreams were turned into nightmares, my ambitions were castrated, my intelligence was mocked, and my love of family, children, friends, and country never had a chance to start. I isolate myself from what family I have; I have only one child, illegitimate, given up for adoption, and I've never seen her; I have no friends; I do not participate in my country except as I'm forced to. Control is a very serious issue for me. I only feel safe when I'm in control. And for me control of my world means staying away from people.

Anne O'Neil sought an external source of control in the religious life:

ANNE O'NEIL: When I went into the convent, there was relief at not having to deal with my anxiety, with that whole terror. I was capable of so completely separating myself from my experiences and my feelings that I would have a momentary feeling and then it would be gone and I wouldn't think about it anymore. It was gone. I had powerful repressive abilities. People who know me now would just have a hard time imagining what I was like. I was a martinet. I had a kind of fierce righteousness. I was my mother's daughter, no question. There was no way anybody could guess what was going on with me. People had the impression that I was incredibly competent, very secure, no fears. I had power because of that as a young woman.

I'm sure it was part of why I was chosen to be a teacher trainer. I just walked around like I knew I had the program. I didn't have any question, any hesitancy whatsoever at telling people what to do. And I usually had an answer. Now whether or not it had anything to do with reality is another question. But you know, I had answers, I was very, very good.

A few years ago I read some of the cards and letters I had written when I was in the convent. It was all about God, God wanting this and God wanting that. There wasn't any evidence of me—no, that's not really true, there was evidence of me because there was a tremendous caring—but everything was filtered through the words of God this and God that. Two years after I left the convent I discovered I didn't even believe in God. More steps into the unknown: I abandoned the world I grew up in before I found another world to embrace.

Karen Seal also built a wall around her feelings:

KAREN SEAL: I didn't cry much as a kid. I was real, real tough. As an adult, I would be easily brought to tears in a loving relationship. It's like my feelings could get hurt so easily by these men. And I would choose men who would do it. That hurts.

Oddly enough, I've done really careless things. I remember going into Mexico City with a friend when we were nineteen, and these guys in the band asked us to go to an after-hours party. Sure! So we took off with five Mexican guys, strangers. What on earth was I thinking? I did some really stupid, careless things.

I was pretty cautious, real prudish, before I got married the first time. But between marriages I'd go out with men I didn't know very well at all, have them come to my house and pick me up—stupid stuff. I won't do that now. A strange man, I'll meet him somewhere. I've got my car and he's got his. But I did some acting out sexually between marriages.

RICHARD RHODES: Some children who were sexually abused are seductive. Was that part of your experience?

KAREN SEAL: I don't see myself that way. I attract men, and I think I'm almost trying to do revenge. It's like I'm real charming, but I don't care about them. It's like I want to make myself powerful vis-à-vis these men. And I think it's got to do with revenge. I've got a real strong tape from my mother, that I'm supposed to be sexually appealing, attractive to men, that without a man I'm nothing. But I don't think I've been sleazy. I've never been, you know, [indicating her clothing] cut down to here or up to here, or whoring around. But I've been indiscreet. When I was married I was completely, totally faithful. When I'm sexual with a man I'm completely exclusive. So, I don't know. I don't think promiscuity has really been my thing. But between marriages, I was really into my feminist stuff—men want to sleep around, so can I. They're horny, so am I. I don't know if that had much to do with the incest. I think it was something about the times. The Sixties were an experimental time. But I sometimes play with men.

RICHARD RHODES: It wouldn't be surprising; your father played with you.

KAREN SEAL: I'm staying in power. I've even asked myself recently if I've ever really allowed myself to love a man. I'm not sure I have. I know the walls are pretty thick. That's what's difficult about the man I'm seeing right now. He's real easy, he just gets right into my heart, and I think, oh, no, this is too scary!

I've been able to be physically close, but emotionally close, that's another thing.

Several of the survivors we interviewed reported making bad choices in partners:

SKYE SMITH: I was very self-destructive then. Very, very, very self-destructive. I was sexually promiscuous. When I was twenty years old I went to Honolulu with fifty dollars and a suitcase. I got a job for a show-business promoter and a place to live that day. I wore the most provocative clothes you can imagine and at that time, believe it or not [*she laughs because she's bone-thin*], I was a 34D bra, I was voluptuous. I had to get away from the mainland, had to do it in Honolulu. I would get on a bus to Waikiki every night, I would look in a bar and would say, That guy, and I would go home with that guy. The next night, That guy. How many nights can you do that kind of stuff? I would cruise the bars; I hung out with entertainers. I went out with Alice Cooper [*the rock star*]. I knew all the musicians who came to Honolulu that summer. I had front seats to the Don Ho show. I'd zone in on these particular men. It got me through.

RICHARD RHODES: It must have given you a sense of power.

SKYE SMITH: Yeah, power and mastery. They wanted me, I'm not that unattractive, that ugly, that awful, that undesirable, that something. It's a very dangerous way to go.

RICHARD RHODES: Dangerous to your emotions?

SKYE SMITH: Dangerous to your everything. I never remember feeling so depressed as I did that summer. It was horrible.

RICHARD RHODES: Have you read my memoir *Making Love*?

SKYE SMITH: No, I haven't.

RICHARD RHODES: Some of us who survived child abuse find a way of dealing with it through our sexuality. By turning very intensely to sexual feeling one can blank out the anxiety or use it to connect with other people.

❖

VALORIE BUTLER: Control, that's a big issue with me, even now. I'm still working on it. The kind of spouse I've chosen, the people in my life, all the way back to elementary school, the people I've leagued myself up with have been hostile, domineering types. It's unconscious, yet the source of my wrath and anger, because I don't want to be controlled. Now I'm happy with being much more aware about that, although it means some hard decisions have to be made. I go back even to elementary school and remember in the fifth grade that I had a conference with a teacher who told me my best friend was the most hostile and critical person in the class. She was talking about my being critical, too. You grow up with a critical person who criticizes and you criticize, you know. There's a little book by James Allen, called *As a Man Thinketh,* very powerful little book. I sit and meditate on the words. It says, We are unconsciously attracted to that which we cherish or fear the most. I realize how, unconsciously, I've been attracted to people who are hostile, dom- ineering, unfree, because I'm patterning my choices after my own past. I'm happier now, because I realize it. Seeing it is freeing.

A more extreme response to child abuse is an attraction to suicide, which almost everyone acknowledged:

JOHN WOOD: The primary suicide method that I think of is going down to Bridgeport or Stratford and getting on a fishing boat. You know these fishing-boat tours, you pay thirty-five bucks to get on board and go fishing all day. And go out there with a little heater in my pocket [*he means a gun*] and lean backwards over the rail and bury myself at sea with a whole bunch of weight.

So, yeah, I've thought of it. When I was going through a divorce, six years ago, I drove my car into another car. I think that was a suicide attempt, because I could have avoided it. That's the first wreck in thirty-five years of driving. Somebody pulled out—talk about suicide, and I've done it since then too—somebody pulled out from the right, a young woman looking to her right. She never looked left. I nailed her right in the door, but I could have put on the brakes a lot earlier. I didn't because I like to come as close to people as I can, see. Wake 'em up. You know, give 'em a little wake-up call. I thought she was going to look left and say, Oh-oh, and stomp on the gas, and I'd go, whew, around the back side. It became obvious that she was not going to step on the gas. She was going very slowly, and finally I jumped on the brakes with both feet. Skidded right into her. We both walked away, but, boy, it's a goddamn miracle.

❖

ALEXA DONATH: I tried to kill myself one day—it was a halfhearted attempt at best. I didn't even break the skin. That's when I left home and stayed with friends of mine. I had just graduated from high school, I was maybe nineteen. It was right before I moved away, before my dear friend Mary and her mother rescued me. My father was eating lamb chops at the table when the police were there. Picture my father eating lamb chops while the police came—this is about as passive you get. Please don't disturb my dinner, I'm eating now. Everything chaos around him.

A less destructive possibility is losing oneself in work:

DAN HAMILTON: Becoming an actor let me put my defensive skills to good use—pretending to be somebody else. It wasn't until my thirties, in my second marriage, that I began to realize that all was not well inside. I had completely closed the doors and accepted that whatever was rotten in there was my problem and would stay rotten. I had no real idea of how much it was affecting other people. I knew that I felt limited in my abilities to love and trust and maintain intimacy and maintain a healthy sexual life. I didn't know why, I just figured that was a given.

In my younger days, in the Sixties and Seventies, it was certainly acceptable to jump from one relationship to another. If anything, in my business, it was almost encouraged as part of a joyful, show-business image. When I first arrived in New York from a small town in California to go to acting school, I was in my teens and this was my first really aware exposure to homosexual life. Here I was in an acting school, taking dance classes and working in theater, and suddenly I was being approached by men. It was assumed that I would want that kind of lifestyle, and it was taught to me that I should have that kind of lifestyle. If I was going to be a successful young actor, it was a requirement to be true to your sexual nature, your impulses and emotions— You can't possibly be a creative person if you don't go to bed with me tonight. It took me about two years of saying no and feeling guilty about it, before I said, No, I really mean no, and I think I'll sleep with this woman instead, thank you very much. Once I made that decision, I was no longer torturing myself as to what I should or should not be able to give other people. It has never been an issue since, in terms of people either hitting on me, or suggesting that I change my choices.

With the affinity I had for feelings, both the quiet ones and the rages, I was lucky enough and talented enough to be able to take that and consciously put it into a profession where it could be nurtured in and of itself. The downside of that was that for twenty years, my only sense of self-worth was my work. Am I working today? Am I doing good work today? If I'm not, then I'm a worthless piece of garbage, and I'll go self-destruct somewhere.

✦

KAREN SEAL: I decided my major addiction was workaholism. During my younger years I would drink a bit, but I would get sick, so I could never be an alcoholic. My addictions were caretaking, people-pleasing, and workaholism. Those are the things that kick in when I get under stress. I've been going to Workaholics Anonymous for almost a year. Actually, I'm not just a workaholic, I'm an activity addict. Anything will do. I'll take up dancing lessons, or go traveling; I'll do anything but sit quietly and just feel feelings. On a day-to-day basis, the core belief that I struggle with all the time is that I am only as good as what I do. I don't get the concept that we are all precious and worthy in and of ourselves, even though my faith says that I am a piece of God. I think, well, that part of me is cool, but the rest of it, you know, it's just . . . I have this sense that we're born with X amount of tread. This behavior has already shortened my life to a certain extent. Getting peaceful and accepting and calm is the only way I can see to ensure a better second half of my life.

RICHARD RHODES: How do you deal with rage? How do you deal with anger?

KAREN SEAL: I don't do it well, I don't do it. [*She laughs, ruefully.*] Sometimes I go into my walk-in closet, close the door, close the windows, turn on the air-conditioning, and scream.

> *Abuse, making a child's life a battlefield, leads to post-traumatic stress disorder in adulthood. Addictions—to alcohol, nicotine, food, or in negative form as anorexia—are a common manifestation of PTSD. In his essay "Prolegomena to an Autobiography," David Ray wrote:*

DAVID RAY: For a time too—all too long a time—I thought my lifeline was alcohol, the goodliness or generosity of which substance I never questioned. I would submit in fact, that alcoholism is a religion, heretic maybe.

❖

CELIA GOLDEN: It's like cigarette smoking; I'm doing the patch now, but I have this dilemma about being healthy. I can fix wonderful food for my kids, my husband, friends, but I won't feed myself. I will starve myself, feeling the need to be sick. It's like I'm repeating all the various kinds of abuse. I want to be healthy because as a kid I was real physically strong, and I remember there's a positive power in being able to do things like ride a bicycle. You feel like there's nothing stopping you, your legs could just go forever. When you smoke, you lose that. I'm playing my mother's game, smoking these cigarettes, just a slow form of suicide.

❖

LOUISE HILL: I was married before I even knew that I was unhappy. Imagine ridiculing your own husband, ridiculing your own children, as my mother did. The way their hair was or something. I thought of this recently. I found out that I'm going to be a grandmother for the first time. My oldest daughter is expecting a child. I thought, boy, I will never do that. It's very cruel. I do remember being ridiculed for how I looked. I was kind of a chubby kid, not all the time. I see pictures in junior high school when I looked pretty spiffy and in high school of course I was interested in boys, but I had a tendency to be chubby when I was little and I will say it's a painful subject for me, that I escape with food.

As a child I would take food to my room and sneak it under my pillow. To this day, don't ever put potato salad around because it's just too dangerous; if you ever want to give me a comfort food, that would be it. But my grandmother would bake challah, which is Jewish bread, on Friday—it was quite fresh—and bake a little one for me. I would cut it up. It was so soft. My mother would make potato salad every Friday. I would make a little potato salad sandwich and take it into my bed at night. It's been a lifelong battle in overcoming that.

I thought I was quite ugly growing up. I will tell you a nice story. When I look back at the pictures, I'm shocked at how pretty I was. I was told that I was ugly and I was fat. I do have to tell one bad story about my father—you see, I don't like to. He was trying to teach me how to dance and I had trouble following him. I said, Daddy, how am I doing? We were dancing around the kitchen floor like characters in a Neil Simon play. My father said, Well, I've driven a Mack truck before.

That did not do me good.

❖

SKYE SMITH: I eat, but I'm wired as an anorexic. That's the way you build a vault around all of your internal stuff, your feelings. That's the way you focus, you don't focus on what a horrible person you are, on how much pain you have inside. It's a neat little system, really. It got me through the 1980s, I would say. You're in control, magnificent control. I'm superior to other people, I do not need these bodily concerns, they do not concern me.

MARIA MAREWSKI: [*Teasing*] Well, you've said things to me lately about the threat that you might become fleshy perhaps.

SKYE SMITH: Yes, fleshy, voluptuous—hips, breasts, womanliness. Anorexia is a way not to be sexual, too. If you look like Peter Pan, you don't pose any threat to yourself—because your womanliness is a threat. It'll get you in trouble. So to stay thin and wear baggy clothes means no body is here, nobody's home, nobody. Yes, you hide out. You do. I've hidden out for a decade now. It's about time to come out.

I bicycled across country one summer to get rid of my feelings, my anxiety. I biked a lot in the last ten years. In fact, my brother, Bob, has taken up bike racing, in Arizona. There really probably aren't too many driven, wiry thirty-nine-year-olds who would want to do that. [*She laughs.*] It's a way to deal with feelings.

Poetry is another way Skye deals with feelings:

Look at Me

Hollow cheeks
scrawny neck
empty bra
What the heck?

Motherhood
lust for life
rich desserts
Too much strife.

I protest
everyday
hate myself
starve away.

Abuse is also a source of nightmares, Michael Davies reports:

MICHAEL DAVIES: My therapy has not gotten me closer to any additional memory recall, except that over the past years I've had a number of very disturbing dreams. They may be purely symbolic in content. Certainly they're echo images I've gotten from my sisters. But they have their own independent life as well and they're very bizarre, they're nightmares. I've reached the point where I can have these terrible dreams and then wake up without waking up crying out like I used to. I don't wake up in a sweat.

Richard asked Skye Smith if she was angrier in the past than she is today:

SKYE SMITH: Was I! I've had a lot of people tell me that my anger is frightening. It was too intense and they just needed to have it back off a little.

RICHARD RHODES: How does your husband deal with it? Is he a calm person?

SKYE SMITH: I think Jack is very calm and calming. He's a good tether for me and I need that. He doesn't get the full brunt of it. The punching bag does, or other things, but he's able to deal with my grieving. He can tolerate it, he's a real grown-up man. He really is. What a mature guy.

✦

KAREN SEAL: I went out, I had a chip on my shoulder and I'd take anybody on. Oddly enough, unless I was married or in some kind of an intimate relationship, I would go out and spill my anger on innocent bystanders. You know, waitresses, people on the freeway. I was filled with rage. The sadness didn't come until I was in recovery.

That victim stuff kicks in around abusive people. Unless they mean nothing to me, and then I can just be enraged. One time Sam [*her former husband*] and I walked into a hotel room in Puerto Vallarta and there were two guys in the room. Ostensibly to fix the air-conditioning, although we hadn't reported it. I felt they were there to rob. And I couldn't believe what came out of me. It was awful! I just screamed at these guys. When my reactions are out of proportion to what's going on today, I know it's old stuff, acting out.

RICHARD RHODES: I can think of many times when I've rationalized not confronting someone because I felt I had so much rage and anger that if I did confront them it would be lethal. Whether or not that was rationalization, it was also true there's that much intensity and anger in there.

KAREN SEAL: The only way out is to vent the anger, the old anger. But somehow I keep dawdling about my mom. It's like I want to be mad at her for a while longer. I'm the one I'm hurting, I do know that.

Anger has its counterpart in depression:

SKYE SMITH: I had a decade of depression, serious clinical depression which included three hospitalizations. In the hospital in Dallas, I'm thinking I'll go to Phoenix, that's where my family is. Of course my husband in New York can't be involved in any of that, because you can't have husbands in my family's system. You can't be sexual, an independent woman, you have to be the child constantly. So I'm making plans in Dallas; my discharge plan is to go to Phoenix, right back into the hornet's nest. At the last minute, my doctor said, No, you're going to New York. I just died. He said, You're all set up in New York; you have a husband, you have a home. But I thought, it doesn't feel right to me, you're sending me off to my deathbed.

I think you need to deal with your pain. I did it to myself with my depression, which is aggressive and violent in its own way. But I just wouldn't think of doing it to another person. I identify with the abuser also and abused myself. That was a neat little system. You don't need family then, it's a one-person world. The problem is that you're never connected with anybody, you're too ashamed.

GINGER RHODES: Everyone in this country has a group that he or she belongs to. Richard and I finally identified ours. We finally realized that we're Martian-Americans. [*Everyone laughs.*] Uh-huh. I see you recognize your heritage. It's a surprisingly large group.

❖

DAVID RAY: It's tough, because I've been very depressed. I guess I'm still a hope junkie. I'll get some project going and throw a lot of energy into it and then be crushed when it runs out. Like mobilizing for a trip to Australia, a real big thing. A lot of good things happened out there and then I came back. It was very hard to come back to Kansas City. I've had a lot of rejections, a lot of professional rejections. I've probably applied for a Guggenheim Fellowship thirty times in a row and I can still con myself into thinking, well, maybe this time. Or somebody else will say, Oh yeah, you have to keep trying. So then you think, well, this time I'll really get it because one recommendation will come from a Nobel Prize winner and another one from God—and it's just more of the same. I still deal with the same thing I dealt with as a child, as the outsider, the unworthy one.

John Wood reported self-destructiveness:

JOHN WOOD: I ran my [*antique*] repair business into the ground. I had a wonderful customer and got rid of that one. He was too good a customer, so I got rid of him by charging him too much, by keeping the things too long to repair, and any other way that I could. [*He laughs bitterly.*] All my life, anytime things get going well for me, I sabotage it, I shoot it somehow. I've got a jillion of those stories.

Behind these other symptoms, Richard told David Doepel, was simmering violence:

RICHARD RHODES: When I was in the boys' home, in junior high school and high school, I used to cross from the school building to the dormitory on a cold winter night and have a recurring fantasy, vivid and real, of the world emptying out. I used to ask myself, What if I were all alone here and there was no one else alive on earth, what would I do? I'd reach into my pockets to see what objects I had that might help me survive. I started carrying matches so I'd have the wherewithal to light a fire. I started adding to the fantasy as I became pubescent that one woman, one girl would be left alive and we would start a new race. But among other things that's a fantasy of murdering, destroying, obliterating everybody on earth except myself and at the same time it's also a feeling of being absolutely alone.

DAVID DOEPEL: Do you remember feeling that way?

RICHARD RHODES: I remember it as a central feeling of that time with my stepmother. Despite my brother's help.

I was also, at the boys' home, destroying animals—legally—with great passion, including most pointedly eight-hundred-pound steers—castrated adult males. I became the boy who headed the four-boy team assigned to slaughter animals for food. I slaughtered those steers with abandon, one a month for two years. Before I headed the crew I was the assistant who volunteered to burn the guts. I would load the guts into a wheelbarrow and wheel them down the lane to a funeral pyre—a concrete pad at the end of the lane, away from the farm buildings on the edge of a pasture. I was supposed to soak them in kerosene before starting them on fire. Kerosene has low volatility and is relatively hard to light. I soaked the guts instead in gasoline from the farm pump, gallons of gasoline. By the time I was ready to light it, waves of fumes were shimmering in the air above this great pile of guts. I'd stand back and light the match, throw it in, and Whoosh! there was this huge explosion. Half the time I'd nearly singe off my eyebrows. I stood there staring at those flames, watching these coils of guts puff up and explode, absolutely hypnotized.

I didn't realize what I was doing until I wrote *A Hole in the World,* thirty-five years later. Then I suddenly connected this odd, dangerous ceremony with a hymn I used to sing in choir in church as an adolescent—"seedtime and harvest, and snow, and heat, and summer, and winter, and day and night shall not cease"—God's promise to Noah that He wouldn't destroy the world again if He was placated with burnt offerings.

DAVID DOEPEL: What were you thinking when you were killing the cattle?

RICHARD RHODES: I knew something more was happening because I felt inflamed. I felt tumescent. I felt horrified and obsessively drawn. The meat-cutting part was a craft and it's a respectable craft but the butchering that precedes it, the killing, the bleeding, the skinning and gutting is a horrible bloody experience. It was horrible to me that it would be asked of someone who was fourteen or fifteen years old. That's what I mean when I say one understands on a farm the full cycle of the universe, which is fatal and yet so green and so alive—and so red and bloody as well. But at the time I only knew I was drawn to it hypnotically. It was an hypnotic experience and I was puzzled as to why I carried it so far, the burning of the guts, this huge explosion. Now I understand. That was my burnt offering. With each steer I was killing my father. Patricide. I needed absolution. Sorry, God, for once again killing my father, cutting his throat, skinning his carcass, bathing in his blood and then eating his flesh. But also: thanks for the privilege. In its own dark way it was therapeutic.

Not long ago I had dinner with Walt Menninger, of the Menninger Clinic. I told him that story. He turned pale, recovered, and said, "Wow, *that's* just barely sublimated, isn't it!"

10

"We Grab On to Solutions, You Know"

T*he quality that most impressed us of the child-abuse survivors we interviewed was the creativity they brought as children to the problem of surviving. It's a quality that often goes unremarked in discussions of childhood victimization. These children, at least, spent very little time thinking of themselves as victims. They had the practical problem to solve of surviving their mistreatment, and they approached the task with great originality.*

Richard asked Celia Golden why she survived when others don't:

CELIA GOLDEN: My therapist has come up with some theories. She says it doesn't hurt to have brains. I'm a little dyslexic, but I entertain myself in my head a lot. As a baby, in the loneliness of the solitary confinement, I learned to entertain myself with games. I would do these mind games. As early as I can remember, I knew I could do things with my mind that other people couldn't do. I had lots of resources, an internal world.

Child psychologists identify resources of native resilience in some child-abuse survivors. Louise Hill was one such "indomitable child":

LOUISE HILL: I look at the pictures of me as a child and there's such life, such spirit. Oh, I'll tell you a story. Yes, I like this story—in fact, I'm using it for an article I'm writing. When I was in first grade, my mother was called to school. The teacher was very upset with me because I was talking too much, talking aloud in class. That [*category of behavior*] was called "deportment." So, as a punishment, I was made to stand in the front of the class, while the class continued, with my back to the class and my face to the chalkboard. I was there I guess for fifteen minutes when I decided to amuse myself—which I would say is just part of who I am. In fact, a student of mine recently said to me, during a trip to Greece, he said, Gee, you're the greatest amusement to yourself I ever saw. He said, You tell jokes and you laugh. I said, That's right. I said, Listen to the song of life.

So I was standing at the front of the classroom and decided to act out Robert Louis Stevenson's "Oh How I Love to Go Up in a Swing." So I started to swing my hands and sing [*she begins singing*], "Oh how I love to go up in a swing, up in a swing so high . . ." This was one of the songs we learned in the first grade. Well, the whole class began to laugh and of course was disrupted. So my mother was called in and for years afterwards and still into my adulthood she'd shake her finger at me. You remember what your teacher said, she'd say, You're a girl that cannot be punished. And when she would beat me up, she'd say, Can't be punished, can you?

Creative play helped Richard, he told David Doepel:

RICHARD RHODES: It was important to seem normal as much as it was possible to seem normal. It was important to get whatever sustenance from adults we could get from seeming normal. The truth is that we *were* normal except for this particular adaptive behavior. We were children. We liked to bike and we liked to read—that's perhaps unusual these days, but it wasn't then. We were good students—both of us. So we had a lot going for us. It doesn't hurt that we were white Anglo-Saxon Protestants. I've always realized how much my red hair—this unusual color, only two or three percent of the American population—helped me. My red hair helped attract adults to me and my intelligence gave me support I might not have had otherwise.

My brother and I didn't accept the abuse we experienced as normal, as children often do who experience it within their family, up from infancy. To us it was clearly abuse. We had lived a more-or-less normal childhood as half-orphans. There had been other loving figures in our life—motherly women in the boardinghouses where we lived and so on. So it was clear to us that we weren't at fault. It was clear to us that something was happening to us rather than that this had always been part of our childhood. The problem for people who have been through abuse within their own families is often the shame of it. The problem of not speaking of it was never something I felt. To the contrary, I've always been very forward about talking about it.

It's hard to recall how I felt when I was ten, but I certainly had a pervasive sense that a parasite had attached itself to what for me was a mythologically wonderful family—my father, my brother, and me.

My brother and I were nerd kids, I suppose. Bright kids who read. I found friends. I can remember one kid who was a scientist-to-be. We boiled urine on a hot plate in his garage to see what sort of residue we'd generate. I remember other kids who lived in houses that were so full of dirty dishes I couldn't imagine how they lived there. There were kids around and they were good kids—we had fun. Stanley and I were always very close, too, which I think somewhat got in the way of finding other friends. We started to divide as we got older and especially as he discovered this system of tunnels under Kansas City, the storm sewer system, where he would disappear all summer. He'd be gone all day wandering around under the city in these twelve-foot-high tunnels that connected through manholes in the streets and storm drains on the curbs. So I had to go make my own life then, which I did, but I remember missing him very much.

The kind of self-nurturing that one has to do as an abused child makes you an adult and a child at the same time. The child was still there, but buried, like the buried baby I once dreamt about in whose murder I was somehow implicated. Still, there were times when I could let go. Increasingly private times. Riding my bicycle down the street watching other families live and play, feeling like a Martian. Nevertheless that was a playful time. The children in the concentration camps still found ways to play as long as they had a little energy left. So did I. So did my brother. Stan was Jean Valjean running through the sewers of Paris—that's certainly elaborate play. He felt as if the whole structure of tunnels was his and that's marvelous play. At the same time, it's really very sad. He felt as if he was totally disconnected from the rest of the city. And so, clearly, if I was compulsively dreaming of riding a rocket to some other universe, I must have felt disconnected too, but that's also play, and creative play.

The fantasy of escaping in a rocket was one I repeated constantly—by drawing and redrawing the rocket. It was certainly a very phallic rocket and yet as I look at the drawing—and I can still draw it exactly as I always drew it—it was also a very maternal rocket. It had skirts—vanes, fins—it was a Buck Rogers-style rocket with skirts. It had an ablated head—it came to a point. Up there in what was a rather pregnant part of the rocket, I drew a little cockpit and drew myself in. So in some peculiar way, the rocket was both male and female. And if I could draw it perfectly—this was the fantasy and I repeated it again and again in school, I filled whole tablets with it—if I could draw it perfectly it would become real and I would become real inside it and we would escape. Of course, I could never draw it perfectly—fortunately, since then the fantasy would have dissolved and I would have realized there was no escape.

DAVID DOEPEL: Yet it was a nurturing fantasy.

RICHARD RHODES: Absolutely. In fact, it connects to what else I did in the way of a very large pattern of escaping and that was compulsively to read science fiction of a particularly melodramatic kind in those days called pulps: thick newsprint magazines, two hundred pages of cops and robbers and cowboys and Indians in space. They were notable, all those stories, for having melodramatic plots involving great monstrous figures called Bug-Eyed Monsters, and they always resolved themselves on the side of destroying the monster. I was so compulsive about reading those books, I read at least one a week and I had to buy them. They cost a quarter, which was the equivalent of at least several dollars today, and I used money to buy them, money I earned housecleaning and baby-sitting, that I might have used for food. One of my stepmother's deliberate deprivations was food. We were semi-starved. We had not enough to eat from day to day. So I made a choice between a nurturing fantasy and real nurturing—between a nurturing fantasy and food.

DAVID DOEPEL: Speak to the extent of the deprivation.

RICHARD RHODES: I baby-sat for my stepmother's daughter, Rowena, who was a nice and decent person, married to a former Navy officer. She would hire me on Saturdays to clean and baby-sit and feed me well. She had a small child and this little boy, infant, had a piggy bank which had quarters in it. I would steal quarters from the piggy bank even though I didn't want to destroy the relationship with Rowena. It was terribly important that I find the money to buy the pulps. Melodrama was just the ticket for me: the monster had to be destroyed.

Some Holocaust survivors attribute their survival to their fierce determination to live to tell the story. Alexa Donath found similar cause:

ALEXA DONATH: I remember being curled up on the floor in my room, thinking, I will never forget this, I will never forget this, I never want to forget this. If I come out of this alive, I won't forget. That's why I didn't kill my mother—because I knew then she'd win. I said, if I kill her I'll spend the rest of my life in jail and I'm not stupid. I'm going to show her, because she's not worth it.

Fantasy is often pathologized as a sign of escapism, but abused children need to escape mentally the intolerable violence over which they have no other control. Richard asked gentle, soft-spoken Valorie Butler what saved her:

VALORIE BUTLER: I think the fantasizing, the daydreaming. We grab on to solutions, you know. Not consciously, it's what we do naturally.

Mine was fantasizing, locking myself into a fantasy world to block out the pain. Especially the pain of standing on the steps for many, many hours. Well, what do you do with that? I don't rebel; my natural personality is to be more compliant and avoid conflict. So, we did not outwardly rebel. All three of the sisters were similar like that. None of us are aggressive. So the natural thing to do is just to go into my mind and find the things in there that were fun. Create my own world, so to speak. I still relapse into it once in a while. I'm aware of when I do it, and I say, okay, what am I avoiding?

RICHARD RHODES: What kind of daydreaming? What is your daydream about?

VALORIE BUTLER: [*Laughing*] Now I've got to 'fess up?

When I was eight, I used to fantasize about Mighty Mouse and Superman. I thought they were just the neatest stars; they were big and powerful, they would save you. Remember the Mighty Mouse song? "Here he comes, to save the day!" My fantasizing changed to correlate with my age as the years went on. When I was a teenager I would fantasize about being popular, wearing nice clothes, and romantic scenes. As I got older my fantasies became more sexual, and that, of course, caused a lot of tension in my body, because if it went on a lot—well, you know.

I think that a part of our life was very squashed. We were made to feel like a jerk when we were kids. We were made to feel like we were filthy and dirty. If we showed any indication that we liked someone, my aunt would make us feel like—I'm a gyp dog, filthy. Here we were children who were virgins, who had had no dating, no contact with the opposite sex at all, but she would talk to us like we were absolutely filthy, vulgar beings. When I analyze this, I remember that she had to get married, and I believe that all those things she was saying to us represented how she felt about herself. She really did feel it. She was pregnant out of wedlock. My uncle didn't marry her right away. She was several months into the pregnancy, and back in those days, those things were not looked upon lightly. I believe she was made to feel like a filthy person, and she was making us feel like filthy people. She's probably never sorted that out. So, the fantasizing, I would lock myself into this world that was romantic-type encounters, things like that, as I got older.

GINGER RHODES: You were able to relieve some of the pain of standing on the stairs by having fantasies?

VALORIE BUTLER: Yes. I blocked it out. I wouldn't be aware of standing on the steps. I might be fantasizing about going to a dance, and I was very detailed about what I liked. I could write a book, in my mind, as a child. I was very detailed about what I wore, what I did. So while that's going on, the other—standing on the stairs—moved into the background.

RICHARD RHODES: Which is what some prisoners do when they're in solitary confinement. They fill up their time mentally.

VALORIE BUTLER: But the trouble with that was it was a safe haven, and I did not want to venture out into life. I could function fine, but it was like a drug. It was just like a drug. It was just as powerful, just as addicting.

Dan Hamilton outed his abuser to protect the next generation of children in his family, including his own son, from abuse:

DAN HAMILTON: I initially broke the ice, and that was when my older boy was about twelve. That was ten, twelve years ago, the first public acknowledgment by anybody in the family. I did it consciously so that my older boy would feel he had permission to come to me if anything happened. And I did it in front of my sister and her daughter; and it was after my admission that my sister's daughter came forward about my father. So in a sense I opened that can of worms. Barbara [*Hamilton, his stepmother*] had never acknowledged it to anyone in the family at that point. It's not that I was responsible, but I certainly was the trigger.

Going back to my experiences with my abuser, I have flash visuals of places. They have no chronological order and no associated dialogue. But I can remember when it stopped and why it stopped: because he started to approach a younger boy cousin of mine, and I said, If you do that, I will tell. I don't know whether he succeeded that time or not with that boy, but he stopped approaching me. I think I must have been twelve, thirteen, or close to fourteen at that point.

GINGER RHODES: Did you want to protect that cousin?

DAN HAMILTON: Very much, yes.

Several of those we interviewed remembered putting a stop to their physical abuse, at least, when they were physically strong enough to resist it:

RALPH KESSLER: The contrast in treatment that I received when I came home from school—sweetness if my mother was home alone and anger and beatings if my stepfather was there—finally woke me up to the understanding that something was wrong. I couldn't take it anymore. If I had gotten the same treatment from both of them, I would not have understood. But I finally knew that I was being mistreated. It had taken some three and a half years to sink in.

Early in 1935, he finally stopped the beatings. I recall the moment when the beatings stopped. Instead of just standing there and taking it, I stuck out my arms. He couldn't get close enough to hit me with his strap. The blows fell on my outstretched arms. I was too big to whip.

❖

ALEXA DONATH: I lost an inch from back operations. I used to be five feet eight and a half. I'm five seven and a half now; all the back operations diminished my height. My mother's really small. When I was fifteen she came up no higher than my shoulders. She also wore glasses. I'm a big girl, big shoulders. I almost killed her, I almost strangled her. I pushed her glasses into her face. I told her, No more! And after that the physical abuse stopped.

GINGER RHODES: You realized that you could overpower her.

ALEXA DONATH: Yes, and I did, and I scared the shit out of her and it didn't happen again. But the emotional stuff continued, and continued, and continued. She's still doing it.

❖

LOUISE HILL: I will tell you another story. The year before my mother died, I was starting to confront her and say, Why did you treat me the way you did? She said, Well, I was so unhappy. When I was growing up, I remember one Christmas my father gave my mother a present—it was shortly before he died. It was the most expensive gift he had ever given her, it was a diamond watch. The box it came in—because I was there when he gave it to her—was this blue suede box. He died shortly afterwards and it was my job then to go to Kay Jewelers where he had bought the watch. He had paid twenty dollars down, it was five dollars a week, and it was my job to go in and pay the five dollars a week on that watch from my dead father until it was paid off.

And that year that I confronted my mother she took this blue suede case out of her bag; she didn't know how to be very warm. She took out that case and all of a sudden she flung it at me. I opened it up and it was the watch that my father had given her, which she was giving me. I still have it. It was Christmas when she flung it at me and it came with a little Christmas tag. I still have the little tag. It says, "To Louise, love, Mother." But she said to me as she flung it, "Now will that do it, Louise? Will that do it?" Will that do what? Absolve her, give me the love I had missed? The answer is no. But she did give me that watch.

With or without confrontation, many of our survivors eventually walked out:

RALPH KESSLER: I heard them talking about sending me away. I was heartsick when my mother agreed. They sent me to my grandparents in Chelsea, Massachusetts. I was there about two months and they shipped me back. The only explanation that I got was that a child belonged with his mother.

I couldn't go back to a home where I was not wanted and I didn't. When I got off the bus in New York, I headed on my own for the open road to make my way in life. I hitchhiked to Camden [*in New Jersey*] and walked across the bridge to Philadelphia and I remember asking some storekeepers for a job. I got nothing. I didn't know how to survive. I got hungrier and sleepier and dirtier. One truck let me off in a small town in southern New Jersey where I was picked up by the police while sleeping in a bus station. I was in their jail for a few days and eventually my mother sent a friend down to pick me up. I have felt all through the years and still feel that if I had been able to make my own way, my family would never have heard from me again. My stepfather's sister took me in for a few months. She had children a bit older than I was and we got along fine.

I stayed with my mother in Hackensack, New Jersey, that summer. When Irving [*his stepfather*] was home he left me alone. The arrangement suited me and I hoped that it would continue while I went to high school. But that fall of 1935 my mother and stepfather left town for the south to live in a trailer while he worked as a salesman. Before she left, my mother befriended a shoeshine boy. He was colored, smaller than I, and she asked him to show me how to shine shoes. I was outfitted with a box and soon enough I shined shoes for a nickel. My mother told me that as long as I had that box I would never go hungry. She was right. It was my ace in the hole. She had left me with a trade.

I lived catch as catch can on my own from that fall of 1935 until I graduated from Textile High School in New York City in 1939. How I did it is another story, a longer one than this tale. Most of the time I lived in a small furnished room on West Nineteenth Street across the street from the school. My mother helped me sometimes with occasional bits of money and food and clothes. I supported myself with a variety of jobs. All I can say is that children were paid less than adults for the same work.

I shined shoes. I worked with a milk driver leaving fresh milk at the door and picking up empties [*glass milk bottles, which dairies in those days recycled*]. That was my hardest job because it was before school and I started the day tired. I sold fresh flowers in the subway system and got fired after signing a union card. I worked as a busboy extra in union cafeterias. To get this job I had to first put time in picketing a striking cafeteria. I was on National Youth Administration [*a New Deal agency*] for six dollars a month. My best job was working as a busboy in the school cafeteria for four periods a day. I liked this job because I could eat before beginning work and also at the end of the shift. I learned to wrap food in napkins and pocket it to take home.

❖

CELIA GOLDEN: As an adult, I would do all the things my parents had wanted me to do to look like a success. Then I would get to this place where it's emotionally empty. So I would go through a period of borderline poverty, not on the streets, but with very little. I would do exactly what I did when I was eighteen—walk out the door with my suitcase, eighty bucks, and a train ticket. That's how I came to California. Every time I leave a marriage I go through the same thing. My ex would get the house, the furniture, the two-thousand-dollar sofa, the TV, the BMW. So here I am. [*She was recently divorced and renting a small apartment in an old storefront at the time of our interview.*] Now I'm saying, I don't need anything, because it's all relationships for me. It's things like music and books and art. I don't need to possess things; things can't make me happy. My kids are real supportive. It's nice.

Michael Davies wrote Richard:

MICHAEL DAVIES: My parents never left me, like yours left you. I left them instead. But I've always felt very much like an orphan, even shared your fantasy of belonging to an alien race that had misplaced, then forgotten me. Floating at the margins, waiting for the rescue ship.

Michael elaborated on his rejection of his past in our interview:

MICHAEL DAVIES: From about the time I left to go away to college, which was in the fall of 1969, until this moment, to the extent that it was possible, I basically tried to bury that part of my past, and I did a pretty good job. I can probably count on one hand—well, two hands—over twenty years the number of times I went back to my hometown in the upper Midwest.

It was a very disagreeable town in my memory, although it was always advertised as a good town to raise a family in. And on the surface it certainly looked like that. It was a conservative, blue-collar–white-collar mix. Nothing terribly exciting ever happened there, but it was very middle-American, however you want to define that. But my memories of the place were so displeasing and uncomfortable and painful that I didn't want to have anything to do with it. And that made things problematic because that meant I didn't see family that much after I got away to college. Basically, I'd written that part of my life off. It felt good to have escaped.

There were good things about it. I can remember good things about it, but the family stuff so colored every aspect of living at that time that there was really nothing left there for me to go back to anyway. So I didn't and I felt good about that. But as it turned out, that's the way I felt about the family as well. I cared about my siblings but they reminded me of what I'd grown up with, so I didn't make a concerted effort to stay in touch as much as I feel like I should have. I think there was some perspective among my siblings that maybe I just wanted to be left alone. So nobody really pushed, not among my siblings, but of course my parents were always hurt by my not wanting to go back and visit. That's still an issue, because, as I said before, we all thought when our father died that finally, you know, finally we would be free.

Anne O'Neil came to feel that repairing her relationships with her brothers and sisters was important. Before that, however, it was equally important to her recovery that she maintain her separation from them:

ANNE O'NEIL: It has taken a lot of years. When Will and I were married, twenty-five years ago, my sister Mary and my brother Pat—the two oldest—both wrote and were highly critical because we were not being married in the [*Roman Catholic*] Church and I had asked my mother not to come to the wedding if she couldn't accept that. I didn't believe in the Church at that point at all, so I wasn't going to base my marriage on a lie. By that time I had found that whatever was going on in my life, if it was something important, I could count on Mary to be critical. So I finally decided that she was voicing my mother's concerns. I realized my brother Pat and my sister Mary were Mother's voice and I decided that I was not going to listen to that. I was not going to listen to my mother's voice and I was not going to listen to their voices. I was going to separate myself, and I did, for a number of years. I had no contact with any of them to speak of, maybe cards at Christmas, that sort of thing, but not much else.

All of my siblings at the time were furious with me because they were all intensely aligned with Mother and Dad. They all talked about what wonderful parents they were and how generous they were with us in childhood and blah, blah, how they did everything for us and sacrificed everything for us and blah, blah. I knew I couldn't articulate my rage. I couldn't speak with them. I couldn't express what I was thinking and feeling in a way that would be positive, supportive, or nurturing. I was angry, I was rejecting, I was determined to have my own life and so I just separated. There was a period of about twelve years. I remember because I did this when my son, William, was born. I realized that I could not attend to William and Will and be in relationship with my family. I could not do it because my mind would be so taken up with small things, like whether my mother sent me the wrong Christmas present. Once she sent a black plastic manikin's hand supposed to be for storing rings. I was so enraged. It took me weeks and weeks to get over it. Finally I said, I can't afford this, I have a baby, I'm going to take care of my baby. I'm going to be with my husband. I'm going to have a family. I can't do both at the same time, so I just did that.

Writing—including writing about their experience of abuse—was crucial
to the healing of many of our survivors:

LOUISE HILL: How did the writing life happen? It's a rather lovely story. Fifteen years later and I was still working for Women's Scholarship. You see—they helped me twice in my life. They came through twice. They were having their seventy-fifth anniversary. They were going to have a celebration in a big hotel in Boston. They wanted to put on a show, Judy Garland style, about the history of this organization. In college I had been a very good public speaker. The scholarship organization would ask me to go around to speak on their behalf to groups—as "the scholarship girl" in quotation marks—and tell about my experience and how I'd been helped. When it came time to write this show they said, Now, who's going to write the show? They said, Well, Louise, weren't you—I remember this exactly—weren't you kind of a writer in college? I guess I was a "kind of a" writer. I mean, I wrote short stories and I did write speeches. Still do, because I work in a university and write my own speeches and enjoy it. They said, Do you think you could write a show about women in education? And I said, Sure, I could do that. I remember going home and thinking, my God, what have I done?—I've never written a show. But I think in some way it was my heart and my instinct that raised my hand and said I'll do it. I must have been ready to break through.

This is another wonderful part of the story. They thought I would take music from other shows, *Oklahoma!* and *Carousel,* take the music and put lyrics to it. I started to do my research and I found out a lot about women in education. (In fact I worked at the Schlesinger Library at Radcliffe and did my research there, which I loved because there I was in a library again.) And suddenly I started to hear the music in my head. Growing up, we did have a piano, and I did have piano lessons like a lot of little kids, and my mother did yell at me because I didn't practice and shortly those piano lessons were canceled. But always as a kid I remember that I could play what they call by ear. I'd go to see a musical in the movies and I'd come home and play the whole score. You could tell me to play any song and I could play it. I could hear the music. So, doing my research for the show about women in education, I started to hear all the music in my head, original music like it was coming from the sky, but I didn't have a piano at this point. So I borrowed a friend's piano and I started to write down the notes in a very, very primitive manner. Then I wrote fifteen songs and they sounded rather wonderful, so I went to someone who could write down music and she said, This is quite good, and she arranged the music.

I wrote the musical. It was called *The Time to Remember*. It was the first thing I ever wrote and I can sing the title song to you. [*She sings:*] "A time to remember a time, da, da, da—it was a waltz—da, da, da. . . ." It had a cast of hundreds, including my own children. We had a big women's vote song in it and it had a very good professional director. It was performed in June at this big luncheon for the Women's Scholarship at the Hilton Hotel.

It so happened that the guest of honor that day was Elliott Norton, who was the drama critic for *The Boston Globe*. A most distinguished, wonderful drama critic. He was speaking on the American Theater— after the musical. I would say that this was just serendipity. One talks about luck in life. It certainly is serendipity. So he had to sit through this whole bloody musical. He had given his speech and we'd done the musical and it seemed a great success. I had a wonderful time. Judy Garland couldn't have been any happier with Mickey Rooney in her barn than I was that day. Mr. Norton came up to me and he said, I would like to see you in my office at Boston University tomorrow; can you make it? He gave me a time and I went in and he said, You are a very talented writer and I'd like to take you on as a special student. I said, I can't afford that. He said, just like that: I'll take you on.

So it occurs to me that we each have to make our own path. We each have to make our own path and it's such a solitary journey and such an exciting journey.

[*Eventually she went to graduate school, wrote, taught, divorced her doctor, met an engineer and married him and moved to teaching and writing in New York.*]

That day we left the house in the suburbs [*of Boston*] and we drove in our car over the hill—there was a big hill that you drove over on the way to New York—I felt like someone who was being born for the first time. I could actually feel skin falling off me as though my body was emerging for the first time. When I arrived in New York—still the sight of the George Washington Bridge sends me. When I drove along that river and saw that George Washington Bridge all lit up, I thought, Oh God, I am home. This is where I'm going to die, because I came to this city and to this Village with such freedom to be myself, to be a writer.

✦

DAVID RAY: I had trouble agreeing to this interview. For a while I was hung up on the feeling that I have a right to tell *my* story, but I don't have a right to tell *their* story. And yet, that's part of what's wrong with the whole dysfunctional family business, that trouble's always blamed on "the identified patient." It's always, "He's the nut." I am the identified psycho of the family. For years, they also thought I was a Communist. Like all those in recovery, I am a threat to my family because I'm the only one who may tell the dirty secrets. And they know that. They've always known that. My daughter had my little book of stories, *The Mulberries of Mingo,* and she panicked, fearing that my mother might read it. She said something, and my mother simply said, "Oh, David never gets anything right." That's one way of dealing with it. In actual fact, they're well protected from the truth. But the guilt is still there on my part.

RICHARD RHODES: Now you're telling us the secrets.

DAVID RAY: Yeah, I'm the one. What would they say now if we had them here in this room? Of some of the stuff, they'd say it didn't happen. I made it up or I imagined it. After my grandmother died, they were saying that I used to chase my grandmother with a butcher knife. Now this is fiction. But it makes me responsible for my grandmother's death. So, here I was like David Copperfield, responsible that my parents are miserable, and are always yelling at one another, and putting us with relatives and so on. I'm even responsible for my grandmother's death.

Ginger asked Karen Seal if she confronted her parents:

KAREN SEAL: Well, I never did during their lives. But I did get to the families. I went to my father's family reunion, two years ago, with the express agenda, not of saying that my father is a sicko, a pedophile, because they wouldn't know what a pedophile was. But I did take aside two aunts that I felt close to, and I told both of them what he had done and both of them believed me. Now, I'm an adult and I'm the star on both sides of the family. I'm the one who has done well, you know, they can point to me. Those aunts believed me, but I think it had more to do with the fact that I'm grown up and I've done okay in the world. But they knew, they knew.

I really wonder about my mother. I went to ask questions of her family, and they stonewalled: Your mother never knew anything; if she'd have known something she would have left your father. I can't get anything out of her family, but there's alcoholism, there's rage, there's cigarette smoking—almost every one of my aunts and uncles have been addicted to nicotine. So, blowing the whistle, that's all I did, but I know once I left that it was tch-tch, tch-tch.

❖

ALEXA DONATH: The last time I spoke with my mother I confronted her about the abuse of my childhood. I asked her to agree to pay for my therapy. She denied any responsibility for what she said I imagined. Previously, she at least admitted to "hitting us because she was alone so much." Now she is in complete denial and has rewritten history; it never happened.

Skye Smith sent a bill:

SKYE SMITH: I fantasized about my father all my life. He's that wonderful, handsome thing, he's fantastic, he really loves me and all that. So I went out to visit him. He was drinking then and sort of left me in front of bars all day while he drank. That was crushing. I could never articulate the depression that I felt, it was so terrible. He gave me twenty dollars to buy a dress because he was supposed to take me to dinner. He had a cast on his arm but he made a bet with somebody that he could swim across the condo's pool without getting it wet. He got it wet and passed out and that was my trip to visit Dad. I've had a lot of terrible disappointment with him. He never offered support, no college help, no nothing.

Three years ago, I wasn't working, I was in therapy and it was costing a fortune. I wrote my father a letter and I billed him twenty-five thousand dollars. [*Everyone laughs.*] I did. I basically said "I need it" and I thought, well, he'll put out or get out. He gave me twenty-*six* thousand dollars, guilt money; he wrote out the check. It was amazing, amazing—amazing that I wrote him, amazing that he came through. And you know, because of that, I wasn't so angry with him anymore.

Anna Lee Traynor decided to sue:

ANNA LEE TRAYNOR: What drew me in was my sister. My sister was becoming more aware of certain abuses that had occurred during her childhood, which I was not privy to ever. She went to a friend, who was a mutual friend of my attorney. Her friend called my attorney and they discussed a similar case in California. I said I would be an outside supporter to the case. Be a witness, give whatever resources I could, but that I didn't want to be involved in the case at all. I had trepidations about her credibility. That was my first trepidation and that has lasted and perseverated through the whole case, credibility.

I never was worried about my credibility. Never in a million years was I worried about mine. But I was concerned about hers and I was concerned that to do this case could lead to a revival of my physical symptoms [*she means her colitis*]. Because the connection of my life and reliving it, I felt, could trigger something else of a pathological nature. I was afraid of that, very afraid. I have to say it was my biggest sacrifice to do this case. I also put myself in a financially vulnerable position because I paid for her too. But to be physically vulnerable was the biggest decision for me. Even my surgeon had asked me, Do you realize what you're going to be putting yourself through? This could have a reverberating effect on your illness. In a lot of ways it did, but I still took that risk.

That was my biggest risk. Not to lose in court but to lose the stability of my health again. Although I hadn't agreed to be a co-plaintiff, my sister and my attorney started to say to me, We really need your case because you're the one who has all the witnesses—there's much more substantiated evidence of what happened to you and it would strengthen her case. I discussed with my attorney right from the beginning my concerns about the credibility of my sister's case. This attorney was my friend, but he said to me, I think you're being very selfish. You're abandoning your sister on this cause; it would help other people and other children. I think you're very selfish just because you're stronger. So it put me in a position where I felt semi-shame, like those old feelings of inadequacy, so I agreed to do it as a co-plaintiff. I felt that I would end up doing this alone. I knew it, I knew it. I knew that the financial responsibility would become mine, that the risk was the greatest for me and I knew that they would compromise their objectives and I would be left with the important aspects of it on my own, which has come to pass. But that's why I did start it.

I went to my surgeon and got what would be one of the more unique evidences to build upon, which was the medical report. I went to witnesses and I really started doing all that discovery on my own. I told my attorney, When you read that stuff, buddy, don't you forget that every memory that I was able to write down, my eyes would close and see what was happening to me. Every kid that you think it's happening to is opening up her eyes in the morning and facing what I'm remembering. I said, Don't you ever forget that. You're reading what's happening *now*.

By bringing suit against her parents, Anna Lee wrote us, she hoped to dramatize the problem and perhaps to change the law that protects child abuses by imposing a limit on how much time a victim has to seek compensation:

ANNA LEE TRAYNOR: The law that would specifically come from this suit would be of a rehabilitative nature. It would eliminate the present statute of limitations that prohibits an adult from seeking justice for past abuses and from past abusers through a civil action. It might be an added incentive to revise and more strictly enforce child-abuse laws on a criminal level. Which would have the more practical and beneficial effect of prevention. Effective prevention in the long term would eliminate the need for abused adult survivors to seek validation through a civil suit, or decrease the levels of abuse where it's recognized at the children's level, and appropriate rehabilitation is provided for the whole family unit. And what better way to illustrate the need for prevention of abuse to children than to legally assess the extent of the damages sustained by this abuse on an adult? Presently the laws don't allow you, as an adult, the opportunity to assess these "damages" or seek judicial or emotional validation from your offenders. So hence we survived the abuse but we remain victims of the system.

The forensic evaluation that I had to go through for my psychological evidence was a terrifying experience. I had to relive hell and then learn just how "scared" I really was. But if I'm going to have to relive hell it will be to help heal me, not to further burn me. The court system is an appropriate way to validate an adult survivor's need to recognize the sins committed against him as not his responsibility and legally transfer the weight of the sins back to their rightful owners.

The trouble is, I have always been acutely aware of my abuse. My introspection of its effects is present, but technically I was aware of all these offenses all these years. So it has been too long for me to have recourse/rights to seek damages for these actions—the statute of limitations has run out. Even though my damages are of a permanent physical nature with correlating emotional effects. And I also have more objective evidence and witness testimony to be accrued. My case is the one they can throw out. That is the legislative change that I would like to come out of this case if we could ever get it to the point of litigation at all. To redefine the statute of limitations specific to abused adult survivors which would allow them the opportunity to pursue a civil suit, without constricting and nonapplicable statutes.

I would really feel more personally successful if the case could be based on the fact that my rights as a child were violated and that the effects of that violation still do presently exist, and not based on how much psychoanalysis I required last week or last year just to get up in the morning. . . .

11

"It Affects You All Your Life"

*A*buse has consequences. It permanently changes survivors' lives. The men and women we interviewed were articulate about how their experiences of abuse changed them—for better and for worse.

CELIA GOLDEN: I've been self-sufficient since I was ten. I've always earned my own money. I don't depend on other people. It's always a gift when people care about me. I'm always amazed when people like me. I wonder why they do.

✦

DAN HAMILTON: I was a charmer. I was a show-off. I fit in well with every group from the motorcycle rebels to the French class to the band to the football players. I was part of every group at some point. I was never close to anyone, and I have no particularly close friends to this day. If you said, What's the name of your closest male friend? I would go, Uh, I don't have one. My wife is my best friend. The people I work with are friendly and close associates, none of whom I will turn to if I need a friend. So if I need a friend it's either me alone, my older son, Josh, or

[*Dan's wife*] Stephanie. Otherwise I just go sit alone somewhere until it's over. I've been far more comfortable with women than men all my life.

❖

CELIA GOLDEN: At one time I went from paying a hundred dollars a month for a room to making more money than my husband did. But I just bounce around. I always feel like I can take care of myself.

GINGER RHODES: You survived the ultimate test—you survived your childhood. Of course you can make it through anything.

Richard suggested to Alexa Donath that it was finally courage that saw her through:

ALEXA DONATH: I recognize it. It gets me through the stuff that I have to get through today. Not being able to bear children, being in chronic pain, losing the life that I thought I was going to have. I know other women who would have been devastated by one of those things. I think to myself, well, just pile it on.

But the capacity for pain has its limits, David Ray notes:

RICHARD RHODES: You've stopped drinking?

DAVID RAY: Oh yeah, yeah. That doesn't contribute to it anymore. But it comes down to simple things like living in the present. I'll get very involved in writing about something in the past and then I'll say I've got to let go of this or I will be right back in the past—there's just too much pain there. So I feel obliged to deal with the pain. I feel obliged to open up my files and get into an old notebook, but it's painful. You can do it insofar as you can mobilize some positive energies, but it's very important to know when you've got to back off. I don't always know because I really get into it. So that limited capacity for pain is a problem. And the shame issue is still there when I'm facing the old script with its attendant terrors.

For several of the women we interviewed, independence meant forgoing children:

KAREN SEAL: I have this thing of being a feminist, and yet I have a highly developed male side. I'm not going to need anybody, much less a man. Which leads me to the other discovery, that my damage was so profound I would not permit myself to have children. I had surgery— tubal ligation—when I was not yet thirty. It was like I didn't trust men with babies and never wanted to be dependent. I've recognized that that's a profound loss in my life.

I had already married Sam, but I told him before we married that I wasn't interested in having children. Now, recognize the timing. I'm just getting this, this very minute. I had told my friend about my father, who told my uncle, who told my mother, and Sam and I got married right in there, and I had surgery a year or so later. It was all in that same time, a really, really high-turmoil time for me. But I'm so anti-dependent. Now, my challenge in recovery is to learn to be interdependent. The man I'm seeing right now is very, very loving, very nurturing, very dear. He is so kind, but I keep thinking, when is the other shoe going to fall? I mean, it's like I can't trust this. It's the same thing— What do you want from me? Everybody else always did.

Richard asked Skye Smith if she was comfortable with children:

SKYE SMITH: Yes, adolescents and I get along. Their issues are so familiar to me: their rage, their optimism and idealism. I really like adolescents a lot. I still identify with them.

GINGER RHODES: But you've never had a child?

SKYE SMITH: No, and that's a big loss.

RICHARD RHODES: Was it a choice?

SKYE SMITH: Yes. I knew from as early as I can remember that I would never have children because they might be as bad as I was. And now it's just not going to happen. It's too late, it really is, and it's a loss. I feel a lot of feelings about that: sadness and rage. It wasn't even a choice. That's what pisses me off so much. All those years, it wasn't even an option. You're afraid to have a child—it might be like you. That's how terrible you feel about you. I should have been aborted myself, so why would I have any?

Valorie Butler has to guard herself against becoming co-dependent:

RICHARD RHODES: You strike me as a generous, loving woman. Do you feel that way about yourself?

VALORIE BUTLER: Yes, I do. I feel that's a gift. I think we all have it in our different ways, but I think it's my natural personality to be warm and outgoing and to care about people. Of course, the problem part of that has been co-dependency, trying to take over problems. I have tried to care for myself more than I did, too. I believe that's real.

David Ray notes in "Prolegomena to an Autobiography" that he found it difficult to accept praise from a distinguished American poet of a previous generation, the New Jersey pediatrician William Carlos Williams:

DAVID RAY: It had been another such attack of shyness that had kept me, in 1965, from using an unbelievably generous comment on my poetry from William Carlos Williams as a blurb to puff my first book, *X-Rays*. Today I am mystified by such unnecessary agonizings and wish the book had been born with the doctor's resounding slaps to assure its success.

Before she broke free, Louise Hill hid out for years in suburbia:

LOUISE HILL: Once I got into college, there was great anger in my family. I was then really no good. I was a bad girl. My father, I can't remember, I think he was so sick by then that he just was quiet. He didn't stick up for me. I can't say he stood up for me. But from then on it was scary, because I really lost any kind of footing in that family. At this point I don't think I particularly thought I was going to be a writer. I was going to major in English. I mean, I was just glad to get out of there and be somebody and I did major in English, a double major in English and philosophy. I was like many people, I got good grades in high school, but when I got into college I found out that there are a lot of other brilliant people in this country. I was just one of many. And it was frightening and I certainly was on my own. But I was gonna make it, I was gonna make it. I had a very influential teacher in college, John Holmes, who is a poet. He said to me, You're a writer, Louise, you're a real writer.

Two weeks after my father died I met the doctor I would marry. If anybody was going to be nice to me I was going to go off with him and of course I married the first person who was nice to me. As if—I'd better catch somebody quick, because somebody like me is never going to get anybody good. I was engaged by the time I was a junior and pregnant by the time I was a senior. I graduated early.

But these were the fifties, the Eisenhower years, and I was a good girl, and the idea was to find a good husband and get married and have a family. I was offered a scholarship to graduate school but I said, No, I'm getting married, and I remember the head of the philosophy department at the time said to me, That's right, that's right, go home and make fudge with the rest of them. I thought about that years later because I ended up not making fudge. But he was dead by that time so I couldn't tell him that.

My first job out, I was doing proofreading and pregnant. So I became a mother and stayed home and had three children very quickly. And for fifteen years I really was in the suburbs. Bobbie Ann Mason [*the novelist*] once wrote a line. She wrote, "Some people can miss their life the way you miss an airplane." I often think that I might have missed my whole life had I not followed my instincts. At one point I did make the break away but then I went back into this suburban life. The whole time I was in it, I felt like I wasn't in the right life. But I didn't know what the right life was. I didn't know where it was and I was so far away from it.

Ginger asked Karen Seal how she explained to herself her decision not to have children:

KAREN SEAL: Superficially, I had read that book *The Baby Trap* that was out just about that time. I said to my husband, If you want to have children, I'll do my nine months, but I expect you to be a co-partner here. If the baby is sick, I get up one night, you get up another night, you take a day off, I take a day off. I really need you to be a partner, because I'm not going to give up my career and be a full-time mother. My husband was one of twelve children and he really didn't care about having children anyway. I also said, If we have boys, I want you to be prepared to take custody if we ever divorce, which is real positive thinking. [*She laughs.*]

I've never missed the experience. I know some women are profoundly sad about missing it. I could be saying, I don't want to feel all that—that could be the reason—but I'm pissed that I didn't even have the choice. Because I feel I did that to protect myself.

I don't really miss being a parent. I'm doing better, a lot better, but the person I don't nurture much is me.

If Dan Hamilton is comfortable with women, he has also been more passive than he wanted to be:

DAN HAMILTON: My pattern—what I learned and what I was really good at—was shut up, cut, and run. Stay quiet. Don't say a thing, it'll blow over. I can endure anything as long as I don't move. And that was very much the emotional reaction to the sexual abuse. Just hold still, this will be over.

I always had the need for contact. I had the capability for contact. So I would reach out, I would touch, and I would get an extraordinary response back because I was so open in my need and vulnerability. Then the door would come slamming down, and people would be hurt and confused and wonder who changed the rules. It took me a long time to even understand the whys, much less learn how to change. Even now, it's there, I just see it coming now.

GINGER RHODES: Right, whoops, it's that old tape, here we go.

David Ray still feels guilt and repetition:

DAVID RAY: Go back and say, Why did I even read those letters from John Warner? Why didn't I say, Another letter from him, forget it? Why did I try to defend myself? [*Speaking as if directly to Warner:*] Oh, you say I had no Honor, you say I'm not Truthful. [*And again to us:*] If you say that, most people will try to defend themselves. Verbally harassed. So, I guess I was his Lolita. He was Humbert Humbert, trying to get me back. And was willing to do anything to succeed.

The script called for me going to my grave with the secrets. That guilt is very, very basic. Right before you came in I thought, oh, I'm about to commit a crime, I'm betraying those people. I should be protecting my mother, John Warner, Nelson Algren, J. Edgar Hoover. [*He laughs ruefully.*] I should be protecting anybody who regarded me as fair prey. And there's guilt, too, about having not fixed it for anybody else. Remember what Robert Lowell said about how his poems hadn't saved a single Jew? I had all my suffering as a child but I haven't saved a single other kid. You know, I haven't gone to one of these orphanages and I haven't—

RICHARD RHODES: But David, you've been a teacher. Don't you think you've helped in that way?

DAVID RAY: Well, you help sometimes. For example, in writing classes when they get into incest or abuse or addiction issues, there are some very meaningful things that have come out of that. I get them to form groups, the ones who have gone through this. It's a way of finding out who they are. Hey, there are a lot of us out there. In the long run, maybe that's one of the most helpful things because the isolation is what's so terrible. If I am the only one this ever happened to . . . In actual fact, it's happened to millions of kids. It is a holocaust. Another guilt is, it wasn't *the* Holocaust, and what are you griping about? They didn't herd *you* into the gas chambers.

But they did hurt us. A Jewish writer objected very strongly one time about the end of [*David's poem*] *Orphans* because I used a Holocaust image. I don't know why he doesn't attack Sylvia Plath for the same crime, except she's a successful suicide, which makes her admirable. Her father, Otto, was not, to my knowledge, a Nazi, though she called him one. But survivors are contemptible. I really believe that. They always say, "*merely* surviving." I see this with the adulation of Plath. We can take her seriously because she killed herself. But somebody who just struggles on . . . You go to shrinks and you write, and you suffer through your broken marriages and you try to get your act together, year after year, but you can't get anywhere, how contemptible could you be? It's beneath contempt. That self-hatred is fed by our society, and I'm in a very abusive profession. I think I couldn't have picked a more abusive profession than writing.

RICHARD RHODES: How so?

DAVID RAY: Elitism and the abusive way one is treated by so many people. There are editors who would never accept my work, regardless of its quality. Just pure snobbery. Snobbery, pure and simple. I try to call it subjectivity, but I feel in some cases it's abuse. I send my manuscripts repeatedly to those editors who are abusive with me, who would never accept my work. Rather than, Hey, there are other people, there are other places! I can't even see them. Because I'm totally addicted to these lousy relationships. It's an addiction, you go back to the abuses.

Barbara Hamilton identifies real, unrecoverable losses:

BARBARA HAMILTON: The childhood abuse didn't destroy my life, but it destroyed certain aspects of it. It terribly affected my job relationships. I would start off just feeling great, that I had made a good impression on the interviewer. A good start. When things would begin to get where

I wasn't quite sure of myself, I couldn't handle it. It would just get bigger and bigger until finally it would affect my job performance.

Little things. This is a ridiculous thing, but it shows that other people I was working with picked up on it and had no idea where it was coming from. I didn't either at the time. One of the things taught in nursing, and when you're giving meds—

RICHARD RHODES: "Meds" is medications?

BARBARA HAMILTON: Medications, yes. You're taught to tri-check your dose. You check the card that the order's on, you check the medicine, and you check the instrument that you're using—the syringe or whatever. You do this three times before you give it to the patient. We'd walked through that a million times in training. Well, some time after I'd finished training and had my job, one of my classmates was working with me. She watched me in the med room one day and finally asked me, Barbara, when are you ever going to get through with this three-check business? She was still doing it, but in the flash of an eye. I was still doing it the way we did in school because I was terrified that I would give the wrong medicine to the wrong patient.

It had nothing to do with sex, but it had to do with my ability to move ahead and cope—because I had no self-confidence. I'd made a lot of mistakes in my life. This was not going to be another one, even if they made fun of me in the med room. I couldn't not do that.

One time there was an emergency at the hospital and I froze. I don't know why, I don't remember except that it scared me so badly that I didn't function as I'd been trained. I wasn't the first person on the scene, but I didn't do what I was supposed to do, whatever it was. It scared me because I felt myself freezing, I felt myself immobile, and I don't know whether it was triggered by something sexual or what. It just had me frozen and it scared me. We had a very good in-service RN nurse who helped us at that time and she was somebody I could trust. I went to her to say that I froze at that particular incident and it scared me, because I had a responsibility and I was glad somebody else was able to pick it up. She said, Barbara, something's troubling you—you're a good nurse, but something is troubling you. She tried to go back to the scenes of that day. To this day I don't know what happened.

But now I do know what the freezing was about, because I got frozen when I was told about my brother abusing one of the children. Then I remembered my own thing of just going absolutely that way with my father. I'm sure that's what happened in the hospital that day, whether the patient looked like my father—who knows what it was, but something triggered it. So I would say definitely it affects you all through your life. It affects all your relationships. You always feel as though it's your fault, that you're out of sync. It's never the world.

✤

DAVID RAY: Some parents just totally want retroactive abortion for their kids. They just totally reject them, don't even want to hear from them. Don't even want to see them. That mystery is always there, you're always going back, saying, Why didn't they love me? That's the basic question. If I see my mother now, it's painful because I feel the rejection all over again. She adores my sister, every move she makes. She has no real interest in me or anything I do. I know that, and she knows that I know it. But it's still very painful. It's painful for me just to look at her face. There's still a little kid in me saying, Mother, why don't you love me? Why didn't you hug me?

✤

DAN HAMILTON: I had assumed that I was bad. That's a given, all my life. I have no conscious memory of my original mother because she left at six months. The only mother figure I had who was in any way warm and nurturing and motherly and comforting was my grandmother, and she died in a car accident when I was about eight. And that shut that door. My second mother died when I was four, and apparently, going back over records and discussions, I felt responsible. She died of Hodgkin's disease, and I can remember visiting her in the hospital and bringing her Hershey bars as a gift, and being told that she died because she had too much sugar. So I felt that she had died out of love for me. Apparently,

I carried that through grammar school, because there are records of therapy sessions in grammar school where that gets poured out. So, early on, I knew I was wrong, bad, and deserved whatever happened. But I also had a strong concern that it shouldn't affect other people or hurt other people. So most of my life as a child and certainly as an adult was give what you can, do what you can not to hurt other people, be whatever they need you to be. You lose all sense of self, obviously.

Karen Seal characterized her feelings of falseness with an unforgettable simile:

KAREN SEAL: I told my analyst that when I think about myself and all my achievements I just feel like icing on a turd.

Many of the survivors with whom we spoke believe the abuse they experienced left them vulnerable. Alexa Donath wrote:

ALEXA DONATH: In June, two months after my sixteenth birthday, my boyfriend raped me. We were alone at his house. We had actually broken up a few weeks before and were together that evening just to talk, to end it properly. We were making out and then all of a sudden I was on the floor and my head was against the fireplace and under a chair. My hands were pinned down—I had been saying no for almost a year and I said no that night. It happened so quickly. When he drove me home all I could say was "Why did you do that, you know I didn't want you to." I was numb, I didn't cry.

I tell this story because after this act I felt that someone had robbed me. I was a virgin. I did not call it rape until years later. But even if I had never called it rape, I knew that he hurt me. Several years later, after high school, I began seeing him again. Had I loved and respected myself . . . I doubt I would have ever had anything to do with this person again.

This is my mother's legacy to me. She violated me for so long, I must have been used to it. She robbed me of positive feelings about myself and I believed her hurtful words.

KAREN SEAL: I never connected at all to my incest history. I just thought, I'm just a high-energy person and am driven because I'm better . . . I was really grandiose. But even as a young kid I thought, what am I trying to prove and to whom? I really couldn't figure this out. I thought, every time I achieve something it's a hollow victory. Maybe that's not it, maybe I should be doing something else.

❧

DAVID RAY: But what do you do to bring these things out in people? Somehow you signal that that's the game you're willing to play. You somehow signal it. It's the self-contempt, it's the lack of faith in yourself, it's the diffidence, it's the—I don't know. But that's the game you play. I've tried real hard to change it. Right now, I'm trying very hard. In three days I'll be sixty years old, which I find unbelievable, because I never expected to be a survivor. I'm trying real hard to start to think of myself as a survivor, not as a piece of human refuse.

❧

SKYE SMITH: When I was in the hospital [*for depression*] the last time, I didn't want my husband to visit me. It's like being a broken appliance. You go into the hospital, get fixed, and then you come home. He wanted to come see me and I remember I couldn't breathe—literally could not catch my breath. I told the social worker, You will not set up a trip with him, he's not to come. In this place you have your phone calls monitored and everything locked, double-locked. It sounds very abusive, but it's not, it's very protective. I had one supervised phone call left—you have to get permission to call specific people—and it was to my brother. I didn't have any phone calls left to my husband to tell him don't come, don't come, don't come, you can't come, you cannot come, you cannot see me here, you can't come.

It was my intimacy problem. I was afraid he would really get to know me and he would see me there all opened up and it was too frightening. I called my brother and gave him orders, Bob, call Jack and tell him not to come. He did call Jack and Jack said, I'm coming. I was hell-bent, I was going to get to a phone and call him and tell him not to come. I didn't have permission to do that and they almost put me into restraints.

It's terrifying. You don't even know what being close to another person is all about when you grow up like we did. You don't know what relationships can be like. You don't know what a world can be like that's not so frightening all the time, not so terrifying.

But despite vulnerability, some have found confidence:

LOUISE HILL: I have a lot of emotional scars that I have to live with and find ways to overcome almost every day of my life. I think it's a miracle that I'm standing. That I've been able to enjoy life as much as I have. That I take the pleasure in life that I do.

GINGER RHODES: That you've been able to allow yourself to be successful, to be good.

LOUISE HILL: Yes. The concerns about prettiness are something I'd like to address. I'm writing an article right now about how inner beauty balances outer beauty.

I thought I was a fat, ugly child. I'm very surprised when I see pictures of me and how pretty I was. I grew up thinking I was quite ugly, quite unattractive. This went on for a very long time—through my first marriage. I married a very unattractive man. I paid attention, though, and by my second marriage I had decided not to do that anymore. My current husband is very attractive. My mother knew him and liked him. She said that he was an exception to the rule.

Two experiences helped me break through. When I was in graduate school I met a writer, a man who was much younger than I, and we were very close. He made me feel attractive and that helped. Then I met somebody else once somewhere [*she means Richard, who met her when they were teaching together in a summer program at Goddard College, before he met Ginger*] and went out for dinner and he said to me, You're a very sexy woman, you're a very attractive woman, and I said, I am? And that was the first time I ever knew that. And so I'm very grateful to that person. I was surprised. I came back home and looked in the mirror and I thought, I am pretty. He was the first person who told me that I was pretty.

GINGER RHODES: How old were you?

LOUISE HILL: I was forty-one. And ever since then I think I've gotten prettier and prettier. Now when I look in the mirror I do know I'm a very attractive woman. I'm sure of it.

✦

DAN HAMILTON: I feel very lucky and in a very good place now. Ten years ago I would have been more pessimistic about where I was going—inside, I mean. But I like who I am inside much more now. Some of that's just growing up, some of it is the process of dealing with this issue of abuse, some of it is the fighting through to make the marriage work, and finding things about me that I liked that were not based on the qualities of me that I had learned very early to dismiss as worthless. You could say that I was talented and charming, and I would dismiss it, because I knew that those were just tricks I had learned. I could get a standing ovation at the end of a one-man show, a thousand people could stand up and cheer for ten minutes, and I would go home that night and just feel like—what was it you quoted one of the others saying?—icing on a turd. It didn't count. I'm getting better with that. Just as this experience this afternoon—I mean talking with you—will be another step for me.

If Dan feels better about himself, he still keeps his distance from his family:

DAN HAMILTON: My relationship at this point is occasional letters through the year. I'm out west once every four or five years and I will go spend a day with somebody. I've chosen not to work very hard at those relationships, to keep my focus here on me and my relationships and my own family and my world, and make these as strong and healthy as I can. I give what I can when I can, but I don't work very hard at it. And I feel guilty about that, because their need is extraordinary. But I don't have any more to give. I'm just staying above water right here. I have to be a little careful about how thin I spread myself. So I have selfishly said I'll try to make me as healthy as I can, given the fact that

that cancer will always be there. I'm sorry that there's not enough to go around. That's the way things stand right now.

GINGER RHODES: That's not selfish. It's realistic.

DAN HAMILTON: I can say that, but it feels selfish. I'll punish myself at some point for it, for not going out and making more of an effort.

RICHARD RHODES: I'm struck again by how many permutations and complexities follow from dysfunction in a family. That Barbara was this rather than that. That you had to deal in the complex ways you have, and your sisters, and the different responses to Barbara's book based on your differing experiences.

DAN HAMILTON: In comparison, if you have to scale these things, my trauma is not as bad as what some of the girls have gone through [*that is, Dan's half sisters, whose molestation is reported in Barbara Hamilton's book— another example of how abuse cascades down through generations*], especially the two older girls who were repeatedly molested as two- or three-year-old children by a group of adults. I don't have that to deal with. I don't have those nightmares to deal with. I'm not trying to minimize what I've gone through. But it's not the same.

Celia Golden still must deal with her nightmares, she wrote in an article on incest survivors:

CELIA GOLDEN: It is no accident that I rejected identification with my mother's gender as a young child and consciously struggled to develop my identity as female. My mother aborted my birthright to feel pride in sharing her gender by providing my initial and most powerful image of "woman." Although I increasingly wear my femininity with greater ease, I am not free from occasional childhood feelings of being an impostor in drag. . . . The victim's reality is challenged by what the perpetrator says is real. My mother says I can't sleep with underpants on because it's dirty. She comes into my room when I'm asleep "to be sure" I didn't sneak them on. I have nightmares that worms are crawling into my orifices.

She was right. There were no worms in my bed—only "worm(an)s." Too, we are frequently told by our mothers that we're crazy, not that their behavior is crazy. My mother needed me to think I was crazy as assurance that I would doubt my reality. By age four I had incorporated her thinking that I wasn't "normal." As I grew older, I decided something was wrong with my mind, that I was slightly brain-damaged or retarded, although I have always placed high on intelligence tests.

My mother told me she thought I was retarded until I was almost four years old. I did not learn to walk until I was two or develop spoken language until I was three. My delayed development is typical of infants whose mothers treated them with extreme neglect and abuse. . . . I can appreciate how threatened my mother was to realize I was more than a mindless object within her total control. It is understandable that she chose to attack my mind as well as my body. . . .

Barbara Hamilton has concluded that it's vital to deal with the consequences of abuse early rather than later in life:

BARBARA HAMILTON: It's important for young people to work on abuse issues while they're young instead of waiting so many years, as I did. Instead of wasting your whole life. It affects everybody and every-thing in your life. I said once, This sucks, and it really does. When you're trying to get compliments or when you're hoping that somebody will say something nice—or if they do say something nice—you put it down, you won't accept it. It sucks, really. Because you're trying to make them praise you more. And you feel like a manipulative little fraud. You've got to shut that out. You don't need to do that anymore.

GINGER RHODES: But would you have the sense of yourself that you have today if you hadn't done the work?

BARBARA HAMILTON: No. I'd probably be in a loony bin. Oh, definitely. I wish I could encourage people to deal with it. It's scary.

GINGER RHODES: It's very frightening.

BARBARA HAMILTON: I was at the bottom. I didn't know it was the sexual abuse. I thought it was my second divorce—failure. Failure, failure, failure, failure. I was a basket case, absolutely. With family responsibilities and everything else, to be unresolved during all that time, when you have so much more that you could have given them. [*She means her children.*] I know I could have. I could have given them a lot more stability instead of losing my temper and throwing bread up on the ceiling because it wouldn't rise. That's the kind of stuff that they saw when they were growing up—this mother that every once in a while would erupt. I didn't hit them, it wasn't that. It was just losing control. I was so ashamed. I didn't know what to do with it.

RICHARD RHODES: Abuse has its aftermath, as much so as war. It's now officially a syndrome with a name, post-traumatic stress disorder. I certainly would have been a much better father if I hadn't been drinking heavily in those years. I was sedating myself as well as acting out, trying to deal with my earlier experiences. I'm sorry. I've told my children I'm sorry. I wish they'd had a better father than they did. But it's also true that we have our own lives to deal with.

BARBARA HAMILTON: And no knowledge. We hadn't a clue as to what was driving us.

John Wood, Celia Golden, and others still feel like children:

RICHARD RHODES: You grew up in Connecticut?

JOHN WOOD: In Newtown. I never grew up. I just look fifty-four. I'm actually fourteen.

✤

CELIA GOLDEN: My voice has grown stronger with practice over the last four years, but I still experience my childhood fear that I won't be believed. I'm forty-four years old, yet sometimes imagine myself as a child sitting on the witness stand in a courtroom filled with adults. My mother's attorney is about to cross-examine me, when he turns to a jury of her peers and reminds them that she's a woman, a mother. He tells the jury, "This is an impossible lie. Mothers don't sexually abuse children! What kind of daughter would accuse her own mother? The mother is the victim."

✤

ALEXA DONATH: My whole life has been spent trying to get over my childhood, every day. It's not there all the time, but it's there in the fact that I still reach for food for comfort when I'm upset. It's there when I spent a lot of years in a marriage letting somebody belittle me. It's there because I don't think enough of myself to really live my life the way people who haven't had to overcome this. My friend thinks he can do anything with his life. He's always thought so. I've never thought that way. I've asked my friend, Do you understand what that means, how lucky you are? Your parents adored you. Do you know what that means to somebody like me? I have no concept of that. But if my parents were reading this, they would say, What do you mean?

✤

CELIA GOLDEN: I was afraid to, but wanted to be a mother. I wanted to have kids and be a good mother, that was really important to me. But I was afraid that I didn't know how to be a good mother. Except for the women who were my baby-sitters, I didn't have any role models outside of my mother.

When my babies were born, I didn't want my mother there. I didn't want her anywhere near my babies. I couldn't come home from the hospital immediately because one of my twins was too little. Then, when we came home, I hemorrhaged and was confined to bed, so my mother-in-law had to come and help. But I didn't want any other woman touching my kids. I didn't trust any woman with my kids. Even in the hospital I kept going to the nursery.

The first time my mother-in-law bathed my daughter, I felt this anxiety coming up, because my mother sexually abused me every time she bathed me. But I knew from the way my mother-in-law looked at, and talked to, and held my daughters that the woman didn't have a mean bone in her body. I watched her like a hawk and learned to trust her. My mother—I never wanted my mother left alone with my kids.

12

"Trying to Get Some Dignity"

More about how abuse changed the lives of the men and women we interviewed.

LOUISE HILL: I was punished for telling stories. I was punished severely for staying in the house. As a writer, I'm amazed that I even get as much done as I do, because I have a very bad feeling when I'm alone. And as we know, a writer has to be alone. I sometimes get the feeling that I'm a "bad girl" very powerfully when I'm alone and writing. The way that I've solved that is, I'll write for an hour and then I'll call a friend. Then I'll write for another hour and I'll do an errand. I'm not able to stay by myself for long periods of time—whether writing or not. Except when I get "tricked"—in other words, when I get so deep into my writing that I forget all those messages.

RICHARD RHODES: What happens when you come out of that trance state that one is in when one writes—do you feel uncomfortable?

LOUISE HILL: Very uncomfortable. It's very painful.

RICHARD RHODES: You lose that focus.

LOUISE HILL: I get the feeling that I want to reach out and find some-body that loves me. I now understand that. My mother would say, What's wrong with you? Something wrong with you? Don't you have any friends? Do I have to pay people to be your friends? Go out in the sunshine, go outside, go out in the light, go out in the light. It's a beautiful day, there's sun outside, sitting in here, what's wrong with you? And what was I doing in the house that she would say this? I was reading a book, probably, or making up some creative game. So being alone was very bad.

GINGER RHODES: Did *she* want to be alone? Did she want you to leave for your sake or for her sake?

LOUISE HILL: Oh, that's an interesting question. Of course, I'm giving you the benefit of an adult understanding that I've only recently come to. As a child, all I knew was that my mother was angry and I was bad. There was no other reality beyond that.

✤

DAVID RAY: I still deal with the same things I dealt with as a child. I will get enough good stuff to keep my hopes going and then I'll get enough crushing disappointment to keep me really feeling hopeless. Re-jection for me is just absolutely routine but I still . . .

And it's this too, you know: you can't suffer a success because you feel worthless. I was reading a biography of Rilke that talks about this problem. Even he couldn't deal with the success because he felt worthless. You can't tolerate failure because you're looking to the outside to confirm that you're worth something, because you don't really believe it inside. So between those two parallels, my life's still pretty miserable and so I keep looking for that outside affirmation, chasing after the ones who won't give it. I'm working on it. But it's not easy. All this stuff has a life of its own and it stays alive.

Louise Hill is strongly affected by her physical surroundings:

GINGER RHODES: How did your mother's behavior make you feel as a child? Were you angry with her, were you apprehensive around her?

LOUISE HILL: I was terrified, I was terrified. That's a good question. I was terrified. I didn't understand anger. I don't think I understood that I had a right to anger. It takes a long time until you understand you have a right to anger. I lived in terror. What I remember is backing into my room with my hands in front of my face—which was, Don't hit me, don't hit me, don't hit me, don't hit me. Sometimes in life, I still find myself feeling, Please life, don't hit me, don't hit me.

There are trails of this stuff that are never, never gotten past, like the problem of being alone. We have a lovely house in the country and I have a terrible problem being there alone. I feel so low and so miserable there, but I now understand it's that feeling of "You're a bad girl," and I'll never be able to get rid of that. Never be able to get rid of that. That's why living in a large city is a very safe place for me because when I look out this window, I see all of these buildings, and that means that there are people there, so I don't have the feeling that I'm a bad girl. I have the feeling that I'm a very good girl in the city. I have to go places where I feel like I'm a good girl.

Anna Lee Traynor's lawsuit triggered feelings she had hardly allowed herself to acknowledge before:

ANNA LEE TRAYNOR: Along the way, I realized that I had never experienced how I really felt. I knew the kind of life I lived made me sick, but somehow I never realized the extent of my illness and what it did to me. I remember the first time I called my new attorney, and he was trying to get a handle on this case from my phone call. [*She imitates herself being terse and impatient.*] I said, *I've got five minutes to get to the bus stop.* I'll never forget saying that [*imitating again*], *And I'll just tell you a couple of things, if you can help me fine.* I was so *crabby* to him. He said, Well, there's a problem with the statute of limitations. I said, *Well, let me just tell you something, if I lived in Wyoming I could bring this as a criminal charge.*

I live with the implications of my abuse every day, so don't you talk to me about statutes of limitations. It's current, it's real, it's tangible, and it's not in my past. It's in my present, it's when I take off my clothes and I look at myself. I lost parts of my body, my body is altered, my systems are altered, and I'm in a state of stable but compromised health. Don't you dare tell me it's been too long.

Abuse disturbed Barbara Hamilton's sexuality, she writes in The Hidden Legacy:

BARBARA HAMILTON: So physical intimacy became a substitute for emotional intimacy, but it did not always lead to intercourse. It never led to orgasm for me. However, since I had heard very little about that phenomenon, I assumed it happened to wives when they conceived a baby. Maybe, I thought, it's what Mother referred to as the beautiful reward for waiting until marriage. If so, I had thrown away my chance to experience it. My arousal responses always faded soon after intercourse began and I just went numb. But I wasn't surprised. Sex, guilt, and numbness were always intertwined. I didn't know that what I really hungered for was being loved, not making love.

Celia Golden felt more generally disconnected from her sexuality:

CELIA GOLDEN: Even as a woman in my early twenties, I couldn't watch gas being pumped into a car without feeling embarrassed. I could not watch it happen. I could not watch anything where something was being penetrated. Sex with a man is a different issue, because I have a whole different orientation to men. My father represented some element of safety and affection, so there are no triggers attached to men. My response is to inanimate objects. It's tools, instruments, hands, fingers, hoses, bolts going into nuts. I didn't want to be around when people were talking about, you know, nuts and screws.

I couldn't use a bathroom if I was at someone else's house. I would lock the door, turn on the faucet, and flush the toilet so no one knew what I was doing. Make them think I'm washing my hands. I learned to pee very quietly. It's like I don't distinguish between the orifices of my body and their functions. I don't think my mother did. When people think of male/female sex, they think of penises and vaginas. When it's women, it's all up for grabs. Women who've been sexually abused by a man only—if it was oral, maybe they've got a thing about going to dentists. If they were sodomized, maybe that's a problem area, but then vaginal intercourse isn't an issue. The way a man smells can be a trigger or the room it happened in. For me, it's all orifices, and nothing that is male-oriented. Going to the bathroom is part of being sexual, it isn't something separate. Eating isn't something separate. I'm a recovering bulimorexic. All those memories are tied together.

✤

ANNA LEE TRAYNOR: My parents caused my illness through stress, through my constant anxiety. My body was always in a state of distress and stress and alert to danger. The illness was precipitated by the work overload.

When I moved out, my physical condition moved with me. So I had the residual emotional scars of the actual abuse, and I also had the ongoing colitis. Along with the acute emotional stress to deal with from the disease process itself and from treatments. Then I had a safe environment, the best physicians, a loving family and friends, but I still had the disease. And it raged on no matter what the intervention.

I was frightened once the colitis started, separately from having ever been abused. You're faced with a disease, your body is in a state of debilitation, and what is called homeostasis—the balance between all your functions—is lost. You then become dependent on chemotherapeutic intervention. You're on steroids, which completely change your system around, and it becomes a vicious cycle. You fear the disease, the disease is exacerbated by your stress and anxiety, and it just eats away.

Then I was dealing with the fact that I was abandoned. I was sent to live with other people. These people loved me, but I had to separate from my brother. I had to keep dealing with the truth that my mother didn't want me, that I'd been abandoned, sent to live with someone else.

Plus, colitis is a very degrading disease. It's degrading because it has to do with your body's eliminations. Who wants to talk about that? Who wants to have a loss of bowel control, bowel incontinence? I had it. When I was training to become a special education teacher, I would drive to college and there would be a total loss of bowel continence. I'd have to drive home and clean myself up. I remember there was a wedding I had to go to when I had to wear a Pampers—baby-sized, which fit me at the time, and I was already twenty years old. So I had to deal with the process of a disease like anybody else does, plus deal with the reason why. It was just one complication after the other. I resented having to depend on medications. I didn't have control. I was out of that home in a loving environment, but still plagued by their offenses against me because now I have this disease. They were there in the disease—I couldn't get free of them.

RICHARD RHODES: It must have been a nightmare.

ANNA LEE TRAYNOR: Yes, it was. Plus, I realized that this disease could kill me and I was angry at that. I was offended—such a poor word—that my mother would have allowed it to go so far that I would end up with a disease with no cure. I was a young girl. Anyone who has this disease will tell you that it's an embarrassing disease. I don't want to use the word, but it makes you feel as if you've been treated like shit. That's what was coming out of me uncontrollably and it almost seemed to correlate with the abuse. I'm strong and a woman of faith, but I couldn't gain control over myself. That was so frustrating.

When I was nineteen, I met my husband-to-be and felt a constant inadequacy because I was sick. So this sense of inadequacy remained with me even though I was out of that home where people told me I was inadequate.

Then my gastroenterologist started preparing me. You're not re- sponding to these medications, he would tell me, so we have to think about the possibility of cancer, you have to start gearing yourself towards a surgical remedy. I didn't want to hear about it. I didn't want to think that I had to go to that length. I was in a state of remission for a few months, but then when I had to wear those Pampers to that wedding, I said, That's it. That's when I made up my mind to deal with the disease and recover from it. Actually, I went to a psychiatrist for a while to learn to deal with the disease. Then I met my surgeon, who discussed all of the pros and cons of the surgery. That was very difficult to deal with. But I developed a familial affection for the man, who's the best in the country. And I was ready for the surgery, because I had made up my mind that that was it—I would not have a productive life, I would not be able to go to school, I would not be of any value to anybody else, let alone myself.

They usually give you a shot to relax you, get you ready for the anesthesia. Well, I refused it. The surgeon came in and said, Why isn't she out? I said, Because she wanted to make sure you were showing up. They all looked at him and he said, Well, I've showed up. I said, Now she wants to make sure you know what you're doing. He said, Put her down and put her out. I had surgery with him more than once. After several rounds, I remember telling him, If your Rolex is missing, it's mine, you're not going back in again. I went to him for five years. I started to counsel people for him for the ostomy [*that is, teaching patients to care for a permanent, surgically created opening into the body*]. As a matter of fact, I said to him, I really think you should leave discussing the surgery to someone who knows what they're talking about, because let me tell you something, buddy, I woke up to a different picture than what you painted and I was very upset. He even changed some of his procedures. So I set a little precedent there.

RICHARD RHODES: Were you seriously underweight before the surgery?

ANNA LEE TRAYNOR: Yes, I was. I was about eighty pounds. Eighty or ninety pounds.

RICHARD RHODES: How tall are you?

ANNA LEE TRAYNOR: Five feet. My normal weight is about one hundred seven to one hundred ten. My lowest weight was about fifty-eight pounds. It did fluctuate with steroids. Sometimes it was one hundred twenty-five, because steroids will do that, but there was a point in the hospital when I never really saw what I looked like. I think I'm bigger anyway than I really am. [*To Ginger, who is five feet four and weighs one hundred twenty pounds:*] I'm looking at you like you're so little, and thinking I'm much bigger.

GINGER RHODES: I commented to Richard how small you are. You're tiny.

ANNA LEE TRAYNOR: I think I'm gigantic. But when I was in the hospital recuperating after one of the surgeries, I used to take walks past the occupational therapy room, which had a stand-up mirror. Walking one day, I saw a woman walking toward me, and I looked to the orderly walking with me and said, Can you believe that they walk the dead, look at that woman!—but don't let her see you looking. I said, How could they bring someone down here like that? You can see her bones. Why don't they just shoot her and put her out of her misery? So we go back to my room and I look at him, he's helping me get into bed, and I say to him, Why were you with that woman? And he didn't say anything. I said, devastated, I'd just figured it out, Because that was *me!*

That was the night that everything started to fail. I thought, this is what I'm reduced to. I was running a fever and they couldn't figure out why. But that's when it started to really hit me: I am just going to give up here. I thought, that's what I look like, that's what other people are seeing. And that night I started to lose hope and incentive and desire to go on living. I could see the changes in my body. I now had the intestines that belonged inside of me, outside of my body. All the wires and the sutures and the pain—I just said, That's it, they won. My mother won. I felt myself start to drift. That's when the nurses came in. I remember hearing them say, I'm not getting a pulse, I'm not getting blood pressure, what's going on here? So another one would come and touch my face and say, Well, she's a little diaphoretic, which means you're sweaty or clammy. They asked me how I felt. I said I didn't feel well and I had a fever. They kept coming in, checking my vital signs.

Then it was like I said, Well, I'm going now [*meaning she felt she was dying*]. That's when I saw the Lourdes water in a little plastic bottle on my table. At that point my room was like a little altar, I had been in there so long, all the Italian stuff and the rosary beads. I decided I wasn't going until I had a drink of water, which I wasn't allowed to have during recovery. And that's when I noticed that bottle. I drank half the bottle. I took the other half and sprinkled it on my incision. I really don't know what possessed me to do that.

Then I remember thinking, If I go, who's going to know? I said, Because you're *evidence*. I said that word, *evidence,* I remember that word as distinctly as anything. I said, You are the evidence of what was done to you as a child and now you're not a child. You have to stay because otherwise no one will know what was done to you. You'll be gone and they'll get away with it. But if you live, they won't get away with it.

So I had to live. Then the next day a black seepage came through the incision, which was evidently poison and toxin. There must have been some underlying blood poisoning.

Now I'm projected into a court case and that's exactly what I am. I'm evidence. We all are, but I'm so much easier to view.

✦

DAVID RAY: Why do other people get better and I don't? That's a tough one.

RICHARD RHODES: The answer may be simply that you were more neglected and abused. You had more to handle.

DAVID RAY: Yes, massive betrayal and so much of it. How long does it take to shovel out a boxcar if it's radioactive and full of shit? It's going to take you a long time. Maybe a lifetime. And maybe you never will be happy like you really want to be. What was it Freud said? Replace hysterical anxiety with commonplace misery? Maybe that's the best you can shoot for.

You forget how bad it was. If you level with yourself, you can't pay attention to what other people will or won't believe. If they want to say your experience wasn't very heavy, that's their prerogative—you know what it was and how hard it was to live, and the bottom line is, you should love yourself for that and respect yourself deeply for that. It's very hard. I find it very hard. Anything positive I discredit immediately. It doesn't register. I won a prize? So what. Put it on the shelf. What do I do *now* to justify my existence?

GINGER RHODES: How do I prove that I'm not really a fraud?

DAVID RAY: I think it will always be a struggle. It will always be the little kid inside, trying to get some dignity.

❖

ALEXA DONATH: I don't see my parents anymore. People ask, How can you do that? Well, I went back and forth for years and years. I would try, and then five years would go by, and I would say, I can fix it, this is going to be different. Finally I said, It isn't about them anymore, it's about me, and I cannot live my life with these people in it. I do not have to explain. It's very, very hard when people judge you when you have to divorce yourself from your parents. I can't tell you how many people have judged me because of it. It's almost as bad as the abuse.

Ginger asked John Wood if his parents were still alive:

JOHN WOOD: No, Allah be praised. Although I suppose it would be better if they were alive, if I could confront them.

GINGER RHODES: They died before you were able to come to terms with them?

JOHN WOOD: Yeah. Well, I buried them, but they're not dead to me. My mother sits right here, saying, Don't be silly.

❖

KAREN SEAL: I continue to have such disdain for my mother that I've never really grieved her. But in a sense, I detached from her when I was about twelve. It was like I felt responsible for her because she was so incompetent. It was like our roles totally reversed when I was about twelve and she became the kid and I was the adult. I wept a bit, but, I don't know. I feel pretty cold about it, I guess.

GINGER RHODES: Did their deaths bring a sense of relief?

KAREN SEAL: Yes, a real sense of relief. I got into recovery after they were both gone.

❖

CELIA GOLDEN: I'm afraid of my mother. I think she's crazy. A lot of my fears are irrational. I'm bigger than my mother. A baby's earliest memory of its mother is someone with superhuman powers, not a flesh-and-blood person. That's what I carry. I have this idea that she would pay a detective to find me, to shut me up if she could. She'd throw acid in my face; there's no limit to what she would do. I don't want to see her. I don't want to know anything about her. I don't want to know when my mother gets sick, when she's dying. I have this sense that her body is what physically keeps the evil, and once she dies, she could be even more powerful without the body, she could just be out there roaming around.

RICHARD RHODES: It's still that terrifying for you?

CELIA GOLDEN: I don't go around thinking about it, but when I do, that's the kind of imagery I have.

❖

LOUISE HILL: When my mother died I had such a mixture of feelings I shall never forget them. She died unexpectedly. She died shopping, which I think is a very good way to die. She just keeled over shopping in Boston. I had a mixture of such grief and such relief. I remember being ashamed of the relief. I remember it being a feeling that I had never experienced before. For the first time in my life I felt free. Nobody could beat me up anymore and nobody could tell me I was bad. Of course, what I was left with was the voice inside that lives in me that says you're bad. But I felt a tremendous sense of relief.

My sister and I went to my mother's house to close up her little apartment and divide the effects. We came into the house and I started to wail and cry in such a way it was almost inhuman. It kept up for half an hour. I just sat there and wailed. I knew why I was crying. The reason I was crying was not because my mother was dead, it was because now I was never going to get what I had always wanted.

❖

CELIA GOLDEN: A lot of my memories are by seasons. In the summer, there are memories when I was outside of the house and away from my mother and there are wintertime memories. But it's more like there's this gray period and there'll be things that stand out. I was depressed a lot of the time. Of the first eighteen years, there wasn't one day until I left my parents' house that I didn't cry. That was a normal event for me. During the summer when I was fifteen and sixteen I lived with some relatives and I remember being nicknamed Smiley. I remember being amazed that I could count the days that I hadn't cried. I thought it was normal for me to cry. So I can chronicle things. I go back and look at seasons and I can remember what I was wearing. I'm a real sensory person. I think that's part of being cut off when I was an infant. It's like when someone's blind, sound becomes more important. Being touched by my sister and my father when I was an infant was real significant.

❖

ALEXA DONATH: The summers were another respite from the pain. My mother was not as likely to carry on her rampages and I was allowed a lot more freedom. It's universal that the ocean evokes serenity, peace, and a feeling of oneness with the world. To this day, whenever I go to the ocean I remember that this was the place where I found some contentment and happiness as a child.

❖

JOHN WOOD: My primary method of coping with life is isolation. I isolate from everybody.

RICHARD RHODES: How did your experience of incest affect your sexuality?

JOHN WOOD: I've always tried to be super-lover. I've not been there when I was making love. I've always been on the ceiling watching what was going on, making sure that she was getting hers. I mean, as the joke goes, Why are men like microwave ovens? Thirty seconds and they're done. As a young man, you normally can't hang on the ceiling for very long. But I did.

RICHARD RHODES: Has that changed? Are you more involved?

JOHN WOOD: A bit more involved. But I'm now at the point where I still love sex, I still love the companionship, and I still love the talk and the stimulation and so forth, but I'm not willing to pay the price anymore.

RICHARD RHODES: And the price is?

JOHN WOOD: Compromise. [*Richard reacts with surprise.*] Yeah, you don't know about it because—maybe you do know about it.

RICHARD RHODES: Two failed marriages before I finally found someone I could be happy with.

JOHN WOOD: What I'm thinking of is being single for an extended period of time. I get up when I want to get up. I go to bed when I want to go to bed. I eat when I want to eat. If I'm driving from here to the meeting [*of his recovery group*], and I decide I don't want to go now, I want to go to the pizza joint, I can do that. I don't have to explain nothing to nobody. I just do it. If I get up at four-thirty in the morning, I get up at four-thirty in the morning. I don't have to sneak out of bed. I don't have to, and it's wonderful. It really is. I mean the price is, I'm very lonely. But I would have done this all my life, I would have been celibate all my life if it weren't for testosterone. There's always been a lady in my life, because I always had to get laid, but . . .

RICHARD RHODES: So control is an issue even within the somewhat mild and benevolent controls of a relationship.

JOHN WOOD: Yup. "Fiercely independent" is how my therapist described me.

✦

MICHAEL DAVIES: I've always been at the margins of mainstream society, I've always been suspicious of authority, I've always been suspicious of hierarchy, I've always been suspicious of the organizational mind-set, I've always been distrustful of people in general, which I know is a fairly common trait for people like myself and my family. With respect to the concept of justice, my mom's victimization especially made me committed to trying to make this a more humane world. It doesn't have to work out the way it worked out for her. I don't understand why we all came out of it—not without scars, but why we didn't transform those scars into abusive behavior towards our children or towards others. I wonder if there isn't some peripheral, unreflected, undeliberate abuse that we're not aware of. I hope not.

✦

ALEXA DONATH: The question of what "survival" means, in the context of child abuse, is very important to me. Yes, I'm a survivor, but when you asked to interview me, I almost said, I can't be a part of this book because I don't know if I survived. I'm only here, I'm a body here. I've had such bad times that I don't know if I can say I've survived. I do say to people that I'm a survivor, and I'm a survivor in any number of things. I've had seven operations in six years. I'm termed handicapped. I have severe endocrine problems. I have a lot of orthopedic problems. I think I got through those because of my childhood. With half of those illnesses, a lot of people would either have become drug-addicted or would not have survived. I thought of killing myself. I used to say to myself, no, you survived that childhood, you'd better survive this. There's a reason why I survived that childhood. [*Speaking to Richard:*] And there's a reason why you survived that childhood. I looked at your dozen books and said, That's the miracle.

✦

BARBARA HAMILTON: I've never asked my children anything. Whatever they want to tell me . . .

RICHARD RHODES: Is that a deliberate decision on your part?

BARBARA HAMILTON: Yes. I was so probed by my mother about anything sexual that I made up my mind when I was raising my children that I never wanted to probe them at all about any sexual stuff. I had felt so cornered all the time. I probably should have brought up some questions, not about their being abused but just about their knowledge of sexual processes and contraception or anything like that. But I was so inhibited by everything. When my book came along, even though I was pulling back from asking questions of my children, then it began to feel right. I understood they knew that I didn't try to get something out of them. They've been going through all kinds of ups and downs in their own healing. So that's one thing that I can't be blamed for—probing my children to get fodder for my book. I never did that.

✦

DAN HAMILTON: In the last ten years, the ability to combine those two aspects, the professional and the personal, has meant for me a great flowering and growth. It coincided with the decision not to be only an actor, but to turn to directing. One of the biggest changes is that I've been able to find and verbalize the things that were holding me back as an actor, which had to do with confrontational skills. I couldn't confront. I was terrific at being charming and coming around the side on any emotional issue. But the ability to confront and the ability to express the rages, the hard-edged feelings, and the willingness to risk not being liked, those three things were missing in me. I didn't have those tools.

So throughout my career as an actor, I was making a living and becoming better known, and in the eyes of many I was a terrific success, but I wasn't moving to the next echelon along with my peers. That led to a great deal of frustration and anger and resentment. My peers were now major movie stars and I was still stumbling around the edges, not moving that big step forward, and beginning to question why. And I was getting angry. Once I dealt in therapy with the reasons why, it still took years to express those three things. Then I realized, okay, I'm not going to be able to use those aspects in my acting right now, someday yes, but not now, but I can take those same weaknesses and turn them into strengths if I turn into a director. Because as a director, your ability not to threaten, but to guide, to pull people together without confronting, becomes a great strength. I can take forty people and make them all go toward the same goal, pull everybody together and achieve something. As a result, the last five years have meant an incredible flowering of confidence and self-worth. Now, if I lose my directing job . . . [*laughing*] we're in trouble. No, I say that in humor now, because now I can. I could act, and I can take a lot of that back to my acting. Just as I can take more of it back to my personal life now. But there's no question that I'm on a journey that's going to take another forty years before it's reached its potential.

✥

ANNA LEE TRAYNOR: Doing the lawsuit has elevated my empathy for other abused people because it forced me to understand the extent of what was done to me. I keep saying I don't want sympathy. Parts of my body no longer exist, and I'm angry that the abuse could have been carried to that extent. I'm angry that they had the right to inflict abuse upon me and get away with it. I'm angry because the child I was deserves to know the reason for what she went through. It's like your life is made up like a Slinky [*that is, the coiled-spring toy*]. You can elongate it to separate yourself from each part that you do or don't want to deal with. I tried to do that. I tried to stay as far away from the feelings of that child because I wasn't sure if I could deal with this case without getting sick again.

But the closer it came to not being able to pursue the case, the more the Slinky closed itself in. The rings tightened together. Because I saw that the *child*—the child I was—was the one who had the strength and the faith to wake up every day in a house where she didn't have a prayer. And I'm saying I don't think I can *do* this? I decided I need the naïveté of her faith and the strength of the future she dreamed of achieving. I just pulled that Slinky together. I'm all together and this is what should get done. And I never let her cry, never let her feel sorry for herself. That's hard when my attorney says, You can't do it this way, or, You can't do it that way. Don't tell me what I can and can't do. You have no idea what I survived. I survived the ravages of a disease. These are merely man-made obstacles.

Richard asked Louise Hill, "Don't you hate it when someone says to you, as people sometimes say to me, 'But look what you've become!'"

LOUISE HILL: Oh, I hate that so much. I hate that so much.

GINGER RHODES: What *else* might have been possible?

RICHARD RHODES: And what was lost? What was distorted? I write about violence. I'd like to write about something else. But I write about violence.

LOUISE HILL: I write about aloneness. I write about sadness.

RICHARD RHODES: I'll never forget, when you and I were teaching at Goddard College, listening to the reading of your play about the plumber and the housewife and weeping through the entire reading. Everyone in the room was weeping.

LOUISE HILL: Yes. Do you remember the speech where the young girl says, "If I danced on a hill and danced on a hill, if I danced on a hill and spit wooden nickels from my mouth, she still wouldn't love me"? "Nothing will fill up the hole" is a line from that play.

RICHARD RHODES: My god. That must be where I got the title for *A Hole in the World*. I hadn't realized.

LOUISE HILL: I know. Yes, it's all right, we gave a lot back and forth to each other. I know that. [*She returns to the subject of distortion.*] Things happen that I don't even understand, moments of pain and isolation that I'll never get over. I'm a very good comedy writer, I have a terrific sense of humor, and I got that from the family. I take great joy in that fact. But

I start to write a comedy and it always turns out dark inside. It's a metaphor for my life—a lighthearted exterior but this part inside that will always be weeping.

Just look at the picture behind you. [*An ample, beautiful nude reclines in a framed oil painting above the couch in Louise's Manhattan apartment.*] That picture was bought with one of my first commissions from a piece. A lot of people ask me, Is that you? It's my idea of me. Now I can look at it and say, That's me. I'm as beautiful as that woman. My body is as beautiful as that woman's and sometimes—she's lying in peace on that lovely couch and really feeling her body, feeling her sexuality, feeling her openness— sometimes after I take a bath I take my towel and lie on that particular couch where the two of you are sitting, under the painting, and listen to music. It's my idea of who I wanted to become in adult life. So there's a writer piece in me but there's also a beautiful-woman piece. I'm still working on that. I'm still working on that. I am still working on that.

I love the moments when I know I'm beautiful. There are moments when I don't feel beautiful. There are moments when the fat little, ugly little, bad little girl exists for me. Like when I get sick—I had the flu last week. I can't tell you how painful that is. I felt bad, ugly, everything bad. I don't feel like I deserve to be sick. I feel like I did something wrong.

Abuse survivors always bear the scars, therapist Alice Brand Bartlett told us:

ALICE BRAND BARTLETT: People can feel trapped in the past. Many people who haven't had treatment feel that there's nothing but the past. That there's no future. That's part of the diagnostic criteria for PTSD [*post-traumatic stress disorder*]—no sense of a future or a foreshortened sense of future.

Some people feel so trapped. It's all they know. They say, I can't be any other way. Some people have left treatment because they couldn't leave an abusive relationship—even when the relationship extended to physical brutality. I think it's hard for clinicians to understand that abuse becomes part of their identity. They can't see anything else. They get labeled as masochistic—a label that doesn't say anything to me. They are just trapped in this past and they have no sense of how to get out of it and they can't take a helping hand. They fear they would lose too much of themselves.

GINGER RHODES: Are they afraid that if they give up being this person who is abused, they'll have no other self? Are they afraid that they have to live this existence or die?

ALICE BRAND BARTLETT: It makes me wonder. Judy Herman in her book *Trauma and Recovery* compared growing up in an extremely abusive family to brainwashing or terrorism. There comes a final stage when you became the perpetrator—when they get you to be a perpetrator. I wonder if these patients who can't get help are people who have turned the corner, as she said, and have done such horrendous things themselves in some way, or at least *believe* that they have, that they just can't accept any goodness. They could also be people for whom it feels like a betrayal—who feel that if they really knew what happened, if they really accepted the truth internally about what happened, then they'd lose everything. They'd rather lose themselves than their family.

The truth is, nothing ever heals the past. Because the past is there. I try to remind people that when we talk about memories, it's only so that we can help you live differently today. The memory-recovery band-wagon has gotten people trapped in the past, which is what you don't want. The main purpose of remembering is to make sure that the rest of your life isn't spent repeating the past. So that people can change, from the present forward. There's always pain attached to those memories and some people continue to have severe emotional and physical trauma symptoms. They have hyperarousal all their lives, at least higher than the nonabused. At least higher than baseline. They're vulnerable to emotional triggers. What they have to do is learn how to manage these symptoms as if they were diabetic.

Child abuse is not only part of the past, Susan Voorhees reminded us; it's a large fact of life in America today—and in the world:

SUSAN VOORHEES: Society can't really support, economically, the level of care that some of these abused kids need. Kids who've abandoned all hope and just don't feel any relationship is worth two cents. Those are kids who are very, very difficult to treat and expensive to treat.

RICHARD RHODES: What happens to them?

SUSAN VOORHEES: They form gangs, and I think they find something in a gang. Gangs provide some sense of family. Gang violence meets some need in the gang members for excitement, however sadomasochistic, however neurotic. It serves some function in that way.

GINGER RHODES: Certainly they get to have emotions.

SUSAN VOORHEES: They can feel they're powerful, they're strong, everybody else is afraid of them. For once in their life they're in control.

RICHARD RHODES: We were struck today by an article about a mass killing. The author, who has written a lot about violence, said, "An automatic weapon is a magic wand." It absolutely, instantly does what you want.

GINGER RHODES: Or in Toni Morrison's Nobel Prize acceptance speech, where she says our children have committed tongue suicide. They've bitten off their tongues and they speak with bullets.

SUSAN VOORHEES: They've bitten off their tongues and we've bitten off their tongues.

Richard told David Doepel about his fugue-state alter ego, Mr. Hyde:

RICHARD RHODES: I published four novels earlier in my career, before I turned to writing history. They were all about men, mature adult men facing crises, usually violent. The men and women of the Donner Party. A gynecological surgeon going through a difficult divorce. A white hunter in East Africa. A former astronaut whose son is kidnapped. Romanticized selves, I suppose. Men whose self-possession I identified with strongly.

But there was another male type who regularly turned up in my fiction. He was monstrous. It's very clear to me that he represented another side of my self that I brought with me out of my childhood. He was my internalized stepmother, if you will: cold, violent, implacable. In my novel about the Donner Party, he was Lewis Keseberg, a real historical figure. Keseberg was the only one in that tragic group of nearly one hundred pioneers who may actually have killed people in order to eat them at a time when they had been reduced to cannibalizing the dead in order to survive. In *Sons of Earth,* the novel about an astronaut, the man who kidnaps the astronaut's son and buries him in an underground cell to hold him for ransom is another Germanic monster. I even equipped him with some of my own childhood memories. My son, Tim, was ten or twelve years old when I wrote that novel—my age during my stepmother years—and I actually built the coffin that figured in the book. I actually went out and bought the plywood and the fittings and made the thing, so that I could accurately describe building it, which Tim found a little uncomfortable, to say the least.

So it's clear to me that I internalized some ideal figure of a responsible, mature father, and at the same time internalized a violent monster, identifying with my stepmother. That character has always been there. I call him a character because he turns up in my fiction. He certainly also used to turn up in my life—in fugue states when I drank too much and blacked out. Then a cold, implacably bitter, contemptuous persona would emerge to rant on through the night. One of my wives called him Mr. Hyde.

I emerged from childhood morbidly shy and extremely anxious, so anxious that when I arrived at college and finally got to see a dentist, the dentist was amazed to discover that the faces of my molars—the outside surfaces that faced the saliva glands in my cheeks—had been dissolved to chalk. That much anxiety expressed as acidity, if you will. The dentist had never seen such a phenomenon before.

I finally came to understand, in thinking all this through again, that I did blame my father, blamed him very much, and that I had clearly blamed him before. Because when my father was dying of cancer, years ago, and I got word that he wanted to see me, I didn't go to see him. I didn't want to go to see him. I didn't want to see my stepmother again. I was still afraid of her—I was twenty-eight at the time. But I didn't want to see my father either. I wrote him a letter. He found it offensive, although I meant it to be sincere. A "Father, I love you" letter. Not to go to see your father when he's dying—obviously I had considerable rage. But I felt strongly that I'd already lost him. I'd hardly seen him since I was twelve years old, since my brother and I were removed from parental custody and sent to the boys' home. I went to see him the summer after high school and he was just an old man, querulous and shabby, still under Granny Annie's thumb, unrecognizable as the father I had idealized.

Another father I jettisoned along the way was God. I was going to be a minister. I'd almost progressed to the point by the end of high school where I had a Local Preacher's license in the Methodist Church. But my freshman year in college I decided abruptly that the whole notion of religion made no sense to me at all. Which corresponds to not going to see my father when he was dying. I wasn't going to reconcile with any father, heavenly or earthly.

The central feeling I remember throughout the entire time with my stepmother was of being absolutely alone and responsible for myself. It was finally not something my brother could help. It was certainly not something my father could or would help. It was not something my stepmother intended to do anything about. At that time in the United States—the late 1940s—there were no hot lines, no social-welfare system available for people to deal with child abuse. So far as I know, most children who were abused were simply left to their fate unless the abuse was so egregious that the authorities couldn't get away with ignoring it. It wasn't something that teachers could help, that ministers could help, that anyone could help. I was responsible for my survival and I think that makes you cynical. It certainly makes you cold. But it makes you resourceful, too.

It also leaves you with a terrible residue of contempt, contempt for the world, contempt for other people, that you have to deal with for the rest of your life. One reason it's very difficult to reach children who have been abused is because, in some fundamental way, they don't believe anything about anybody. They've learned not to trust. They've learned to be hard. Even when you *do* believe, at some more basic level you *don't* believe. If you're lucky, later, maybe you turn that around so that at some even more basic level, below the level where you *don't* believe, you find a level where you do. If you're lucky.

13

"What Do Normal People Do?"

*V*arious forms of therapy and group work helped, and continue to help, many of the abuse survivors we interviewed. Theory seems to have been less important to the success of treatment than the presence of a listening, supportive adult whom these men and women could trust.

Menninger therapist Alice Brand Bartlett distinguishes the psychological consequences of abuse from other forms of psychological disturbance: the abnormal visited upon the normal—upon children:

ALICE BRAND BARTLETT: With torture, the goal of treatment is not to pathologize the victims but to tell them how normal their responses are to abnormal events. You do the same thing with people who have had chronic trauma, but it's harder and it takes longer. You want to help them normalize. To say to them, "The way you responded is the way most people would respond—of *course* you don't want to think about it; of *course* it sometimes intrudes and you have nightmares. The goal is to try to manage it, to talk about it, to find ways of coping with the knowledge that this happened to you, so that you can live beyond it." It's a straightforward treatment, but it does take years sometimes, even if treatment begins immediately. Here I'm thinking especially of adolescents, where there's a lot of chaos simply because of the stage of childhood they're going through. For adults, the healthier the person, the less severe the trauma, the quicker the recovery comes. Of course, the better the support system, the quicker the recovery.

Some survivors arrived at therapy obliquely; for others, it hasn't yet worked:

DAN HAMILTON: During my present marriage, there was pressure and difficulty and pain between the two of us. My wife insisted and I finally agreed to joint marriage counseling. In the first several months, the focus was primarily on talking about the marriage and the problems. Then, in the midst of one session, I used the phrase, "If I hold still it will pass," and tears, totally unexpected, began streaming down my face. The therapist, who was obviously good at his job, picked up on a totally different reality. He said, Excuse me, Stephanie, I need to talk to Dan. He immediately realized that there was a much bigger issue to be dealt with than I had acknowledged up to that point, and that was the beginning of separate therapy for a long period of time.

It began the opening of doors, not so much in terms of my suddenly remembering things, but my ability to suddenly connect those past, distant things to my patterns and emotional life now. It wasn't that I was unaware. I think at that point we had already dealt with the issue of my talking to the family, so it was not that I was particularly even hiding it at that point. But when people asked me, What happened in your childhood?, it was one of many things that I could fairly easily talk about, that I had thought was safely and unemotionally detached. I had no idea how alive the emotions still were.

❖

MICHAEL DAVIES: I've tried some therapy, not over a long period of time. The longest I've gone is a few months. I thought the last guy I had was pretty good. He knew the literature. So he was a good person to talk to. I think he was a good therapist, but I told him—and he agreed at some point, several months down the road—that I had to be closer to my pain before I was really going to make any progress in therapy. Because we'd never get anyplace. It was good to talk, but that basically was all it was. I didn't feel like I got any closer to understanding myself or my family.

✦

ALEXA DONATH: I had therapy early on and my therapist said, Get over it. It was the early Seventies and that's what they were doing.

RICHARD RHODES: It's called the Rubber-Band Theory: Snap out of it.

ALEXA DONATH: That's right. That's exactly what he said.

✦

JOHN WOOD: I married an incest survivor.

RICHARD RHODES: Was she aware of that when you married her?

JOHN WOOD: No. But she was very suicidal. One time I came up from the workshop and she was sitting off in the woods right near the house with a shotgun in her lap. I had lots of guns around. I was a gun guy. Why the hell I escaped being one of these guys who goes into a restaurant and blows everybody away, I will never understand. But I did. I escaped.

RICHARD RHODES: Is that how you feel?

JOHN WOOD: I can identify with the guy who drove a pickup truck into the restaurant and blew off those—what did he call them?—he called them female vipers. At the time I said, I know where that guy's coming from. Give 'em hell, Bruce, or whatever his name was.

Anyway, I found my wife sitting cross-legged with a shotgun in her lap, and I said, "Cut the shit, will you? Give me the fucking gun! Christ! Stop the playacting!" That was not playacting. Shortly thereafter, we were invited to a party at a neighbor's house. A famous neighbor, Alexander

Calder. She said, I can't go to that party. What am I going to say to those people? I said, Shit, they're no different from the rest of us. I'm going to the party. So I went to the party and it was very embarrassing. Everybody said, Where's Janet? I don't know what I said. I probably said that she's not feeling well, which is what my mother used to say about my father when he was drunk. Janet was a drinker. Janet was probably plastered shortly after I left.

Anyway, I got home and she had taken up residence on the couch with sheets and blankets. I said, fuck that, I'm going to bed. Pretty soon I heard, John? I said, Yup? and she said, Good-bye. She opened the door and walked out and shot herself in the head. She didn't die instantly. She blew half her head off. I called for an ambulance. She was taken to the hospital and there was a neurosurgeon who worked on her for a couple of hours. And she died. Actually, I said to him, Look, if she's going to be a vegetable, let her go. I had the presence of mind to say that. I don't know if he—you know, she died. It was a very difficult time. At the funeral, her college roommate came up to me, and said, John, we all knew that she was going to kill herself someday. Her roommates used to wonder when they would come home and find Janet hanging from the chandelier. God, everybody knew that she was suicidal except me.

I went to an ACOA [*Adult Children of Alcoholics*] meeting where there were close to eighteen people, three or four of whom were men. It was in somebody's home, in a room rather like this, in fact. Everyone was sitting around this great room, quite low light, in the evening. Six of the thirteen or fourteen or fifteen women shared that they were incest survivors. There was a young girl there, about seventeen or so, and she shared about how her brother was sexually abusing her, raping her on a couch in the living room. Her mother had walked in and stopped that incident, but she never stopped the sexual abuse. I felt some compassion, I felt some anger, and I wanted to kill the mother, you know, that kind of anger.

The woman I was with was crying in the car on the way home, and I said, "Are you okay? Would you like to go back and talk with the woman who was leading the meeting?" "No, no, no, it's okay, just, you

know, nothing happened to me but I just feel so bad about those kids."
She was crying all the way home. So I got home and I didn't feel anything.
I never feel anything. I don't feel anything; if you don't believe me, just
ask me.

One or two weeks later, a sixty-two-year-old man who was at that
meeting was sharing in another meeting that he had felt really uncomfortable when those six women shared about incest, and he talked about
it. By the time he was done, I was sweating, I had a heartbeat, I felt
clammy, I felt cold inside, and I didn't need a Ph.D. in psychology to
figure out that maybe there was a little something I needed to investigate.
That was four years ago. So I thought, now what do I do? Shortly after
that, I heard another woman at an Al-Anon meeting, a young gal sharing
about incest and that she had gone to the Stamford Rape Crisis Center's
nine-week program. So I buttonholed her after the meeting, and I called
them up and they were really sweet. They said, Yes, we've been running
a program for two, three years, but we don't have a program for men.
We also want you to be in therapy on this topic for a few months before
you tackle incest in a group context. I figured those gals have got to know
more about it than I do so I'll take their word for it, so I asked them,
Who do you recommend? They said, Well, there's this guy, Paul Espos-
ito, who's on our Board of Directors. I figured if the guy is on the Board
of Directors of the Rape Crisis Center he's got to be cool, so I called
him up and I've been seeing him ever since. I just came from there, from
him, to see you. So I've been working on it ever since. I've also been
doing work with John Bradshaw's tapes and books.

In the beginning, when I first started going to meetings—as soon as
I caught on that there was really some serious shit that I had to deal with
and as soon as I caught on that I didn't remember anything and that that
in itself is serious—I figured I'm probably pretty sick, maybe I really ought
to do something serious about this. Well, in Alcoholics Anonymous they
tell you to do ninety in ninety: ninety meetings in ninety days. I thought,
okay, they probably know something about what they're talking about,
so I'll try that. So I did and I went to a meeting every day for the first
ninety days. Then I kept going—seven meetings a week on six days, two

meetings on Sundays, and Al-Anon, Adult Children, Co-Dependents Anonymous.

There weren't any meetings around here at that time for sexual-abuse survivors. So I started one. The Stamford Rape Crisis Center didn't have anything cooking, but I badgered Paul until we got something going. I announced at the meetings I went to that we were starting a group for men who were sexually abused, and that if you want to know more about it, speak to me after the meeting. Well, the first time I announced that, when I stood up, I literally had rubber knees. I was awful glad there was a chair under me when I sat down. For months—it took me two or three months—I would announce this before the big meetings. There must have been at least thirty guys who came up to me and said, Well, I probably should do something about that, where is this meeting held, can I call you? Only six of them showed up—six of us showed up. I cried through the whole meeting. I was shaking. Paul kept looking at me, asking me, Are you okay? I said, I'm okay. It was scary as hell.

RICHARD RHODES: When did you start recovering memories?

JOHN WOOD: Right about that time. In fact, the woman who turned me on to the Rape Crisis Center said that her therapist had got her to the memories through dreams. She remembered dreams, and that's how I started remembering. I had a dream of being sexually abused by my mother.

RICHARD RHODES: Were you?

JOHN WOOD: Yes, absolutely. The memory is clear. In fact, I called my brother about it a few months ago, and when I said it to him, it became crystal clear as though it happened yesterday. Always before that I was a little unsure that it was a real memory. The woman who wrote *The Courage to Heal* said, We're not too sure about these memories, sometimes you're not sure if you're making them up or marrying different stories with memories, but this was crystal clear. I cried when I talked to my brother. I could hardly speak to him. I was crying, shaking, it was happening again. See, that was the fear—of it happening again.

GINGER RHODES: How did you feel the first time you said out loud that you remembered being sexually abused?

JOHN WOOD: The first time I said it out loud I said it to a therapist, which isn't really saying it out loud. I guess the first time was when I announced in the Co-Dependents Anonymous meeting that we were forming a nine-week program for men who were sexually abused.

RICHARD RHODES: So by announcing that you were forming a group, you were also announcing that you were a member of that group.

JOHN WOOD: Yes, to the world. There were a hundred, probably a hundred fifty people in that room, and that was real scary. A couple that I had become friendly with came up to me afterward and said, Boy, it really took courage to do that. I guess it did.

Richard asked Karen Seal when she realized that her father had sexually abused her:

KAREN SEAL: I always knew that it had happened. I mean I have this knowledge that it happened with some regularity, but I only have a few vivid memories—well, two under hypnosis, and three others. It went on until I was twelve, any chance he got. I know that it happened a lot, but I don't know exactly what happened. I have a memory like this: I remember having a little T-shirt with semen all over it. All of my life, I cannot stand to have sticky hands. It still goes on. I mean, I still can't stand it. And it has affected my sex life, too. I can't stand to lie with semen, you know, I just can't stand it.

RICHARD RHODES: So you were aware that you had been sexually abused, and then you reached a point where your marriage broke down and you realized you needed some help?

KAREN SEAL: But it didn't have to do with the incest. It had to do with my frenetic activity level. I was teaching full-time, overtime, managing real estate, handling our investments. Sam [*her former husband, a college administrator*] was on the career ladder, and we were doing a lot of entertaining. I was a super-achiever, taking on the world's problems, and was getting migraine headaches, two or three a week. I would go to stress-reduction classes and try to meditate, but how can I meditate when I've got so much to do? I think what finally brought me to therapy was a combination of my physical condition and my troubles.

Therapy of course deals with childhood. In therapy, I happened to mention, Well, my dad, it's kind of weird, but he flashed at me when I was a kid, made me touch his penis, but it's no big deal. My therapist said, What do you mean? This is major! She said it only takes a split second to destroy a child's trust.

✦

CELIA GOLDEN: I went into therapy for the first time when I was twenty-four. I couldn't accept my father's death, couldn't accept the loss—I had to pretend he hadn't died. He was the person I thought loved me the most. My therapist always wanted to focus on my father, and I could never understand why people thought I should be angry at him. But I refused to talk about my mother. I always felt that they would discount what I said about her, because they would hear that this *man* beat me, but they wouldn't hear that this *woman* beat me. They would tell me that what my father did was emotional incest, but they wouldn't hear me giving them clues that I was physically—sexually—abused by my mother. So I would go in and out of therapy.

I was thirty-seven years old before I told my therapist, "I think my mother molested me." I expected my therapist to vomit on the spot and throw me out of her office—as though I were the perpetrator. If she had raised one eyebrow indicating shock, repulsion, or disbelief, she would never have seen me again. I remember watching her face. She was real calm, but I immediately changed the subject. She said she could never get me to open up about it again. It took two years and a nearly fatal suicide attempt before I was ready to discuss the issue. Before I could say, "My mother sexually abused me."

Six years ago I attempted suicide. I quit drinking after that, and then

I couldn't go back to where I was. I had to talk about my mother. The suicide attempt happened just a few months before I acknowledged my sexual abuse to my recovery group. Everything initially was really traumatic. I can tell what things are more significant for me because when I would talk about them, I would have different responses. When it's something that had to do with my mother, when I would lead towards things that had sexual significance, I would just start shaking like a leaf. I have the same reaction to worms. I have an immediate response of just wanting to puke and run. There was a program on public television several years ago on the suffragettes in England, and there was a scene where they had strapped this woman down in bed and they were force-feeding her. I had the same response to that scene. The rage was coming up and I started to scream and turned off the television. I wanted to run out and had nowhere to go. When the person you fear the most is not a stranger, is someone who is there every day, so that you can't get away, you have to transfer that fear onto something else. Worms were safe.

❖

SKYE SMITH: I think my last depression set in because I had the audacity to move away from my mother and stepfather, to go to New York. That's very clearly when it began—the last long, long haul.

I've been so depressed I couldn't get out of bed in the morning. Twice I resigned from teaching jobs. It's horrible to just shut down. Curled up in a fetal position is how my husband described it. He said, I will never forget you like that, coming home and finding you in bed in fetal position.

The only thing you can do is not eat. That's the only thing you can do that shows you have some kind of control over something. You can't control your depression. All those voices come back: you lazy slob, get to work, snap out of it, what's the matter with you? You try everything. It's bigger than you are by yourself. Psychotherapy helps. You get connected to somebody and then you show your real self and your feelings and let some of that pain out. You begin ventilating and then you are able to connect with people.

RICHARD RHODES: What did you do with your rage?

SKYE SMITH: In the hospital I used to punch the hell out of a punching bag with a plastic baseball bat.

RICHARD RHODES: [*Laughing*] Where can we get one of those?

SKYE SMITH: Oh, it's fantastic. Those big fat bats, plastic bats. I would give the bag people's names, scream at it, whatever, until my hands would bleed. It was so great. I have to do physical things and hitting is good. Racquetball's okay but it's not as direct. Bicycling helps me with the rage. I used to bike every day. I'd yell while I was biking. I'd get worked up and say this and that and tell certain people off.

RICHARD RHODES: I once heard Thomas Harris, one of the founders of Transactional Analysis, speak. He said that when patients called him and said they were thinking of killing themselves, he always told them to get outdoors and walk—use those big skeletal muscles. He'd shout over the phone: PLUG IN THE ADULT! Not that that's enough—but it's true, using your body helps. It's not only the release of endorphins, but also the existential sense that you exist when you use your body, instead of being disconnected, rattling around in your head.

LYNDA DEROBERTIS: I scared one therapist away. It was remarkable because at that point I didn't know what the proper procedure was for terminating our working together. I was distraught; my mother had attempted suicide and I was really flying with the feelings that were coming up. I called the therapist and said, Look, I need to come back into therapy. So I went back in and apparently she got very uncomfortable with my affect. I was all over the place—understandably, when I think back on it. She said, I think you need to be on medication. I said, You know how I feel about medication. I come from a family where drugs were abused constantly. I have an aversion to drugs and she knew that. But she said, I really think you need to be on medication.

The experience actually turned out to be very healthy for me. We set up an appointment with a psychiatrist to prescribe the medication. He comes in, this big, disgusting-looking person, and I say to myself, How healthy is this guy that she's handing me to? She's sitting there with me, but silent throughout the whole procedure and right away he starts writing out a prescription. I said, What's that? He stopped writing and I said, I have to tell you, I doubt I'm going to take it because I don't want to take medication. He said, What's the matter, you got something against feeling good? I said, Yes, when it's not real, I do—I prefer to feel my feelings.

My therapist didn't say a word. She just sat there mute. So right after, I went into session with her, and this is the God's honest truth, I said to her, I really feel abandoned by you. I said, I thought you just sat there and sold me down the river to that guy, and I think I need to leave therapy. She said, You know, you're absolutely right—good-bye and good luck. That was after a year and a half with this person.

SKYE SMITH: I threw my purse as hard as I could at one psychologist I saw for a couple of years. He couldn't help me. It made me so mad I just fired up and WHAM! I wasn't trying to hit him. I was just making a statement above his head. But you know, he wasn't helping me, he wasn't competent, so it's a wake-up call, pal. You're not doing your job.

Yeah, lots of rage, tons of rage, volcanoes. I'm past the worst of it, but only after years of *When do you think it will stop?* There was an endless supply. Once you start, you can just go, and go, and go. It goes for a long time. You can feel the rage even when you're thinking about your garden or calling your friend. But it gets triggered. When I sense injustice being done, that triggers it.

RICHARD RHODES: Does it have something to do with your decision to go into social work?

SKYE SMITH: Probably. A means of correcting the rage. Therapy was a healing experience. I felt saved. I'm a caretaker and it goes along with that. It saves lives, therapy does. For the last four years I've been in therapy with someone I like. He saved my life. He's wonderful, he's phenomenal.

He believed me. I had the feeling that here's a person who believed it was a very painful, awful childhood, even though it didn't sound so terrible to many people.

GINGER RHODES: A lot of people seem to do therapy as a sort of crisis intervention. They get to a certain point, blow up, go get some short-term help, and it works for about eighteen months.

SKYE SMITH: Shores you up a little.

GINGER RHODES: They "graduate" from therapy and say, Oh, I'm fine now.

SKYE SMITH: Yes. That's the way I thought—I don't need this. I'm fine, just get on the bike, I'm fine.

MARIA MAREWSKI: Sometimes that's all you can tolerate.

SKYE SMITH: I don't know. I think if it's the right person, you want to unload that pain.

RICHARD RHODES: It still has to come at the right time.

SKYE SMITH: Yes. You have to have exhausted everything else.

GINGER RHODES: Or at least be able to afford emotionally letting it out. You have to have some sense of security.

SKYE SMITH: Four months into therapy, I started asking my therapist, When are you going to kick me out?—I should be cured now—I'm retarded, I'm retarded—I'm not doing it fast enough.

My second time in the hospital, my father wrote me a letter, saying, I want you to have the fastest, speediest recovery on record. You can get out of there in record time if you just work harder. I thought, okay, I'll cry more. When you're with the group every night, cry. That'll do it, cry a lot. Punch the punching bag more.

How do you force healing? How do you do it fast? It takes time.

GINGER RHODES: I probably asked my therapist a thousand times, Are other people like this? Do other people feel this way? Do other people do this? What do real people do? What do normal people do?

MARIA MAREWSKI: That's what's so great about this project [*she means this book*]—so many people wonder that. People who know something is wrong with their lives but who haven't admitted to themselves that they need help.

Valorie Butler's special gift has been to integrate therapy and personal recovery into her deeply held religious faith:

VALORIE BUTLER: When I was twenty-five years old, about fifteen years ago, I realized that I had to embrace the pain. I was basically unhappy and intense. It was just something I carried around with me all the time, tension and anxiety and fears and daydreaming. One day I said to myself: I'm not happy, I'm going to be happy today. I just arbitrarily told myself that. But it didn't happen that way. Then I heard about someone who was seeking counseling, and I thought, I need to do this. I had thought about it a few times before. I was very nervous, but I decided to dial the number without thinking about it. I would just get in contact with a counselor before I decided not to do it. So I picked up the phone. From that point on, I believe, a slow road opened toward healing.

Things were happening subconsciously even before that. The tension was mounting and so was my awareness of it. A depression was coming, I think. I probably had been living with depression for many years, but a deep, climactic depression was coming. I was doing things like pacing without even realizing I was doing it. I was pacing in my office one day and my boss said, Are you doing your exercises? I was talking to myself. A few weeks after starting to see this counselor, I landed in the hospital. She talked about depression, and I wondered what she was talking about. I know I'm bothered by things, I told myself, but I'm not depressed. Of course, I was very depressed and didn't realize it.

RICHARD RHODES: You were admitted into the hospital for depression?

VALORIE BUTLER: I'd never acknowledged the pain of my past, never much talked to anyone about it. I didn't feel anger and hate. Those were no-nos. The pain was so great that I went to the hospital, but the recognition of the pain came later. The right to be angry, the right to feel these feelings came over years. I'm still probably somewhat depressed. But at the time of my hospitalization the depression was so great that I wasn't functional. I couldn't cope with anything. I needed medication.

A lot of healing has taken place outside of therapy, because I like to introspect. I like to think about things. I like to read. I found quite a bit of healing in a couple of books I read: *Where Is God When It Hurts?* and *Forgive and Forget.* Forgiving was a big issue with me. I thought I should forgive my aunt. In my estimation, she was the biggest abuser—she was responsible for the largest part of the pain. Now I realize through therapy that my uncle was responsible, too. He had his own part in it, more silently.

RICHARD RHODES: We always try to ask people what or who helped you survive. So many people who've experienced violent abuse *don't* survive.

VALORIE BUTLER: A counselor talked about my strong will to survive. Strength of will, she said, is something that goes back eons and that we don't completely understand, but some people are gifted with it. She said I had an innate, strong will to survive. I look at that as a gift from God. I don't think that He looks down on someone else who *didn't* survive, either. I just believe that all these different levels of suffering have meaning. I believe that we must see how we hurt one another—my sisters— you know. It's a message—this is how it affects people. I don't believe God is the author of the evil. We talk about original sin, that's all very mysterious, but God is not a controller. This is why I love Him. Control is a big issue with me. He does not control. He allows free choice. That was something He gave us in the first place, and that's why people are free to choose to do evil as well as good. I believe that He does not control these choices, but He does not interfere with the consequences of them either. If we didn't see the results of our doings, we'd never know or never learn.

We have free choice. That's so special to me, free choice. Very special.

GINGER RHODES: You've spoken of going into your "sanctified imagination." When you do that, do you feel Jesus to be a brother, a father? How do you characterize him?

VALORIE BUTLER: When I talk about sanctified imagination—I have this time in the morning that's my time, about an hour or so, that I set aside for my spiritual time, to study, to read, to meditate. I spend a certain portion of it trying to hear Him, so to speak. I don't hear anything audible, but whatever thoughts I have that mean something to me, I take to be Him speaking. I can go into my imagination and see Him as someone who loves me and think about my pain.

I thought about my sister recently. Trust is an issue I'm working on with her. I happened to have a vision—not the kind of vision that a prophet has, but in my sanctified imagination. I saw Him holding her and petting her and loving her. I relayed that to her. And that was special. She's a person who's suffering with her mistrust, with her sleeplessness and with other problems.

At other times I see myself beside Him, with Him, with His arm around me and mine around Him.

RICHARD RHODES: Is there a connection between the times that you feel are sanctified imagination, and your ability to fantasize as a child? Here he comes, to save the day?

VALORIE BUTLER: Yes. I think it's the gift that was always there. I went through a period when I thought that I had to block the fantasizing, I had to cut it off because it was bad. Now I believe that perception is incorrect. I see that being able to visualize is a gift and that I can continue to do so in a positive way rather than to block out. I believe it's a natural thing to do, but when I'm doing it to avoid confrontations or to try to avoid dealing with pain in my life, that's when I need to stop.

RICHARD RHODES: You really are using meditation as a way of thinking through experience. There's an old tradition of meditation in Christianity. Monks used to be taught how to meditate, in a very different sense of the word from Eastern meditation. They started with a Bible verse. Then they imagined the setting of that verse, then the people in that setting, and so on. There were books on how to meditate. Eastern meditation is emptying the mind. Christian meditation involved filling the mind with an imagined drama—a vision, if you like.

VALORIE BUTLER: Right. It was the salvistic part of me when I was younger, and it will still continue to be a healing and a growing part of me. I plan to keep my imagination. I was ridden with guilt about it for many years, I think because sexual subject matter came to be involved. Even learning to accept my own sexuality has been a big struggle.

GINGER RHODES: Something that you're still working on?

VALORIE BUTLER: Yes, very much so.

RICHARD RHODES: Do you actually visualize Jesus, as a person?

VALORIE BUTLER: I have a hard time visualizing God—and the Holy Spirit, that's even worse. But my idea of Jesus is the Semitic person that He was—the earthly Jesus, so to speak. Tallish, dark skin, dark long hair, very kind, nonjudgmental, with that unconditional love that we all want very badly. Someone I can talk to about anything, no matter how embarrassing or gross it may have been. All the weird thoughts that go through my mind, all the thoughts I have struggled with for so many years. I can take it all to Him. Physically, He's a strong, bronze color from the Galilean sun.

GINGER RHODES: Handsome?

VALORIE BUTLER: Yes, lean, tall, like the pictures that I've seen of Him. When I see a blond Jesus, it just blows my mind. But He came here in the human form, too. That's how I see Him. But very kind.

GINGER RHODES: Does your feeling about Him as a physical presence connect in your mind with anyone whom you knew who was alive and real in your life? Is He like someone you once loved?

VALORIE BUTLER: I don't think so. It's separate. It's through reading and contemplating Him by Himself. I don't think I relate Him to any particular person. Of course, I have connected people—loving people— with beautiful things from Him. I might use the expression, I see Jesus in them. But physically I haven't connected them, because I visualize Him the way they dressed back then—His robe and so on. I could just imagine, if He returned today, He might have on a pair of slacks, you know?

I believe that Jesus was probably the very best psychiatrist who ever lived. He was so free and yet so secure in who He is. I think that's what He wants for all of us, too. I feel freedom to be myself, much more than I did before, but it takes a lot of courage to be free.

For me, as a child, religion was a monster in the sky that was ready to zap you. We were told to kneel and pray when we did something wrong. Or, if they wanted to know the truth about something, they would make us line up and get the Bible out. You would put your hand on the Bible and swear that you didn't do it. We would tremble in our boots fearing that we were going to hell.

But God isn't up there in the sky, He's right in here, inside. He felt the pain when my sisters and I were standing on the steps. I believe in His omnipresence, which I don't understand and don't claim to—I just feel that He feels hurt, too. And of course in the person of His son, He certainly demonstrated that. He feels much closer to me, because He was with my pain and in my pain and suffered in my pain. I believe that. With all this suffering, God is not just out there looking at it, He's in it, in that He feels the joy when I feel the joy, He feels the pain when I feel the pain. So that was meaningful for me, meaningful and healing for me in my relationship to God, because of the kind of God I grew up with, the cop in the sky.

In the Adventist Review, *in an article titled "Song of Valorie," Valorie wrote:*

VALORIE BUTLER: Indeed, I am not the child who was thought to be retarded. Today, I am not addicted to a fantasy world; today I go into my "sanctified imagination" to be with Jesus. He invites me to His side, and in imagination, I see myself beside Him with His arm around me and mine around Him. Humans have and will hurt me again, but He will never hurt me. He allows me to see others through His eyes; and now I can look with compassion upon those who have caused me so much pain. Thank you, Jesus, for healing me.

And so I pray that you too will find that you can trust Him with your pain and find healing as I have.

☙

ANNE O'NEIL: I once participated in a communications training where they did a lot of work on the parent/child. They had us beating a chair with our fists. I swear I didn't think I would ever stop sobbing. I just went on and on. The trainer was furious with me. He said I was too dramatic. They had no idea what my history was. They don't deal with people like me every day. Most people like me don't go into training that way. I realized later that he was just at a loss. He didn't know what on earth to do with me. But it was the first time that I had ever fully *expressed* my rage about my childhood. There was a tremendous amount of residual sobbing all locked up inside. Later in that training I discovered the terror beneath the rage: that my mother could have killed me.

GINGER RHODES: We're survivors.

ANNE O'NEIL: And beyond. Thriving.

Children sense that something is odd. Certainly there is evidence that we sensed that something was wrong, because, for one thing, we never,

never would have admitted that our mother was giving us those enemas. So clearly we felt shame about it. I was in analysis every day for three years before I mentioned the enemas. And then, only once. Now that's wild, wild. I was supposed to be free-associating! Which isn't to say that I didn't know about what happened. I did know, but I wasn't going to speak about it again. Because of the shame of betraying my mother and father.

It took a lot of work because I thought for many years that the key was to be perfect. If I could just be perfect, then great, I'd have friends, I'd have my career, I'd have a lovely marriage—but the question was how to be perfect. How to be better than I was. I didn't know that being better than I was meant being vulnerable, honest, willing to experience pain. When I first heard that idea I was totally blown away. I could not imagine anything more revolting. I was forty-one years old and I could not imagine a more repulsive idea than to show my vulnerability.

But I started chipping away. I started looking around in a different way. I saw movies in a different way, I saw art in a different way. Everything looked different from that perspective. I can sit and listen to music now and feel it, whereas before I heard it up here in my head. I had a lot of musical training, but my experience of music is entirely different now. The problem with a model like that, the perfection model, is that even though you know that's not it, you don't know what is. Plus, with that kind of training and perfectionism, it's so painful and terrifying to endure the process of learning. It's completely different from what Thomas Edison said his mother told him. His mother told Edison that learning is exploring. Simple. Don't you love it? To learn without pain, without resistance, is my goal.

After she left the convent, Anne trained as a Montessori teacher and then became responsible for training other Montessori teachers, a responsibility she eventually rejected:

RICHARD RHODES: What happened to your martinet persona?

ANNE O'NEIL: I just took it apart. There were things that I really, really wanted to do and one of those was to work with people. Not to boss people, not to be the boss, but to be with them. I didn't want to spend my whole life feeling isolated. I didn't know how to break out of that cage, but I knew there had to be a way. I wanted to use my gifts productively, to make a difference. I couldn't do that if I was terrified all the time that if I took one slight step in the wrong direction, another person's life would be ruined. If I made a mistake in training teachers, for instance, then they would pass on that mistake. That was the sense I had in my Montessori work, that if I made one false move, I would destroy the lives of children. I was absolutely terrified. I watched everything I did.

Of course that's all a false sense of power, an unrealistic and grandiose interpretation of what responsibility is. I was not that powerful, but at the time I didn't see that. That was why I laid my career in Montessori to rest. Then I thought, well, now what am I going to do? Obviously I need to work. So I decided to renovate our house. I figured, at least I'm working with *materials* and if I make mistakes, the materials don't hurt the way people do. So I was starting to allow myself to make mistakes. My husband, Will, was my support in that. He was always encouraging.

It was very hard for me to endure those mistakes. Even though I wasn't hurting another human being or destroying a life, I often felt that it was the end of the world if I chose the wrong color. It was all over for me. No hope. Doomed.

The bathroom was the first decorating task I took on because it looked like a manageable task. I could do this one little bathroom, the smallest bathroom in the house. The work amounted to choosing color for the paint and choosing fabric for the window and shower curtain and so forth. I got the paint and it was wrong. I was aiming for a blend, two tones of paint, each one somewhat lighter than the existing wall tile, and neither of them was right. I thought I would die. My husband said, If you look at that not as what you were intending for it to be, but as what it is, it's really very pretty. And I looked at it with a new eye. I trusted Will to help me to look at things with a new eye. Then I saw that the colors were beautiful and I went out and I found fabrics that had those tones and those colors and it was lovely. Far prettier, far more subtle than it could possibly have been if I just used lighter tones of the same color.

RICHARD RHODES: How extraordinary that you chose a bathroom to begin with. Bathrooms were places the enemas had stained.

ANNE O'NEIL: [*She's surprised at the connection.*] How very interesting. It was no accident. Bathrooms had to be transformed. Houses had to be transformed. And I wanted to transform myself.

Decorating was a safer way for me to go about living and learning. Teaching was too close, too terrifying. I was afraid I'd hurt a child.

RICHARD RHODES: There's a realistic basis for your sense that one false step could have lasting effect. That's an accurate representation of how the world might have looked to you as a child with a mother who had great capacity for inflicting lasting suffering.

ANNE O'NEIL: Yes, it was reflective of the terrible devastation we had endured at the hands of our mother. I knew that.

After that first bathroom renovation I continued on my path, working and studying and learning in all these different ways, and now I'm at a different place. That's one reason why writing my memoir is so terribly important to me and why creating a public forum for my thoughts is so vital, because it's the result of all the work that I've done, including Montessori, about learning to be creative. Learning to endure and hopefully to enjoy the creative process, which is full of chaos and confusion and mess. In my decorating/renovation work, over and over again I have chosen to arrange the process so that I had to live for a period of time in an area under construction—a direct and deliberate attack on my perfectionism. To teach myself to endure and even to enjoy it. To enjoy it by enjoying the mess, to enjoy the chaos, the confusion, the not knowing, to enjoy not knowing when not knowing had been so dangerous to me as a child. That's one of my challenges.

RICHARD RHODES: And then to bring order into life.

ANNE O'NEIL: And find the beauty in the process itself.

RICHARD RHODES: Beauty? Not just order?

ANNE O'NEIL: No, but order is part of beauty. A sense of well-being, a sense of serenity, a sense of joy and liberation and respect for people.

RICHARD RHODES: Are you happier than you were twenty years ago, thirty years ago? Or is it something you don't think about?

ANNE O'NEIL: [*She hesitates, estimating.*] Interesting. I don't know. Yes, I have great joy at times. I have great sadness and great joy, and quite often a simple sense of well-being.

RICHARD RHODES: But you can feel both extremes, which probably wasn't true of the martinet.

ANNE O'NEIL: Oh no, feelings were not part of the picture. It was all about ideology. It's not like that now. Now it's, I'm living. I don't filter my ideas or my feelings through others. I say, This is what I think, this is what I feel. Which isn't to say that what other people think or feel is unimportant or wrong. My process in life has been to insist over and over and over again, no matter what, that there are always different perspectives on everything. As many people as are in the room, there will be that many different perspectives and every one of them will have a certain legitimacy. If I can take in each one, I can see a huge picture.

RICHARD RHODES: Your mother's point of view was that there's only one truth.

ANNE O'NEIL: But now I can assess whether I agree or not, based on my own experience. And I can learn. That's very different. Before there was none of that process. It was as though I didn't really have my own experience. I lived life through my mental constructs. You understand what I'm saying. It's astounding. I'm so different!

Richard asked David Ray when he started writing:

DAVID RAY: Well, I guess it started in high school. Then it became a very desperate thing. I used to carry a lot of poems around. I published a little bit in the high-school newspaper. A poem or two. Then I would carry these poems around with me and work on them all the time.

RICHARD RHODES: Why poetry?

DAVID RAY: I suppose because that's where you most spill the feelings. Because I was trying to get my feelings straight. I think I wrote to keep my sanity, not as a conscious intention.

GINGER RHODES: How did you make that discovery? Writing as a way of keeping your sanity—how did you make it work?

DAVID RAY: I don't think I made a discovery, I just did it. There had always been an obsession, and there's still an obsession about writing things just to get them straight. Just to understand them.

When I was in college, I wound up in the hospital. I made two serious suicide attempts and got into psychiatric treatment. I saw that doctor, Alvin Suslick, for years. I had no money, so I paid all of a dime a week for a long time. But he saved my life. There's no question about it. One of these recovery books says, you have to find somebody who believes in you. Alvin Suslick believed in me. I don't know why he did, but I think he pulled me out of the pit. And it was a long haul, I can tell you. Because I was almost unredeemable. I was terribly bitter and terribly in pain.

In The Hidden Legacy, *Barbara Hamilton writes:*

BARBARA HAMILTON: In looking back, I marvel at the healing process I found in writing my way through despair; how I have been turned around and put back on track by insights from within. Alone in my mountain room one night, I wrote:

"Sometimes as the waves of anger and sorrow rush over me, when I remember the pieces of my life that have vanished, I sense a push from an unseen force. It's as though something is trying to erase me from the universe, is trying to deny me my sense of belonging here and is obscuring my rightful place in the scheme of things.

"My mind tells me this is not so, but when I'm tired my strength ebbs and my inner self can't ignore the question. Perhaps I need these crushing waves now and then to stiffen my resolve; to dig in my heels in defiance; to get on with my work and to finish it, despite all setbacks.

"Suddenly I don't care anymore who knows what about me. I will write freely and continue to use my own name. My life belongs to me!"

During our interview, Ginger asked Barbara if writing her book had helped her:

BARBARA HAMILTON: It helped me a lot. I tried to describe in the book the difference for me. It was exciting, it was so validating. Because in spite of all the pain that I was dealing with, one of the biggest pains was the confusion, the not knowing. Understanding my own childhood behavior. For instance, getting down on all fours out in the yard to see if a neighbor's dog would mate with me. Right out in the open, out in plain sight. Anybody who knows anything about psychology, which of course I didn't as a child, knows that has to be a cry for help. The whole neighborhood could have seen me. But in those days, who recognized anything except that this was a really bad seed, a creepy kid?

I've gotten burnt out on the term "the child within" because everybody uses it, and I think it probably irritates people who don't have the vaguest idea of what you're talking about—

RICHARD RHODES: Yes. I've used it in a book or two. Reviewers can get very testy about the phrase.

BARBARA HAMILTON: —but it's very real, and without using that expression, I opened the book with a flashback [*to a memory of her father's head appearing over her in the dark when she was small, leaning over to kiss her erotically on the mouth*], a way of inspiring or stimulating the reader to feel as a child. To experience as a child. To try to get some sense of the horror. My father was not a big man, but to little me that head was enormous. That flashback only occurred in 1985. That was something else that the writing and working through did—it stimulated flashbacks, and also stimulated these miraculous pieces of the puzzle that I call floaters—insights, connections, flashes of how things are related.

RICHARD RHODES: The process you call "floaters" is exactly the way I find material for a work of fiction. I start out by making random notes and let my unconscious do the original creative work. You reinvented the process for yourself.

BARBARA HAMILTON: It just hit me. I was in therapy at the time and that stimulated my associations. I'd be scribbling down floaters and sticking them in my pocket, pulling off to the side of the highway to write down something, because I knew by the time I got home I'd forget it. You have to do it right now. In a restaurant or wherever. I had papers everywhere. I'd put them all in these envelopes that had very weird headings because I still didn't know I was going to write a book. But I felt, well, if I look at these things . . .

I had a double bed at that time, and one day I just took out all these little pieces of paper and spread them around, made little piles. Wow, I began to see a real flow there. And that when you're ready, your subconscious lets go of it and lets you deal with it.

The first draft I wrote was just ridiculous. Nobody would have ever published it. But I had to just write and write and write without cutting myself off. After I got through with all that stuff, I wanted to put more happy times in. I said to myself, people will think I was totally miserable, so I wanted to alternate with some of the good things I remembered. But it would have dissipated the strength. So to stay in focus, I kept with the abuse and with the effects of the abuse. That was plenty. That was a milestone for me, too, because it helped me say, the happy memories are fine, but you don't have to excuse what happened. It was like I was on an adventure. It wasn't that I was seeing anything very pleasant, but it felt like I was finally getting some keys to understanding what was wrong.

Therapists also have feelings, Susan Voorhees told us, and need support:

SUSAN VOORHEES: When you agree to work with abused kids you agree to walk in a world that we work very hard to deny and ignore. You agree to consider that very nice-looking people, very reasonable-sounding people and very caring people at times, can do horrendous things to children. That's a struggle for therapists too.

RICHARD RHODES: How do you keep up your strength?

SUSAN VOORHEES: Partly because I hope that I can give something to these little kids. Partly because I try not to overload myself with too many cases at once. So I'll treat other kinds of kids. Sometimes I just want a regular kid. A regular kid who is having problems in school, perhaps. And it's delightful.

But also, there's something in the children. There are times when I don't want to talk to an attorney, I don't want to talk to a father, I don't want to talk to a mother, I don't like any of them. But this little kid will come in and there's something so wonderful about that child. Maybe it is my wish to rescue them. But suddenly, it's worth it. Even if they're not allowing me to see the abuse and not allowing me to do what I think the job might be. But we spend an hour playing in the dollhouse, or if they're a teenager we spend an hour trying to figure out what kind of hairstyle is a reasonable hairstyle. They've allowed me to be some part of their world, and if they can carry that with them to give them some strength to deal with something terrible in the future, then maybe I've done something to help.

Richard told David Doepel:

RICHARD RHODES: What was most important to me in my seven years of therapy, working through the abuse and other issues with a wonderful analyst, Jerry Ehrenreich, was his model of poise and maturity and his understanding that my anger had a place. That finally the rage was part of the person I had become and his sense that it simply needed direction toward the real work of the world. He put it much better than that. He said, It's okay to be angry, because there are things in this world that are worth being angry about.

✤

ALICE BRAND BARTLETT: We see many people who are trapped in their past and we can help them move. And they can move a long way. If I can be so bold as to interpret a little bit, the woman you mentioned who went into her closet or her car to scream [*she means Karen Seal*] found herself a container for her feelings, didn't she? When it's spilling over, you need to have a container. So she's in her car, she's in her closet—I think that's what treatment is for a long time. It sounds simplistic, but it's somebody to sit with you so you don't have to be alone with your feelings. Somebody to go through it with you, metaphorically, so that you don't lose connection when you work through these painful memories of abuse and of betrayal. And to help you find positive memories as well. I always make a preface statement at some point—when it seems right—that we will probably be talking about many feelings about your father or your mother and I hope that you will feel able to tell me all of them, because as horrendous as parents might be, they're never just that. I guess there are some Hitler parents in the world. But I try to say that sometimes there are pockets of goodness as well as horrible badness. Trying to put those pieces together is what I think treatment is about.

14

"The Kids Have Priority"

*T*he *quality of their insights, more than any other factor, led us to interview the men and women you have come to know in this book. In this chapter and the next, we bring together some of that hard-earned wisdom.*

MICHAEL DAVIES: My father was usually drinking on these occasions of abuse. But he could be very demeaning and mean-spirited and bullying even when he wasn't drinking, simply because he had to have control over every aspect of our lives. He kept us close at home. He was terribly afraid of not knowing where his kids were.

GINGER RHODES: Because you might be out there telling on him?

MICHAEL DAVIES: He was a very scared man. A guy who believed strongly in insurance, which he later sold, after he left the company. He was one of these people who always thought that bad things were going to happen, so he had to be prepared for the worst. But, you know, it's really difficult to grow if you feel that everything is threatening. He was not the kind of father who encouraged us to take chances, who encouraged us to take risks, who encouraged us to try to do something difficult.

He always wanted to hold us back, ostensibly to protect us, but really because he was afraid of what was out there and maybe a little bit about the world finding out about his deficiencies as a person.

In my memory, my father is not so much my father as a guy who was hired to run the family, the guy in charge. He was not a mentor. He taught me by example, but it was negative example. He taught me what I would never do in my own life. That may have been his best legacy for me.

✦

ALEXA DONATH: It would be easier if I had some tangible reason for my mother's abuse. If she drank or she took drugs. If you want it tied up—which none of these things ever are—it would be easier to say, yes, she was like this when she drank. But you can't say that about my mother. I can say that she should have been out working. That she would have been much happier. But my father made her stay home. That was a fact of life with a lot of women in the fifties, but they didn't beat up their children.

✦

SKYE SMITH: I was called ugly all the time. By everybody. You're bad, you're ugly. Ugly, ugly, stop being ugly. That was their word for misbehaving—"Don't be ugly. You're being ugly." I was so stubborn. I think stubbornness was my attempt to hold on to myself and who I was. I remember from earliest memory on: I never cried when they beat me. Never. And that enraged them— We're not getting to her.

RICHARD RHODES: Not crying was something you did, rather than something they ordered you to do?

SKYE SMITH: Oh yes. They're not going to get all of me. I've got some power over them. No matter what the cost, I'm not giving in to them. I'm holding on to myself. I think they really expected total subservience. I get this feeling around my mother—I haven't had contact with her for several years now, no contact—that she wants my life, my blood, my essence. Whatever will make her alive inside, because she's dead there. I can't give it. I feel guilty about it but I can't give it all away.

I have a hard time justifying why I don't speak to my mother now, why I can't have contact. But it's my mother or it's me. It sounds dramatic but it's the truth. One of us will live. I cannot be with her, cannot have any contact with her or she will suck the life out of me. I can't do it. Several years ago, the last time I was in Phoenix and saw her, she set me up again. She's constantly saying, I never get to see you. So we made plans to see each other. In fact, I ended up renovating the bathroom in their house. It's so fitting that I would be renovating their house for them, doing all this sweaty, hot work. I get over there, she's late coming home from work—which she never is—and I'm stuck talking with my step-father, one on one, which I'm nervous about anyway. She gets home, and it turns out she's got an appointment to get a permanent, she'll be gone for hours. She was gone for about three and a half hours, leaving me there with my stepfather. All this after telling me she never gets to see me.

So I'm working in the bathroom and my stepfather is standing across the doorway and I feel trapped. I was just sweating it out, thinking, What's an exit, which tool can I use when he comes near me?

It's one or the other, me or my mother, and it's going to me. I choose me, for the first time in my life I choose me.

Celia Golden discussed her mother in the context of a longitudinal study of male rapists she had reviewed:

CELIA GOLDEN: I see a lot of parallels. I don't see that the gender makes a difference. The study comes up with three categories of rapists. There's the pedophile, whose intention is not necessarily to cause pain. There are people who respond out of anger and that anger takes the form of sexual abuse. And then there are the sadists. My mother falls into that category. A lot of women, contrary to the literature, fall into the sadist category. I've talked to other survivors, male and female, and my impression is that it's more common for women who sexually abuse to be sadistic than it is for men. And for women to be very angry when they sexually abuse children. What the existing literature would like us to believe is that when women sexually abuse, it's an extension of their nurturing and that they get confused. They're gentler, they're teaching about love and affection and they don't know what they're doing. That's not it.

But it's hard for people to hear the truth. Our truth is so contrary to what the literature says that it's a little overwhelming to go against it. People like me get silenced. It's like pissing in the ocean. I grew up with these attitudes about not talking about sexual abuse. If I talked about the way I really felt, I'd be burned at the stake.

❖

SKYE SMITH: It helps to get as realistic a picture of your abuser as possible, which requires years and years of therapy, distancing, and emotional working through. Just see them for what they are.

MARIA MAREWSKI: Sometimes you realize that all that drama wasn't necessarily about you, it was about them. It was their show and you just happened to be in the wrong place at the wrong time. You don't feel that way, because you had to participate in the drama, but finding that separation can be healing.

❖

CELIA GOLDEN: Boy, if there's one place where a woman can feel powerful, it's at home. You go out into the workforce and there's going to be someone smarter, more savvy, with a better education, better-looking, better-dressed, I mean, it's competitive out there. But in your house, who's to see . . . ? Women have more time alone with a child than most men do, unless he's staying home taking care of the kids. Women have always had the greatest opportunity to abuse kids. No one wants to look at the statistics, that the majority of physical abuse of infants and small children is by women. If physical, then why not sexual abuse? If we're willing to say that women historically have been the targets of child sexual abuse and abuse begets abuse, then why don't you follow the argument through?

In an article in Matrix, *Celia wrote:*

CELIA GOLDEN: I didn't encounter the term "mother-daughter incest" until I was in recovery and began to research the little literature available. My research did not produce an existing vocabulary describing female-perpetrated abuse, however; my vocabulary is borrowed from the experience of victims of the Holocaust, of the Vietnam War, of political imprisonment. These are the experiences that more clearly describe my childhood: a state of imprisonment in which my captor had total control over my existence and unlimited access to my body. But unlike adult prisoners, I had known no "safe" time prior to the abuse. For me, sexual abuse was an extension of the generalized abuse I'd known from early infancy.

An infant has no words to order her universe; a child must find the words outside herself. My mother certainly didn't give me a vocabulary that could be used against her. And I didn't find a vocabulary in my research, either; the vocabulary that accepted experts use is incomplete and replete with misnomer and myth. It is a misnomer, for example, to refer to same-gender child sexual abuse as homosexual.

❖

SKYE SMITH: I wanted my father to love me, so I did just what Mother did— Don't say anything and he'll love you. Then I wrote him an eighteen-page letter and told him the story of my life: what happened after he left, and that it wasn't so great. He sort of responded to that but then backed right off. He had a heart attack and I went out to see him. I thought: there's unfinished business here, I think I need to see him another time. He's doing fine now. He's running marathons and doing great on the treadmill again. He's a storyteller, he's charming, he's the life of the party. He has this incredible energy, he's funny. But that really gets old when it's your father. You don't want a stand-up comedian all your life. For an hour and half he's very amusing and funny, but okay, now what? He gets out his photo albums of his fighter-pilot reunions that he attends around the country. Pictures of these middle-aged strange men who were really something back in the war, but now, who cares? The crowning comedy is the picture of the medals the guys got for being shot down.

My father's friend flew five hundred forty-one missions over North Vietnam. If you put that together, five hundred forty-one missions means he killed a lot of people. My father's glorifying all this stuff and he just doesn't get it. I thought we were so similar and we do have similar temperaments and all that, that's genetic, you can't help that. But we're not similar at all in any other way. He's about as deep as a sheet of paper. There's nothing about the man that interests me. He's very macho, he's still into his 1960s fighter-pilot air force. He was only in the military a few years and he's hanging on to that. It's pathetic. You think there was one picture of me—his daughter—in those albums? No. Not one. So I'm not involved in his life and he's not involved in mine.

During my visit, there was no mention of anything difficult. I was in bad shape for a long time, hospitalized, but my father didn't even mention it. But when the car was packed and we were getting ready to leave, and it was safe, he could say, I'm really proud of you. [*She laughs.*] He's so predictable. So I get in the car and bye, it's been nothing. I can't even say it's been real. But at least I see it. Not that it's okay, not that it's great, but that's what it is with my father. I see the truth. We have nothing in common, he's not interesting to me.

So I married a pilot. Yeah, found a man in New York who I thought was the exact replica of my father. I thought he was a dead ringer. But it turned out he was really a great guy. He's sensitive, he's a grown-up, wow!

❖

CELIA GOLDEN: The problem is that the family has been traditionally so sacred, so-called, that within that circle it's a law unto itself. In many ways it still is. That's what the family values debate was about. That's why Hillary Clinton infuriated the family-values crowd when she suggested that children had some rights in this world.

GINGER RHODES: We can't all be king and queen but within our own little fiefdom we can. Off with their heads!

❖

DAVID RAY: Nobody makes the judgment even today for the child. It's always the parents' rights that are considered first and foremost, and with a very narrow and biological definition of parenthood.

❖

BARBARA HAMILTON: Social-welfare agencies don't ordinarily take children out of homes where there are two parents. One of the awful things that happens these days is that they put them back. I know it's hard for agencies with such limited funds, but they're not really thinking of the kids. They con themselves into believing they are, by claiming these families can heal. I say, What family? Those children never were in a family. They were in jail with two abusive adults. They were in jail.

RICHARD RHODES: Bystanders demonstrate a universal truth about violence: that neutrality isn't neutral to the violent. If bystanders don't show their disapproval, if they try to be neutral, the violent take that neutrality for approval.

BARBARA HAMILTON: It's a green light. And justice doesn't want to be just. They want to protect the male animal, I guess, since most of them are males. They get all tangled up in their priorities.

It's so simple: *The kids have priority.* All this business about protecting the perpetrator's rights is appalling.

❖

SKYE SMITH: I can't imagine hitting a child. Can you imagine picking up a belt, a big red belt, and smacking a three-year-old, over and over? How can they do it?

RICHARD RHODES: All sorts of people do it every day.

MARIA MAREWSKI: I'm not sure people think about what they're doing. You see people do amazing things in public. You realize they have no shame.

SKYE SMITH: They think they're doing the right thing. They think what they're doing is what a good parent does.

GINGER RHODES: I used to look away and pretend I didn't notice. I still can't walk up and say something, but I watch them shouting at their child. I watch. I want them to know that there are people out there, that we're watching. We're paying attention to what you're doing.

MARIA MAREWSKI: Sometimes I think those people are confused about whether you're disapproving of *their* behavior or their *children's* behavior. As for motives, some people do it because they're aping their parents. It's all vented on the child; they blame the child for the whole scene.

LYDIA DeROBERTIS: They become embarrassed that their children are reflecting badly on them in public and therefore they feel justified in hitting them.

MARIA MAREWSKI: The children are "making them" hit.

SKYE SMITH: They're all-powerful beings, aren't they, those two-year-olds in the cart there?

❖

DAN HAMILTON: Our family kept the doors to communication shut. We were all taught that that's how a normal family worked. In addition to the experience of physical abuse and sexual abuse, we were taught that example of total noncommunication and role-playing. We presented ourselves to the community as a terrific, healthy family. We were active in the church. We had foreign students living with us; we had three African students for five years. We were just this great, liberal, together family, and all of us knew it was rotten at the core. We went out into the world to get away from it. And as we all got into relationships, we thought, what do I do, how do I do this? I don't know anything about how relationships work.

GINGER RHODES: For years, I did the same thing that you did—until I met Richard. I would get involved in a relationship and at a certain point—the point at which you have to start negotiating how you feel with another human being—I couldn't make it across that gap because I never learned negotiation. My family didn't communicate, so we never had to negotiate. I cycled through relationship after relationship, and never managed to communicate with another human being about how I felt about myself, or how I felt about him, until I met Richard. I understand what you say about your wife. He was the same for me—another human being who finally looked me in the eye and said, I care about you enough to hurt through this with you. Let's hurt through it together.

DAN HAMILTON: Yes. Even now, that's probably the most difficult thing to deal with.

✦

CELIA GOLDEN: When women abuse children, they have more of an investment to cover up, to protect their feminine image and their image in society. Even if they're full-time career women, there's still value to being a mother, so they've got a greater interest in covering up their abusiveness than a man does. I also think that they prey on babies and younger children who are preverbal. The statistics bear that out: women are the primary physical abusers of infants and small children. The male figures in when the children reach the age of about eight, where they begin to be able to defend themselves against a woman because they're physically closer in size. I remember, as a child, hearing women say, I can't deal with you, your father's going to take care of you. So you call in the armed forces and you get to play the little lady.

In the Incest Survivors Information Exchange, *Celia wrote:*

CELIA GOLDEN: I am a feminist but I am first and foremost a humanist. Society's unwillingness to acknowledge female perpetrators is reflected in the lack of literature on the subject, in the many references that the incidence of female-perpetrated abuse is "rare," and in the sexist language that assumes perpetrators to be male and victims to be female.

I do not support sexism, racism, classism or any other form of prejudicial thinking. Just as intellect, creativity and leadership are not determined or limited by gender, neither is sexual abusiveness. I believe in equal rights for all—and equal responsibility.

Valorie Butler told us people don't always believe her when she tells them about her childhood abuse:

GINGER RHODES: Why do you think that's the case?

VALORIE BUTLER: I think some people are not even aware that these things exist, they don't believe they exist. Just like people still don't believe the Holocaust happened—and I find that incredible. My perception is, for these people it's so big a shock that they think you've made it up. They did not experience anything like it, or they did not know other people who did, or they're not perceptive people anyway, and they may not even want to be in touch with something that horrible.

✤

DAVID RAY: The last person you can forgive is yourself. A lot of Holocaust victims—I'm straying onto sacred, sensitive territory here—but they, too, blame themselves. It's very hard, because basically you're still saying, something's wrong with me or I wouldn't have been treated that way. The abusers had the power, so they must have somehow been right, I cannot question the validity of their all-wise judgments. You read a book that says that sometimes there's pleasure in the abuse. So you blame yourself for that, though it might have been a mere tingling of nerves or an involuntary orgasm. An outsider would say, You must have wanted that, or it wouldn't have happened. Hey, I was barely fifteen. But they reply that you're practically an adult at fifteen, you could have protested. So there's always a way of delegitimizing what happens to somebody else. To cut them down, to find a way to discredit them.

In one of the many letters we exchanged, Anna Lee Traynor wrote:

ANNA LEE TRAYNOR: I never really cried for what happened to me in my life. Or over spilt milk either, since the two seemed synonymous to me most of the time. I didn't cry when I read over my narrative [*the document she prepared for the lawsuit she brought against her mother and stepfather*]. I actually thought my attorney might not think it bad enough to even pursue a complaint. . . . It's easier to cry for someone else's sorrows than to face the fact that the extent of your own could be so painful— to feel such despair for yourself. That seemed so selfish to me. But this time, when I cried for Stanley and Richard [*after reading* A Hole in the World] I finally knew that I was crying for myself too. It hurt and felt good all at the same time.

❖

ANNE O'NEIL: I think it's important to acknowledge how very, very difficult it is not to buy into our fears. Because terror was there for a purpose. It was to protect us, and that's one thing we *will* do—protect ourselves as human beings. That's the survival level. But living well isn't possible when our terrors isolate us from others. How could I live well, trapped in the cage of my own fear?

GINGER RHODES: You're right, healing is in relationships.

RICHARD RHODES: And there's healing also in creativity, as you well know. I was in tears when you said you realized you couldn't continue Montessori work because of the terrible responsibilities, but that you could try to work with materials. That was extraordinary, to see that creativity involves destruction as well as creation. In fact, some people who have written about creativity point out that destructiveness is a necessary part. Even if you're only going to use paper, you have to cut down trees. If you're going to work with clay, if you're going to work with paint, destruction comes first and then the forming and building. That's the way the natural world cycles as well, so it's not surprising that the cycle has power.

ANNE O'NEIL: I'll never forget the time when I was a child when my brother Leo took me out onto the back porch and showed me how he had carefully opened up a fish and laid out all the parts. He was just full of wonder about it. He loved the wonder of the fish and how it all fit together. I stood there and loved my brother's wonder. He was meant to be what he is, a surgeon, who destroys, meticulously, in order to restore.

❖

LOUISE HILL: I now realize that I was quite a creative liar as a kid. But of course that's what made me a good storyteller. In fact, I became a writer because I realized that instead of telling all these creative stories to fifty people one at a time over the phone, I would just tell them once on a piece of paper and it would save tremendous energy.

❖

KAREN SEAL: I have to say I'm really amazed that I've not had a lot of hatred for men. Even though I'm a feminist. Some women, some people think feminists hate men. I identified with men, because they're powerful.

Anna Lee Traynor wrote us about the progress of her lawsuit:

ANNA LEE TRAYNOR: Can you believe that halfway through my mother's deposition, their attorney discussed a settlement!?! Our attorney informed him that my sister might consider a settlement, but forget me. Ten million dollars wouldn't be enough. He told their counsel that I'm determined to take them to court. And if dismissed, I'm going to pursue through appeals. I told you I had a good case based on the medical reports and also testimony from witnesses. Those are the elements usually missing from other cases of this nature. As well as a strong plaintiff. Too many are like my sister. They give in before they have the chance to realize that this is finally their opportunity to be fully realized for the valuable child that they were and the adult they are now. I look forward to telling you how it is to go through this kind of a suit. It's very, very difficult to bare your soul. The most difficult part isn't when you allow yourself to be revealed to the public, but when you first have to bare your soul to your own self. To face what you've wanted to remain "faceless" is so painful.

❖

KAREN SEAL: When my father died, I really grieved. I've heard that you grieve hardest when you didn't get what you wanted.

❖

SKYE SMITH: As an adult, on a visit home to Stearns, I felt compelled to go to the theater where we'd lived when my brother and I were kids and look in and go upstairs. It's not used for anything now. My soul was in there somewhere. I think I was trying to find it.

❖

ANNA LEE TRAYNOR: This lawsuit is part of my life. It's the reason I'm bothering you with my story. Otherwise, I could care less. I'm just one in a million.

❖

DAVID RAY: You're still holding on to the fantasy that they love you, the hope that underneath it all, your mother loves you. You can't face it that she didn't love you. We've been talking about the abuse issues, but it's not just those. It's grief as well, because basically you're saying, Yes, I lost. I lost a parent, I lost all kinds of things. Those are grief issues.

In his essay "Prolegomena to an Autobiography," David wrote:

DAVID RAY: When parents die, they are mourned. The wound heals over the sacred introject, a stone near the heart. But when they live on, mourning can be even more intense, awakened again and again, enraged by new reunions that don't work out.

❖

DAN HAMILTON: Even now I've never really expressed that rage except in my work. It's an immediate and terrific button in my work, which is a nice, safe, as-if, pretend environment if I'm performing or acting. You know, if a page in the script says, "He enters in a rage," oh! [*he laughs*]— piece of cake.

I'm not good at being angry. I'm not good at letting it out safely. It tends to build up and build up until it's out of proportion.

RICHARD RHODES: I've always been worried that I have more anger than I could handle.

DAN HAMILTON: Oh, *I* could handle, but certainly nobody else could. Nobody else could possibly handle it. Nobody could love me. Nobody could possibly deal with it. I will just destroy anyone around me. The arrogance of that—thinking that nobody has got the strength of love to deal with my rage.

Barbara Hamilton wrote in The Hidden Legacy:

BARBARA HAMILTON: Long ago, when Dad put his molesting hand on me—his child—he reached ahead through time to molest his great-grandchildren not yet born. And his legacy still remains, partially hidden. It will never be fully uncovered. I have written about some of the abusers and some of the survivors, but not about all of them; there were several boys among the victims. All of us growing up in three generations of dysfunctional families during a span of nearly seventy years were adversely affected. Assaults included pimping, rape, and sodomy. Abuses that were not physically painful and were seductively masked as expressions of affection produced unnatural emotional bonding—a nearly impenetrable block for young victims to overcome. The most painful experience for some was being thrust aside and ridiculed, scorned, or hated. Many of the survivors have spent months, even years, in various types of therapy, working to find the wholeness we lost when our childhoods were stolen from us. Aftereffects include several suicide attempts by at least two victims, illegal drug abuse and sexual promiscuity, and a number of broken marriages. We heal slowly—not steadily—and the scars will never completely disappear. They are a permanent part of our history. Our goal is to transform them, to keep their aftereffects from running us as we learn how to break old patterns and take control of our lives. . . .

I know that this book has caused pain, especially to those who knew and loved the principals. The pain of disillusionment, betrayal, awareness of duplicity, and tarnished memories can be loaded with anguish, rage, and heartache. It feels as though it will never end. I have experienced all these feelings and I would not wish them on anyone else. But blind family loyalty cannot require its members to protect those who dishonor the family.

All I can say to the outraged who may be angry with me for exposing these skeletons is, you have a right to feel outraged; and I must suggest that you redirect your anger to the crime and the abusers. . . .

In his "Prolegomena" essay, David Ray wrote:

DAVID RAY: The quixotic do-gooder instinct which had led us to try to clean up the greasy rodlines [*of oil-well pumps, when his sister lost part of a finger*] has often got me into trouble in adult life as well, for I have too often tried to fix the world up, and have had difficulty accepting it as it is. The world has little tolerance, though, for Don Quixote.

Richard asked Skye Smith how she feels about herself today:

SKYE SMITH: I'm working on it. It's better. I grew up thinking I was really dumb, incredibly dumb. Bob's the smart one in the family and I'm ugly and dumb. My whole goal was to not outshine my family, which was kind of tough. [*She laughs.*] My mother is the pretty and artistic one and my brother is the smart and athletic one, so what's left for me, the failure? Quitting jobs and depression felt good. I was being a good daughter.

❖

ALEXA DONATH: So it's not like, just get over it. I want to say *wise up* to society. People don't understand that what we're dealing with here is everything, everything: it's all the kids who never grow up. I saw brilliant kids who were dying before my eyes.

❖

CELIA GOLDEN: I think there's been too much pressure for people to focus on forgiving the perpetrators. That's a problem I have with AA [*Alcoholics Anonymous*], the idea that you take personal inventory, make amends to those people you have injured, change those things you can change, and let go of the past. In essence, we're being told that the crimes of the past are the crimes of the past. What someone did to you, we're not going to address. What you did to someone else, we're not going to address. It's from this day forward. So if I'm a perpetrator, my kids are supposed to say, Well, you're a recovering alcoholic, or, You found God, and now I have to deal with you as you are. If I don't, you might drink again, or use drugs, or commit suicide or whatever because you're so fragile that I have to protect you. So the kids never get to have their rage. I as an alcoholic am not supposed to get angry, because I may go out and drink. On the other hand, if I don't get angry, I might go drink. I think that our whole society has been about taking care of the perpetrators instead of really looking at the damage and doing something about the kids of today and the kids of the future.

❖

BARBARA HAMILTON: It never occurred to me to turn around, go back and try to win my family back, or win them over, or try to do anything with them. If we had had anything really strong and supportive there in the beginning, it would have kept us together, allowed us to face this together, but it didn't. So good-bye. I hate that *forgiveness* business.

RICHARD RHODES: I do too. I wondered how you felt about that.

BARBARA HAMILTON: I think it's a bunch of patriarchal B.S. from the pulpit or wherever they promote this idea. Forgiveness—I get really angry because I've been challenged on that, too. I try to make it very clear that I can't forgive abusers of children.

❖

VALORIE BUTLER: I can be angry and understanding, all in the same ball of wax. But my aunt's not released from accountability. She's still very much accountable.

❖

DAVID RAY: I made a few notes of points I wanted to remember. . . . When you try to live in the present but your true loyalty is to the past—

RICHARD RHODES: Why so?

DAVID RAY: I think kids are brainwashed. But I do not adore this guy [*who molested him*] who's alive out in Colorado. He called here a few years ago and I was still in his will. His lawyer sent me a copy and he called here and I said, No, I don't want to have anything to do with you. I'm sure the lawyer got a call right after that. I'm sure I'm not in the will anymore. [*David has since learned that John Warner died not long after these calls.*]

I do feel disloyalty to my mother in speaking of this. Yeah, I should be protecting her. I should be trying harder to forgive her. That's the thing. If you don't forgive it, then there's something wrong with you, it's your fault.

RICHARD RHODES: Do you feel that way?

DAVID RAY: Well, there's all this official literature that we're exposed to and all this bullshit we're exposed to, you know. Maybe there's some kind of serenity to be accomplished by forgiving. I'm not sure, but I think in a way it's a cop-out. Should the Jews forgive the Nazis?

David summed up his feelings about forgiveness in a letter to us:

DAVID RAY: Forgiveness is easy to recommend by those who have little to forgive.

In The Hidden Legacy, *Barbara Hamilton writes:*

BARBARA HAMILTON: A conversation with myself:
Will you ever forgive him?
No, I wasn't asked—not once—not ever. He never said he was sorry. He never asked my forgiveness. He never acknowledged his responsibility. I feel absolutely no need to forgive him.
Nine days later came this floater:
"I don't believe it's necessarily appropriate to forgive the abusers of our children. I don't forgive the Nazis and I'm not Jewish. I don't even know anyone personally who has told me about losing someone in the Holocaust—and yet I don't forgive the Nazis.
"My children are alive, but they were cruelly scarred. To forgive their abusers is to extend their betrayal and denigrate the suffering they've survived. It is out of the question.
"If being unforgiving is a mark of self-righteousness, I do not shun its stain. Forgiving is for lesser crimes than those committed against helpless, trusting children."

Celia Golden wrote in Matrix:

CELIA GOLDEN: In the words of Octavio Paz, "to explain is not to justify, much less excuse." I cannot excuse a perpetrator of child sexual abuse because she's a woman any more than I'd excuse a man.

During our interview, Barbara Hamilton told us:

BARBARA HAMILTON: I started writing in 1980. The years were running out. I was beginning to get a lot of flak from the family. I was also beginning to get the feeling, especially from the negativity of my brothers, that I didn't want this to be a feminist thing. I wanted the book to be meaningful not only to women who had axes to grind for whatever reason. It's not that I'm not empathetic, but this must be carried forth by all of us, must be inclusive of men. Men have the capacity to help turn other men around in a way that women don't. Men can change laws and confront and show some of these fellows that this just doesn't go.

GINGER RHODES: They're the power brokers.

BARBARA HAMILTON: Yes, definitely. I mean, it's going to be forever until that changes, if it ever does. Little things, they give us a pat on the head here and there, but that's about it. It's funny that since the book came out, I've been contacted mostly by women's groups. There are all kinds of ways that they want me to channel into what they're doing. That's not where I am. I'm not an organization kid. I don't want to confine child abuse to another woman's issue.

GINGER RHODES: It's larger than a woman's issue.

BARBARA HAMILTON: My brother, the one who's not an abuser, couldn't hear it from me, but he might hear it from a strong male personality. It's the ones who could do something whom I'm trying so hard to reach.

The night one of my articles came out in the local newspaper, the phone rang. The very first person who responded was a young man. He told me, I've been an abuser; I was caught and served my time; I'm in counseling and would like to talk to you. Only he didn't say it that directly. He was much more hesitant. He was afraid I'd hang up on him.

I think he must have gone all day trying to decide whether to call me or not. I said, I'd like to know something about you. Well, I'm in therapy, would you like my therapist's name and number? I talked to his therapist, who was supportive and said it would be all right.

We met in a restaurant, and after we talked and talked and talked I brought him home. I didn't tell any of my friends. A child abuser, a jailbird. They didn't know anything about it and they would have been very surprised. Well, his coming here and meeting with me was quite interesting, because he kept coming back. He would come every few days. One day he brought Chinese dinner. In the article that I had written, I had referred to Andrew Vachss's novel *Blossom*. He wanted to know about that, because it was about boys who were abused. He borrowed it and had a terrible time reading it. That book and my articles had brought so much up for him. I'll never forget him saying—he was standing right there where you're sitting—saying, Barbara, you're tough; you're really tough. That was the best thing he could have said to me. He wanted to know what I thought of him. He said, I want to marry someday, I want to have a child. I said, You want to know what I think? I don't think that abusers should ever be alone with a child again. I don't care how much therapy they've had. He said, I've paid my price. And I said, No, you paid what the State required of you to pay. But that child is still suffering.

They've already blown it in my book as far as their chance to be responsible is concerned. It's not worth any child's one moment of doubt, with or without a hand on them, for him to be reassured that he's cured. Because he's not.

GINGER RHODES: So you're really talking about the risk.

BARBARA HAMILTON: I'm talking about the risk to children. I'm sorry about the abusers—how they got that way, what happened to *them* and all that. If they were children and were abusing, there might be a chance if you could get them early enough. But adults who abuse children—in my book, they've blown it.

ALEXA DONATH: It's beyond obscene. It's like when you're talking about the Holocaust—you can't deal with it anymore. So when a friend of mine says, Get over it, I say, Do you understand how many damaged people there are walking around out there? It isn't just that it colors everything in *my* life. I think it's what causes violence in our society. When I saw children who had cigarette burns on them and came in smelling of urine, I knew that in ten years, those children were going to be in jail. In ten years, half those girls would be pregnant.

I was in the hospital when a fourteen-year-old came in who used to be in the program where I worked and I didn't recognize her. She said, So-and-so has a baby, and so-and-so, and so-and-so. I just started to cry.

It isn't *us,* it's not *us.* It's not that *I* have to get over it, it's that it trickles down. It trickles down from everywhere and if you work with the kind of communities I worked with, if you see the kind of children I saw, if you study alcoholism and drug abuse, you know they don't come from a vacuum. That's why I know there's got to be some reason for my mother. If you want to hear a kosher pig story, you've got one. There are no kosher pigs.

15

"If You Don't Have a Heart, There's No Limit"

The insights we heard from the men and women we interviewed included insights into their abusers. Who would know them better?

LOUISE HILL: My grandmother came from the old country. She came from Russia. Now that I think of it, she was probably a very angry woman also because her husband was having an affair—which I found out about years later. It was my aunt who told me. He was a tailor. One of the most horrible moments in my aunt's life was walking down the main street of Boston and seeing her own father walking hand-in-hand with his seamstress. She was very pretty. Like my father, my grandfather was carrying on with somebody, so my grandmother was a very angry woman. How things get passed on, anger to anger to anger to anger.

❖

ALEXA DONATH: My mother didn't drink. She used to say to me when she was in a rage, Am I such a bad mother, am I a whore, am I alcoholic? Years later I thought, Gee, I would have loved it; I could go to meetings of children of alcoholics. I can't say alcohol or drugs caused her violence, so there's no place where I can go. There's a secret, there's a secret way back, something in her past. I don't know what it is, and she's never going to talk. This sort of abuse doesn't happen just because she was afraid of being a mother or because she wanted to be a career woman again. This sort of abuse happened because somebody hurt her or something happened to her. I know and I can feel compassion for that, knowing it, but I can't forgive her because she hasn't asked for my forgiveness.

Richard told Dan Hamilton: "Some people who were abused grow up and become abusers. One of my immediate relatives was abused as a child and then was abusive in turn to his children. But others who are abused grow up feeling the way you do, the way I felt: determined that not I nor anyone else would abuse my children."

DAN HAMILTON: But the rage is there in me, and the pattern is there in me, the responsive pattern. When Josh was a child, twenty years ago, I knew that I had the capacity to be physically abusive. Intentionally or unintentionally, I was taught that there's a point at which the physical expression of your anger is allowed. If not accepted. And when Josh was two or three, there were times when I would hit him way out of proportion to whatever the issue was or the discipline was. One reason for that divorce—although I don't think I could have said so at the time— was that I couldn't deal with my behavior, I had to get away.

I knew the pattern was still there when the question came up of becoming a father again, all these years later. For years my second wife and I had mutually agreed that our careers were enough, but as we got older, she said, No, I think I want a child. So we tried for several years and found that our immune systems were incompatible; she would carry and lose it and carry and lose it. We finally realized that we would have to adopt. I said, Okay, there's a rule—because I know this about myself and she had learned about my family history in therapy with me— When I say, I need to leave the room, I mean I leave the room *now*. When I say, I can't take any more, I mean it. I'm not just playing power games or demanding that you be the parent. Because I can hurt him, and I don't want that.

I don't know if that ever leaves. I have the ability to deflect the anger and go with humor. I can usually defuse a situation very quickly. But if I haven't slept enough or whatever, I will very quickly get to the point where my gut-level reaction is to reach out and hit.

RICHARD RHODES: What enabled you to change the behavior?

DAN HAMILTON: Two answers come to mind. I don't know if they're universally valid. First, understanding how much that kind of abuse hurt me made me understand that I can't do it to anyone else if I can be in control of it. Second, I was lucky enough to be loved by enough people along the way that I knew there was a better choice. It may be that you combine those two influences. Some people are more sensitive and aware as children—aware of other people's feelings. Maybe that capacity, combined with the experience that people can be gentle and loving, whether as a child or as an adult, allows you to find control.

GINGER RHODES: Which people in particular in your life?

DAN HAMILTON: The first who come to mind are the two women I married.

In Matrix, *Celia Golden wrote:*

CELIA GOLDEN: I was in a psychotherapy group twenty years ago with six women who'd been sexually abused in childhood by men. I didn't disclose that I'd also been a victim of child sexual abuse. It was difficult at that time to even minimally reveal the emotional and physical abuse in my childhood. The only perpetrator I dared speak of was my father. The other perpetrator, the one I dared not name, continued to be protected by my silence. And I continued to be trapped by the same silence, afraid to hear my voice, to see the effect of my words on someone's face.

It wasn't until sixteen years later, when I met another woman trapped by a similar silence, that I was willing to break my own. I identified with her self-abuse, her multiple addictions, her attraction to suicide, because these were the patterns that had brought both of us to the same treatment program. Listening to her allude to plans of suicide one evening was the turning point that brought my anger to the surface, where I could direct it at the perpetrator instead of myself. My friend's life was more important to me than my silence, and I saw my voice as the means to free us both. If I would dare to speak and risk the consequences, she might be encouraged to find her own voice.

Suicide is no longer an option for me as escape from the refuse of abuse. Today I confront my fears and tell people I was sexually abused by my mother. The more I speak, the more I realize what a well-kept secret female-perpetrated child sexual abuse is. The most common response is, "Your mother. It never occurred to me that a mother would do that."

✦

LOUISE HILL: When I had children I made a vow that no matter what, they were going to know that they were loved. That was the most important thing to me, because it's clear to me that I wasn't. I could try to go back and say, perhaps I was but in a different way. But I wasn't. My mother was too angry and too bitter and too pained and too confused to give out any kind of love. So I made a tremendous effort with my children, and I do know that they feel loved.

You so much don't want to turn into your own parent and you're so sure you're not going to. I never physically abused my kids, but on occasion I can be very mean. On occasion I can be sharp. Today I was sharp to one of my daughters and I was so pleased that she called me on it. She said, You ridiculed me. No one ever said that to me before, and now that I think about it, I did. Why did I do that? My only answer is, I guess I learned it from my mother. So I guess I'd better unlearn it.

Celia Golden, writing in Matrix:

CELIA GOLDEN: We also need to ask how a woman learns to nurture and protect her children from abuse if her role model was abusive or failed to protect her from abuse. Researcher Selma Fraiberg considered mothers to be the key in breaking the cycle of child abuse. The nonabusive and protective mother who was abused in childhood is worthy of study and applause as proof that women can break the cycle of child abuse when they choose to be responsive and responsible.

Richard raised the question of the identity of violence with David Ray:

RICHARD RHODES: One of the mysteries that fascinates me, and that I don't yet understand, is the identity of violence at every scale. What happened to you happened to Jews in the Nazi camps, happened to the disappeared in Argentina, happens to small children all over this country in every social milieu, and the patterns are identical. The pattern of abuse involves taking away your privacy, humiliating you, depriving you physically and psychologically, and inflicting physical violence. It's as if there's a standard set of methods for degrading and controlling and humiliating a human being and every abuser figures them out. But to arrive independently in different cultures and different power relationships at the same set of methods seems far-fetched; it's more logical to suspect they derive from a common origin. Do they originate commonly within the dynamics of the family? They certainly look as if they do. The leader of the nation is the great father and so on. There's some metaphoric parallel that people follow.

DAVID RAY: Maybe, in a perverted way, it's just problem solving. After all, if you decided, I want to control this person, how do I do it? How many ways are there? They're very good at it, very good. I think that they're ingenious at knowing the limitations or the sicknesses of the society—at knowing how much tolerance there is, how much they can get away with. As I say, I could have gone to the police. I could have got this guy sentenced to prison. Looking back on it, I think maybe that was a possibility, and yet, he obviously feared no such thing. He obviously had no fear of my telling my mother or the people in his social circle in Tucson.

To Anne O'Neil, Richard commented:

RICHARD RHODES: I worry about people who are emotionally inaccessible, because those emotions get expressed in terrible ways. It was "rational" defense intellectuals who managed to figure out that Vietnam was a good idea and it was "rational" arms strategists who figured out that you could destroy millions of human beings with nuclear weapons and called that victory.

ANNE O'NEIL: It's very scary. What I discovered with my mother—and this was one of the gifts that came out of my childhood experience—was that anything can be rationalized and justified. You can get to any conclusion intellectually—any conclusion. Both peace activists and people who worked on the bomb are interested in your book. [*She means Richard's history*, The Making of the Atomic Bomb.] Our thinking can take us anywhere we want to go, anywhere we're inclined to go. But the *inclinations* have a whole lot more to do with our childhood experiences than anything else. And what we do with them. It's very scary. If you don't have a heart, there's no limit to what you can do.

❖

LOUISE HILL: I always wondered why some people survive abuse and why other people don't survive abuse. I often wonder why I did. I've never come up with a good answer. I think it must be a certain genetic endowment, a certain spirit, a certain character, why some rise and some fall.

❖

DAVID RAY: It's a mystery how I survived, it really is. I think that's part of getting a little crumb here and a little crumb there. It would have been a lot easier and it might even have been fun at times if it hadn't had to be so deadly serious. In one book I read, the author talks about how victims are so deadly serious all their life, how they can't have any fun. That's one of the legacies of this stuff. You can't have fun. You can't. The effort to survive by putting together a little bit from here and there is defeated by the suicidal behavior, the destructive behavior, and then drinking and so on. If you could only be your own best friend, you could get through anything. The reason survival is amazing is that you were not your best friend. You were your worst enemy. And yet, you somehow survived. That's the mystery of it.

RICHARD RHODES: You're speaking about the adult time of survival. But as a child, aren't you your own best friend in the sense of being clever about finding something of what you need?

DAVID RAY: There's a part of you. Yeah, there's a part of you that's your best friend.

In a letter to Richard, Karen Seal wrote:

KAREN SEAL: What I see that is common between you and me is that we both turned to "super-achieving." You, of course, are far more famous and successful than I; but in my own way I "overachieved." I am still the only one in my father's family to have graduated from college (I went on for a Ph.D.), even though he was one of eleven and I have thirty or forty cousins and untold second cousins on his side. There is only one other family member on my mother's side to have graduated from college (and Mom was one of eight children).

I worked addictively, prospered in the material world, but felt empty and awful in my core. Finally, after my second marriage collapsed, two years ago, I decided to find out what was wrong with me; why was I so stressed, so outwardly successful, yet feeling so unfulfilled? I entered twelve-step recovery for co-dependence and incest abuse, and I am feeling a thousand percent better now. As I gather more experience in recovery, I have noticed that those of us from abusive homes seem either to try desperately to be good enough or we give up and turn to crime, victimhood, or we drop out in some way.

In our interview, Karen added:

KAREN SEAL: I've often looked at people from happy childhoods and thought, well, okay, I'm glad they're happy, but they're really not trying very hard, are they?

Michael Davies wrote Richard:

MICHAEL DAVIES: There are many mysteries here. Not the least of which is how we [*that is, Michael and his siblings*] managed to survive in the face of these depredations. I think that deep down we still credit our mother (an Arkansas native, like your own) with keeping the family together. For a while, however, a divide has opened up between my mother and her two daughters who felt that keeping the family together was an act of surrender to a sadistic tyrant.

✦

ALEXA DONATH: I thought, if there was a God, then why me? There can't be. Then we come back to the camps. It's why I identify so much. There's nothing else when you're in such circumstances: that's your world. [*To Richard:*] You wrote *A Hole in the World*. That was your world. This was my world. In order for me to survive it, I told everybody what was being done to me. That was my way of surviving. Otherwise I would have splintered. Otherwise I would have been Sybil.

I remember thinking to myself, that could happen to me. I could split. There would be relief in multiple personality. This hurts too much, I remember thinking; the next time she does it, I'm going to let somebody else take it. But when the time came, I didn't. I just decided I was strong enough to take it myself.

RICHARD RHODES: I understand about the splitting. I used to try to make myself invisible when I was being beaten, because then my step-mother couldn't see me.

ALEXA DONATH: So we could have splintered. We could have. I used to go down into the basement to read and listen to music. I really believe that books saved my sanity and perhaps my life. Losing myself in the fantasy world of literature was a healthy alternative.

When I worked with children, I did something that you're really not supposed to do. When children came in and told me about abuse, I'd sit down on the stairs with them and say, I was too. Their eyes would get so wide. They couldn't believe it. I'd bring them over to my apartment. Sixteen black kids getting out of a van—my landlady used to love that! I showed them that you could, in fact, survive.

I have read every bit of Holocaust literature. When something like *Sybil* was on television and I'd see it for the ninth time so that I could find the courage to live my life again, my husband would say, Why do you do this to yourself? Because I need to do this, I told him, I need to be a witness. He said I sounded like a Holocaust survivor. I am. And I will witness again. If we don't bear witness, if I don't use my own name now, then what am I saying? I'm saying that this can go on, and on and on.

We just keep coming. They can't comprehend. I was listening to Elie Wiesel the other day saying, No one could comprehend this, and the Nazis were banking on it. Parents who abuse their children, who commit incest with their children, they're banking that no one is going to believe it. Don't tell, because no one will believe you. My mother was banking on it.

I'm a survivor, yes. People say, Oh, are you working? I say, No, but I'm walking.

❖

DAN HAMILTON: Sometimes, in discussions like this, I think, what about the good times? What about all the good times? What about all the good things they gave? Because somebody made me this way. I didn't do it by myself. Some of it may be genetic, some of it may be environmental, and some may be gifts from outside the family, but somebody inside the family gave me the ability to laugh, the need to give, the ability to give, to listen, to feel. Somebody taught me. It wasn't all dark.

What allowed me to turn these corners as opposed to putting a needle in my arm and dying at eighteen? Endurance. If you say, Tell me one thing about yourself you know will not change, I'd say I can endure almost anything. I've not been in any great physical pain. I don't know about torture. I've not had to face life and death. I did not serve in Vietnam. I've never had to kill anybody. I never had to watch anybody be killed. I've lost friends a thousand other ways, but not through immediate physical violence. But I can endure that kind of pain. That's my strength.

I've usually felt that people loved me more than I loved them, and the inherent power that gives you, I think I've been aware of, and often more lonely as a result of it. But not in a manipulative way. I would like to think I don't play games about that.

I'm pretty good at being alone. I can get depressed and self-destructive, too, but I can find an activity to pull me out of it. I do physical work. We have a farm upstate, and I can lose myself in that. Computers, books, astronomy—through the years there has always been something I could channel the aloneness and loneliness into. As I get healthier and healthier, I can put it into my family. Now we have the very obvious focus of raising a child. That takes up every waking moment. I don't have an hour a day of being alone.

RICHARD RHODES: These are all traditional signs of good health, you know. Work and activities. Being involved with your family and loving them. Has enough change come that you feel much more fulfilled?

DAN HAMILTON: Yes. Yes. I feel very lucky and in a very good place now. Ten years ago I would have been more pessimistic about where I was going inside, regardless of what happened in the career world or the personal world. But I like who I am inside much more now. Some of that's just growing up, some of it is the process of dealing with this issue of abuse, some of it is the fighting through to make the marriage work, and finding things about me that I like that were not based on qualities that I had learned very early to dismiss as worthless.

Finding the words was hard. One of the joys of acting was that somebody else gave me the words—all I had to do was let go of the emotions. Acting gave me a way to make a living and to be well thought of.

RICHARD RHODES: I would guess that there's a high level of abuse in the background of a lot of people who act.

DAN HAMILTON: I've found it so. In the last several years, with Barbara's development and my decision to step forward and say, Yes, me too, I've been able to guide creative processes dealing with this issue. For the past two years, we presented a story line on the soap opera I direct about father-daughter abuse. I was able to help the two actors shape and perform that story. From our sixty million viewers we got tremendous response and support. All of that I was able to do very much out in the open and out front. That's been my deliberate public acknowledgment. I want to do what I can with my tools. We took the poem at the end of Barbara's book and incorporated it into one of our scripts. The actress who played the part of a girl who had been abused by her father sexually read the poem. We acknowledged it as a real poem from a real book, and then read it as a statement of healing. We got a great deal of response: people calling the network and various affiliates all around the country asking for the source.

GINGER RHODES: Barbara mentioned that in her last letter.

RICHARD RHODES: She's wonderful.

DAN HAMILTON: [*Surprised, recoiling*] In many ways, yes. He said with a cold eye. [*We all laugh.*] Yes, I have great admiration and respect and caring and empathy for what Barbara has gone through and what she's accomplished in her therapy and healing, as well as the achievement of her book and getting it into publication. I saw early drafts when the book was far more an instrument of anger and revenge. Working with a good editor, she was able to focus it so that it was more than just a release. I admire that greatly. But it's conflated in my mind with the experience of having been raised by a woman who was trapped in her past. Raised by her long before she was aware of what happened or acknowledging what happened. So a lot of the resonances of my childhood have to do with a parent who was completely shut off and unable to deal with parenting, communicating, loving.

That's still part of the equation. Our relationship is communicative and open but still tangled because there's so much history involved. I don't think I could live with her because of the history, and as much as she's grown, there are still great blocks in the way that she will never be able to step across, including her very valid and strong hatred of men and inability to trust them.

Richard asked Skye Smith if part of her surviving was choosing the man she married:

SKYE SMITH: Oh yes, one hundred percent. Yes, absolutely. It's enriched his life, too. His life has a depth and a complexity to it now that he freely admits it wouldn't have had otherwise. I guess he'd go through it again. I think so. It's not easy, though. Not easy when you send someone out to a psychiatric hospital and you don't know when they'll come back, if ever. He had a lot of doubts whether I would make it. Whether I could survive the pain that I had. I don't know how I did. It's awful pain.

MARIA MAREWSKI: You knew you survived it once when it happened to you, so you could survive it again.

SKYE SMITH: I know I'm on my way now, no suicide, no self-destructive stuff, no doubts.

RICHARD RHODES: So you learn to handle the pain?

SKYE SMITH: It's like the skin grafts have taken, finally. A little protection here, a little comfort.

GINGER RHODES: Believing in yourself.

MARIA MAREWSKI [*To Skye*]: Yes. Such a radical idea, huh?

RICHARD RHODES: Put on a few pounds?

SKYE SMITH: [*Laughing*] *That* we're working on. . . .

MARIA MAREWSKI: She's made progress. I've seen her in something sleeveless.

SKYE SMITH: I did. I went sleeveless. . . . I'm just being born. I just got out. It's really great.

Anna Lee Traynor wrote us:

ANNA LEE TRAYNOR: In having to reflect on my past for the lawsuit, I have finally come to an honest determination of my impression of my life, from child to adult. Even so, I still feel fortunate and grateful to have survived relatively unscathed, as compared to others. I fully realize that feeling this gratitude now is somewhat displaced. My ability to survive comes from my own tenacious emotional character and my personal physical capacity to have endured the colitis, the corrective surgery and the continued daily challenges, both structural and metabolic, that the surgery provokes. I'm grateful for these elements of the person I am. The reasons for the necessity to have survived I am not grateful for. I should not have had to survive this psychic and physical pain. I should not have been abused in the first place to have needed to survive anything.

Richard told David Doepel:

RICHARD RHODES: Writing *A Hole in the World* left me with a great deal of sadness. I felt something lost. Maybe I just finally recognized that something *was* lost. It's taken all these years to come to that acceptance. I didn't really want to accept it. When I was twelve, what I felt I needed was unbounded love. Whether or not that goes all the way back to my mother's suicide and abrupt disappearance from my infancy, how much it relates to the horror of my stepmother's torture, I can't quantify, but what I looked for in adults, especially teachers, was unbounded love. It was a long time before I understood—in therapy—that there's no such thing in adulthood, and that if there were, one probably wouldn't want it, because it comes at a price, the price of being treated like a child, or worse. Adults who are willing to treat other adults as children usually have an agenda of their own.

Since the book was published, I've heard from many people who survived childhood abuse, some of it far worse than what my brother and I experienced. One of the most charming, to me, was a woman who said she survived by saying, *I'll show them*. Similarly, the resolution of the anger I feel about what happened to me as a child is to use it as a source of energy to deal with the violence that continues to infect the world. That's a wonderful revenge, sublimating violence against violence. It's why I find the idea of the death penalty so heinous. To kill because someone was killed is rage and revenge, but understandable. Old as the hills, really, the way it's always been done. But *not to kill* because someone was killed is remarkable, and will finally be the only way out of the cycle of violence. To find ways to *prevent* further killing because someone was killed would be extraordinary.

In any case, I have plenty of unconverted anger left. Anger and hatred aren't the same. I feel enormous anger. I write about nuclear weapons. I write about abused children. I write about the exquisitely scaled and detailed, infinite varieties of inhumanity that man visits upon man in this world and I write about it from the perspective of how to get past it. Of the possibility of hope. The possibility of sustaining some degree of dignity and strength in the midst of the violence. I understand very well that life is fatal. But I also understand that it's all that we are and have. Perhaps that's one reason I find it difficult to be interested in religion. This present life is so remarkable, the more so because I feel like such a survivor. And I feel a responsibility as a human being to try to find ways past all that violence.

Therapists Susan Voorhees and Alice Brand Bartlett both looked at abusers in our conversations with them—and looked beyond:

SUSAN VOORHEES: I just testified in an abuse case that involved custody. The question was raised whether the stepfather abused his stepson. I wasn't able to say one way or the other. This little boy had been questioned a lot and a lot was riding on what he said, and he's only five, so he's pretty little. The little boy has said that his mom watched his step-father sodomize him—watched and allowed that to happen. One of the attorneys asked me, In your heart of hearts, can you believe that this man would do that to this child? They wouldn't let me answer the question because "heart of hearts" is not a standard that's admissible in court. But I went home that night, I told my husband about the question, and later we happened to watch a program on television about the Holocaust Museum in Washington. And my husband turned to me and said, I hope that attorney is watching this, because in his heart of hearts he evidently believes that people can't perpetrate violence on innocent people.

But if human beings can murder six million or more people, of course they can do horrible things to little children.

✦

ALICE BRAND BARTLETT: I don't personally have a history of abuse, so I have to listen to my patients who have shown me what is possible. People who have survived abuse have to find some meaning in their life. Judy Herman calls it a survivor mission. I don't know if it has to be a survivor mission, but they have to find some meaning—grab on to religion, grab on to their work, try to create something better for their children, whatever they can find, something that makes their life worthwhile. That, I think, is the end stage of healing—the stage of healing that gives you resonance.

RICHARD RHODES: Love and work, Freud's holy duality. What everyone needs to be happy. So you're saying survivors reach healing when what they need for happiness becomes indistinguishable from what everyone needs for happiness.

ALICE BRAND BARTLETT: There you go.

RICHARD RHODES: But you're right. Finding meaning is everybody's problem, but it's especially a problem for—especially important to—abuse survivors.

ALICE BRAND BARTLETT: Because otherwise, it's hard to find a reason to live. Knowing what happened to you, knowing how cruel the world can be—and you know better than anyone else because you can't deny it as other people can—how can you go on? That's basically what I tell my patients. The rest of us can push it aside, at least for a while, but you have to live with it every day. So you have to find a reason to go on in spite of it.

16

"As Much As We Can Hope For"

Viktor E. Frankl, an Austrian psychiatrist who survived Auschwitz, wrote what we consider the best of all the books about surviving abusive experiences, Man's Search for Meaning. *To explain the essence of his approach, which he calls logotherapy, Dr. Frankl quotes Nietzsche: "He who has a why to live for can bear with almost any how." People need reasons to live, Dr. Frankl explains, especially people who are suffering. All of the survivors you have come to know in this book found reasons to live. Another name for what they found is hope.*

CELIA GOLDEN: My daughters were so beautiful and so lovable that it seemed to me anyone could love them as much as I could. That allowed me to think about suicide. But when I did, I'd tell myself, I'll hang around until they can talk. That was critical to me: once they could talk, then they could tell people if someone was hurting them. Then I thought, well, I'll hang around until they're about eight years old. Then, no, they still need me. As if everything hinged on whether someone needed me, whether there was a reason to stay around.

✤

SKYE SMITH:

Tough Enough?

I be tough
& I be mean
I delight in
lookin' lean.

SpaghettiOs
& pies & cakes
For this tough girl?
Give me a break!

Sweat & guilt
and feelin' bad
is my life's work
It's all I've had.

Trust & hope
and sex divine
Can this be part
of me & mine?

With help, support
& pain galore
Could my life change?
Become much more?

Soft I be
and girly sweet
and fleshy hipped
Nocturnal treat.

I don't know
It's scary stuff
Put on a pound?
Be tough enough?

ANNA LEE TRAYNOR: I don't want to lose sight of the fact that this case [*her lawsuit against her parents*] is for the children. I would be lying or deluding myself if I didn't admit to wanting to feel some relief. I have to feel a little short-term satisfaction to support the effort—I want to feel good too, because being a martyr isn't healthy either—but I also want to see it happen for someone else. I would like so much to have won this for me and for other children too, a case that could be studied and used as a precedent for other cases. I would be very happy with that.

❖

DAVID RAY: The emotional roller-coaster was especially destructive. The parent shows up and promises the kids a bucket full of gold and then the next week leaves them in an unlocked apartment without any food. That's the way it is, that's the pattern. Then the big fantasy, longing for them to show up again. I'd be sitting by some dusty road. If only my father would come driving down the road. Then one day in this little town my father does show up. He shows up with a girlfriend in a Pontiac and says, "Come on, let's go to California." I really wanted to. But once again, that loyalty. I didn't want to stay with my mom. Things were getting bad. But it would have been disloyal to go with him.

Karen Seal wrote us:

KAREN SEAL: I am growing stronger and more serene each day with my therapy and my twelve-step support groups. I do believe I am "over the hill" and am on the downside of all of this. I know that I will carry scars for life, but I am growing in confidence that healing *is* possible.

During our interview, Karen explained:

KAREN SEAL: It's getting better, because I'm willing to sit with a little more calmness, really quite a bit more. I'm not traveling, because that's another hyperactivity for me. I'm just being quiet, staying home more, doing a lot of journal writing. I go to four meetings a week. I go to Al-Anon, which is for me wonderful—it's teaching me how to be an adult and how to interact with people. I go to a support group for incest survivors, to Workaholics Anonymous, and then I go to a spiritual group. So I have four a week. I need that kind of reinforcement to retrain and reparent myself, because there's so much faulty thinking in there. I still don't know if I will be able to commit again, to a relationship. That's a big one for me.

❖

ALEXA DONATH: Reading about others in difficult circumstances, I gained courage, hope, and the will to go on. When times seemed so desperate that I didn't see any point in even trying to hang on, I remembered that books and music would be there for me.

❖

CELIA GOLDEN: I've always wanted to be loved, and needed to have someone to love. There are people that cut themselves off from life or feel like they can't deal with any more pain. They say, I never want to be vulnerable again, I never want to be hurt again. Yet, I feel like with me, I got some significant satisfaction from my father early. It's this dream that I don't want to let go of. Maybe I made poor choices in my life, but I don't see myself as ever being willing to totally close down.

GINGER RHODES: Where are you now in your life?

CELIA GOLDEN: I'm in a relationship and we leave for Thailand in February. I feel like I've dealt with a lot of my fears. I may be totally off, but I'm not interested in the middle-class lifestyle. Material things don't mean much to me. I have some things—gifts, my books—that I'll keep. But the furniture, my house, none of this stuff is what's important to me. I want experiences and I want to be happy. I would really love to travel, I would really love the freedom to write. I love to read and I like to meet people. I would like to be the kind of person I've met where I think, it would be wonderful to have the experiences she's had! I'll be fifty in four more years. So my friend John is in Thailand. He paints, and I'll write.

❖

ALEXA DONATH: I made a final break with my parents. I'm forty-two and I was letting it happen—they were still lying to me, they were still manipulating me, they were still trying to hurt me. I told myself: you are not a child anymore and I won't be hurt anymore.

❖

DAVID RAY: There is still so much shame and guilt bound up with this stuff, the feeling that it's all my fault. That's where David Copperfield started and that's where I started, with How can I fix this? If we were better, they wouldn't be like this. My father wouldn't be leaving or these things wouldn't be happening.

GINGER RHODES: We keep trying to rewrite it and make ourselves part of a happy family, with loving parents.

DAVID RAY: You keep going back over and over and thinking you'll make it come out differently. Thinking I'll fix this and be better and they'll have a good marriage because I'll be a lovable child. Then all this other stuff won't go wrong. All this other stuff won't happen. I am totally addicted to going back over these things. Writing about them, thinking about them. I think at the base of it is always this—that it would come out differently. That it wouldn't have happened if I had been worth more.

In a letter to Richard, Michael Davies mentioned his reaction to Empire of the Sun, *the J. G. Ballard novel of an English boy in a Japanese prison camp, from which Stephen Spielberg made a popular motion picture:*

MICHAEL DAVIES: I suppose *Empire of the Sun* hit close to home for me because the movie also reminded me of a friend of mine who survived the Bataan Death March and endured the unendurable throughout his own series of prison camps. He told me how, at the moment of liberation, he ran behind one of the prison barracks where no one could see him and bawled like a baby. As a true survivor, he's been an inspiration for me. He never gave up. Despite everything, he never gave up. And he was rescued. His story, other stories, and your own story—all give me hope that someday I (and my family) will be rescued, too.

Richard told David Doepel:

RICHARD RHODES: I think of a nightmare I had many times in therapy in various forms—that I was about to be discovered to have been implicated in the murder of a baby. Bulldozers were knocking down a garage. The baby had been buried under the floor of the garage. In the dream I was absolutely certain that what was happening wasn't a dream, and I had the most overwhelming terror that I had done something irrevocable—murdered the baby—and that it would be made known. I was thirty-five years old the first time I had that dream, and I walked around the next day haunted by the certainty that in fact such a murder had taken place and that I would be found out and that my life would be ruined.

It was finally clear that the baby in the dream was the child I was, the child I had somehow had to bury, the child who had been nearly murdered, soul-murdered, with torture and abuse and neglect. Then, at the end of writing *A Hole in the World,* all these years later, I dreamt that Ginger and I had a child—in fact, we haven't had children—and the child was the baby from the nightmares. It was in its crib. It was small for its age, but it was alive and it was happy.

❖

VALORIE BUTLER: I have something now that no one can take from me. Inner strength. They can't take that from you. That is my space, I can have it, and I don't care what anyone might be doing to me physically. I can see someone in a bare cell, bound down, restrained, but she can go into her mind and have something that no one can take away.

RICHARD RHODES: What about the pain that your aunt inflicted on you? What context have you found for that?

VALORIE BUTLER: Yes. An innocent child. Let's say God didn't allow people to hurt children. That's not nice, they shouldn't do that. And of course it isn't. But if their freedom was limited that much, He would be controlling, for one thing, and for another, we wouldn't see how ugly it really is. If He controls anything, we would only be held responsible for that much, we would be more like puppets. But if we're allowed to hurt deep in our guts and then resolve it if we can, we can feel more, and be more autonomous and help others.

GINGER RHODES: So the meaning of your suffering as a child is . . . ?

VALORIE BUTLER: Because of that suffering—because of facing it and coming through it—my awareness is much greater than it would have been if I'd had a perfect childhood with no pain at all. I'm in the real world here, it's very painful, and there's a lot of suffering here. I believe God says He's sorry that this happened to me. I don't believe He planned for it to happen or anything like that, but I believe He puts his arms around me and says, Now that this has happened to you, what can we do with it? I believe I could take the mud pie, so to speak, and make a flower grow out of it.

When Richard answered Michael Davies's first letter, Michael responded:

MICHAEL DAVIES: I was very pleased to receive your letter. I have to admit to having had second thoughts after I mailed my own letter to you. Rereading it, I was pretty convinced that I'd gone overboard, said too much, said it too melodramatically. I wondered how on earth you could respond to a letter like that. Upon further reflection, however, I realized it really did, after all, express what I wanted to say, even if the words were woven into an elaborate mask that could only symbolize, not convey, the essence of our family's experience. . . .

I want to do whatever I can to help expose both the hypocrisy and real potential of "family values" in our society. We've allowed the family's sanctified status, its image as sanctuary and refuge, to hide its darker dimensions as a totalitarian microcosm, a prison. That darkness has to be confronted if we're to make any progress.

❖

BARBARA HAMILTON: For years, I felt unauthentic. All my life, and even through a lot of the therapy. It was just horrible when I began to learn that my children and grandchildren had been abused in their turn. How could I not have protected them when it had happened to me? [*To Richard:*] I don't know whether you did this or not, but when you met somebody, would you compare yourself to them and find yourself always less than they were? They were always smarter or prettier or they dressed prettier or people liked them better or they got better grades or—it just goes on and on and on.

But it does go away. I like where I am now. Things kind of fall into place as to what's important. Suddenly you realize that what you're doing has value. You don't have to have your husband, in his love, tell you that. That's great—you appreciate others telling you, but you get to the point where you *know,* inside yourself. Even if everybody in your world is a denier—and certainly they're not welcoming my book with open arms. Certainly not my family.

It sounds egotistical, but I know it isn't. I know it's just me, finally coming through and saying, This is what I'm supposed to be doing. I'm about fifty years late, but this is what I'm supposed to be doing—so do it.

❖

ALEXA DONATH: Every relationship that you're in, if you're an abused person and if the other person really doesn't know what they're doing, they're going to blame you again, all over again. But that's not what it's going to be about for me anymore. I used to be a victim and now I'm a volunteer.

There's a difference between being selfish and acting in your best interests. "I used to be victim but now I'm a volunteer" isn't original with me, but it's something that helps me stay on the road I need to be on. It means I choose as an adult not to have someone hurt me anymore. I had no choice as a child. But I choose right now, as a forty-two-year-old woman, not to allow it to continue.

❖

ANNE O'NEIL: I've needed to learn how to give to myself. There's a lot more for me to learn about that. It's still such a struggle to take care of myself and sometimes I feel very tired of the struggle. But then, I always get back to saying, Okay, what am I going to *do* about it?

I want to be a gift, you know. My name means gift. Anne means grace. That's my calling. That's what I'm called to do—to give. That's what I'm happiest doing.

❖

ANNA LEE TRAYNOR: I'm very angry about this case. When I set that fault line, I really didn't mean so every person over thirty can say, Oh, good, I can sue my parents. Absolutely not. But making parents responsible would eliminate abuse eventually through prevention. Through funding and social intervention and revision of court processes for child-abuse and neglect cases.

It's an issue that we'd better start acknowledging. It's a daily condition, a fact of life, for many children, and in plain English, that's *crap*.

❖

RICHARD RHODES [*To David Doepel*]: In relationships with other people, for many years, I lived with a great deal of contempt, for people and their beliefs and anything that differed from what I believed that week. It's still easy to fall into a contemptuous mood if I feel hurt, if I'm having a conflict with my partner, if something doesn't happen the way I want it to. I'm sure I learned the contempt during the years with my stepmother. She had contempt in abundance, and so did my dad.

But the contempt extended beyond simply disliking people. It extended to a nihilism about the world. The phrase that comes to mind, from somewhere in the history of natural philosophy, is "gray and scurrying matter." There was a time, when I was younger, when that seemed to be all there was to say; now I understand that it's one perspective on the reality of the world and not the only perspective. That it's perfectly valid if you're thinking of physics, even though it's something that many human beings spend their lives trying hard to deny, a brute fact about the world that many of our great cultural systems—religion in particular—were invented to deny: that life is ultimately death and dissolution. That's the way the natural cycle works. Yet even as I say that, I feel equally strongly, more strongly now than when I was younger, that the natural structure of the world, the natural cycle of life—fathers and sons and mothers and children and so on—is great and deep and secure and comfortable.

Maybe I can sum it up best in a story. I was talking about *A Hole in the World* to a group of teachers a few months ago and I said that going to the boys' home and farming introduced me to the cycle that is built into farming where things are planted and they grow and then are harvested and killed and eaten. The destruction is painful, but it's part of the same cycle—and it *is* a cycle, coming around again to renewal, seeds collected and planted, manure spread to fertilize, sunlight and new growth again. I said that always felt benevolent to me, and was healing. A teacher came up to me after the lecture and said, There's a reason why it feels that way, because the universe on that level *is* benevolent. She's right, it is, and it was a great realization for me at the time.

There's a complementarity to all experience. Even nuclear weapons have their good side, as it turns out—they make it suicidal to wage world-scale war. In my case, the particular complement to my stepmother's violence was my brother's love. He may have been responding to a beating when he ran away from home and went to the police, but when he faced the court he insisted that I be allowed to escape with him. He took me with him. It's not something he had to do. So whenever I think of my stepmother and her cruelty—I think of my brother and his love. In this opaque universe, it seems to me, that's about as much as we can hope for. It's quite a lot.

Envoy

From conception to conclusion, producing this book took six years. When we sent our contributors their edited texts, in late 1995, we asked them to let us know their situation today. Here are their responses. In every case they evidently continue to heal, confirming psychoanalyst Karen Horney's famous observation, "Life itself still remains a very effective therapist."

ALICE BRAND BARTLETT: I'm beginning research on the effect of childhood abuse on the experience of self and others in adulthood. My husband, Tom, and I just finished renovating a small 1888 Victorian house. I continue as Edward Greenwood Professor and associate dean in the Karl Menninger School of Psychiatry and on the faculty of the Topeka Institute for Psychoanalysis.

❖

VALORIE BUTLER: My life since our interview has taken quite a change for the better. The sanguine side of my personality has blossomed quite a bit as a result. In April 1993 I was separated and I was divorced in July 1994. This needed to happen for many years. It was a painful time. Now the "fun" part of my life is developing. I even wear a little jewelry. I can even think about God having a sense of humor. It's great to feel in charge of my life. No more thinking like a victim. Now I can quickly resolve inner conflict, and I am decisive about what is right or wrong for me. The boundaries are intact.

❖

MICHAEL DAVIES: To be honest, it's still a mystery to me why my siblings and I survived as well as we did. Our mother's amazing courage and endurance seems a likely candidate. As a survivor and despite enormous costs, she set an extraordinary example, showing us how love and determination can overcome the worst of circumstances. But things are not that simple.

There were levels of abuse in our family that remain only partially addressed, which raise troubling questions about the nature of our survival and even about the fundamental nature of both social and physical reality. Whatever I survived pales before the experiences of my sisters and makes me feel like an impostor here. And their survival owes as much to their own strength of character as to our mother's.

Strength of character, hard work, a strongly developed sensitivity to injustice, a spirituality not necessarily tied to organized religion, and an ability to contain the pain of our memories have allowed us to go forward and make something of our lives. I have much to be thankful for in both my professional and private lives, including a woman who's taught me how to live in the present and hope for the future.

❖

LYDIA DEROBERTIS: I am currently in private practice with a concentration on family systems. I'm still healing—aren't we all.

❖

ALEXA DONATH: I have made a promise to myself not to listen to the people who "don't get it." Distancing oneself from those who hurt and diminish us is always a healing thing to do. Now I try to put positive, supportive people in my life, those who recognize my struggles, appreciate my gifts, and celebrate my victories. No longer do I use my humor only in a self-deprecating manner. I cherish my assets. Recently I received a devastating diagnosis of a chronic illness, and though I often wonder "Why me?," I know the strength is there to overcome it. Trying to change your life is like crabs in a basket—every time one tries to climb out, another crab stops him by jumping on his back, making him fall down into the pile again. No matter how many get on my back, this crab will make it out of the basket alive.

❖

CELIA GOLDEN: My mother died last April. I had reestablished relationships with my older sister and brother two years ago, and so was aware when my mother became seriously ill. It was gratifying to realize how much more realistically I saw myself in terms of being an adult, and my mother being a very weak, physically fragile, prematurely aged, dependent adult. And it was a relief to know that she was finally dead, that she could no longer hurt me in any way, and that her evil power did not become unleashed, nor did I suffer from nightmares. My sadness was for the innocent child she was at birth and the destruction of that child's natural goodness and beauty by abusive and neglectful adults around her.

❖

BARBARA HAMILTON: For several years I have felt as though I was on a continuing journey, with some of the positive changes flowing along with me. For example, I never feel fury surfacing over unimportant annoyances anymore—fury that was difficult to contain and never accomplished anything positive. My true anger pushes and guides me as new evidence of child abuse appears. Although I still sound off in frustration occasionally, I am finding ways to express it more usefully by writing to those in positions of power who must act, without exception, for our children. *The Hidden Legacy* continues on its journey too. It has brought letters from all over the country (including a women's prison). Dan produced a beautiful audio version of my book, and a documentary film, *The Healing Years,* is in process and for which I have been interviewed. So the messages so many of us have to share are being powerfully told. I find this encouraging. It must be said, however, that the evil horror of child sexual exploitation continues to increase all over the world, especially in Southeast Asia. My hope is that the numbers of those who join the war against all forms of child abuse will reach everywhere a child of the Secret is still hanging on and waiting for us. *We must use our strength and courage beyond our own healing.*

❖

DAN HAMILTON: I've recently completed producing and directing the audio recording of Barbara's book. I commissioned original music for it and will do the final mix in Los Angeles. This project, as well as participating in the documentary David Doepel and his associates have been developing from *Trying to Get Some Dignity,* have filled the past year with much thought, productive communication, and a strong, positive feeling for the future. I continue to direct at *As the World Turns,* trying to make movies on a daytime schedule. My wife, Stephanie, just received her second Writers Guild award for her work on *General Hospital.* We are exhaustedly raising our five-and-a-half-year-old wunderkind, Dylan. My parents and siblings continue their own journeys in growth and understanding, somewhat painful and slow for some, but steady. I think we all agree that to protect and nurture the next generation is paramount, and ultimately personally rewarding.

❖

LOUISE HILL: The interview was a gift because it made me reflect on the trials and gifts that have been mine. We excavated some old battlefields and honored them. Going forward with a brave spirit—that's how my life has changed. I understand it all, or almost all.

❖

RALPH KESSLER: The permanent cloud of my mother's betrayal was lifted on my seventh-fifth birthday. I got a call from a dear aunt, Manya, who is eighty-four. She was a close confidante of my mother. I had written to her asking her why my mother and my grandparents would not give me a home. Manya's wonderful birthday present was to answer my questions. She said simply that my mother suffered from ulcers, had a husband who did not want me around, felt that she needed him to assist her, and so she gave me up. My grandfather decided to return me to my mother after two months, Manya said, because he was sick with headaches and at age sixty decided that he didn't want to raise another child. The people who took me in and then asked me to leave were responding to my stepfather's failure to pay them the money my mother promised them for my board. When I learned all this, I went to see a therapist for the first and last time. She smiled at my story and said that the best therapy was when the patient understands and solves his own problem. I feel at long last like the village crier who shouts at the end of the day, "Twelve o'clock and all's well!" At least for today.

✦

MARIA MAREWSKI: I have founded and direct a nonprofit organization which is committed to giving children a voice. The Children's Media Project puts the tools of communication directly into the hands of kids through workshops which teach them to make their own films and videos. We encourage kids to look to the events, observations, dreams, and experiences of their own lives for the raw material of their movies. In retrospect, I can see that I've been driven to create the very lifeline to healthy creative expression which I so desired as a child. This act of creation has become my own lifeline as an adult.

✦

ANNE O'NEIL: Since completing the first draft of my autobiography, I've taken time out to study the art of memoir writing. I study voice and musical-theater performance privately with a view to developing original musical-theater pieces, and I continue to work in the field of interior design.

✦

DAVID RAY: My wife, Judy, and I have moved to Tucson, Arizona. We travel widely and give poetry readings, lectures, and workshops, independently and together. Recently we spent a season in France, where I was a fellow at the Camargo Foundation. I'm completing a book of memoirs for Dutton/Signet as well as new collections of poetry, fiction, and essays. With the help of therapy and medication, I continue to deal with depression dating from childhood.

❖

KAREN SEAL: What a jolt to read my words from five years ago! I was still very angry and distrustful of men and into revenge and hurt. I'm happy to report that those feelings are almost totally gone today. My "program" has brought miracles to me, in particular a much more trusting attitude, because I have come to trust *my* ability to discern what is good and not good for me and to trust that I can and will do what is best for me (notice that I had to change here, not others). I feel the serenity that comes from letting go of the past. I have been in a stable, loving, safe relationship with a wonderful man for nearly two years. We're learning and growing together. I don't think about the incest much anymore. It feels quite healed. I can't stress too much the wonderful healing that has come from finding a spiritual path. I lean on God in my life today, and find He/She/It *never* lets me down.

❖

SKYE SMITH: My father died last year and my brother's actions in the aftermath of that loss forced me, agonizingly, to "fire" him. At the time, I thought the pain engendered by those losses would kill me. But it didn't. My therapist told me some years ago that living well is the best revenge. I'm well on the way to carrying out his prescription. There's an emotional safety net under me now that's securely held in place by my expanding family of choice: individuals who appreciate and love me for who I am, not for who they need me to be. And who I am is interesting, I'm discovering as I go about claiming formerly threatening, cast-off aspects of myself such as my intellect (I'm currently pursuing my Ph.D.), my artistic vision (I've created public gardens at work and at my local library), and my prodigious energy, now largely freed from exhausting combat duty. I love my work as a clinical social worker. My husband also facil-itates and encourages my growth. I'm discovering that love doesn't hurt, demand obedience, or clip wings. I feel excited optimism about ensuing life chapters where, truly, the sky is the limit!

ANNA LEE TRAYNOR: In September 1993 I took my first step toward becoming a public advocate for children's legal rights. Faced with the possibility of a settlement of my lawsuit, I personally informed the presiding Superior Court judge that I adamantly refused to acquiesce to any agreement that would compromise my freedom to pursue revisions in child-abuse and protection laws. No financial offer of settlement could shake my decision. My sister chose the money. I chose to continue on with my original goals, which were to seek physical protection, emotional relief, and spiritual emancipation for today's children and the innocent souls of those yet to be born. Through the continued support, patience, and expert legal advice of my friend and attorney, James Vigliotti, I have redirected my energies into volunteering as a legal advocate for domestic violence victims in the court. Recently I attended a national child-advocacy conference in Washington and began working with congressional staff on framing more effective national child-advocacy laws.

❖

SUSAN VOORHEES: I left the Menninger Clinic in March 1995 to establish a solo private practice working primarily with children and adolescents, many of whom are abuse victims. I also do child-abuse evaluations and consult with courts and community agencies on child-abuse issues.

❖

JOHN WOOD: Since my interview, I started and trashed an auction business. I'm now buying and selling real estate and doing well. This allows me to isolate—to deal with the fewest possible people and still earn money. I've been in a loving relationship for three years. Not a healing one, of course; that would be boring. Oh well, we aim for progress, not perfection.

SEEKING HELP

Organizations differ from city to city and state to state. A place to begin wherever you live is the blue pages of your telephone book, which list government agencies. Call your town or city government for referral to help an abused child or adult or to seek help yourself.

SOURCES

Contributors referred to the following books during their interviews:

Allen, James. *As a Man Thinketh*. Various editions.

Bass, Ellen. *The Courage to Heal*. New York: HarperPerennial, 1994.

Frankl, Viktor. *Man's Search for Meaning*. Boston: Beacon Press, 1992.

Hamilton, Barbara. *The Hidden Legacy*. Fort Bragg, Calif.: Cypress House, 1992.

Herman, Judith Lewis. *Trauma and Recovery*. New York: Basic Books, 1992.

Miller, Alice. *Prisoners of Childhood*. New York: Basic Books, 1981.

Rhodes, Richard. *A Hole in the World*. New York: Simon & Schuster, 1990.

————. *Making Love*. New York: Simon & Schuster, 1993.

————. *The Making of the Atomic Bomb*. New York: Simon & Schuster, 1986.

Schreiber, Flora Rheta. *Sybil*. New York: Warner Books, 1989.

Smedes, Lewis B. *Forgive and Forget*. New York: Harper, 1991.

Vachss, Andrew. *Blossom*. New York: Alfred A. Knopf, 1990.

Yancey, Philip. *Where Is God When It Hurts?* New York: HarperCollins, 1990.

ACKNOWLEDGMENTS

Thanks first of all to Claire Wachtel, our editor at William Morrow, for sharing our vision of this book when it was still only a story we had to tell. Tracy Quinn kept the lines open.

Thanks to the many people who wrote to Richard following the publication of *A Hole in the World,* especially those who agreed to be interviewed but whose paths we failed to cross.

As always, Mort Janklow and Anne Sibbald encouraged and supported as well as negotiated.

David Doepel and Barbara Connell at Echo Bridge Productions generously made Richard's interview available. Helen Haversat did her usual outstanding job transcribing the miles of tape.

Thanks most of all to our contributors, who bravely and painfully opened their lives to us and to all who read this book: Blessed are the merciful, for they shall obtain mercy.